A SMOKY MOUNTAIN BOYHOOD

I remember, I remember
How my childhood fleeted by,
The mirth of its December
And the warmth of its July.

—W. M. Praed, "I Remember, I Remember"

A
Smoky Mountain
BOYHOOD

Memories, Musings, and More

Jim Casada

The University of Tennessee Press
Knoxville

Photographs are courtesy of the Casada family collection or author unless otherwise noted.

LIBRARY OF CONGRESS CATALOGING-IN-PUBLICATION DATA

Names: Casada, Jim, author.
Title: A Smoky Mountain Boyhood: Memories, Musings, and More / Jim Casada.
Description: First edition. | Knoxville: The University of Tennessee Press, [2020] |
Includes index. | Summary: "This book comprises the recollections of one man, Jim Casada,
who was born in Bryson City, North Carolina, and has had a long career as an outdoorsman
and author. Casada gathers his reminiscences on Smokies life in four parts: holidays, seasons
of the Smokies, mountain childhood, and a concluding section where special memories blend
with a once prominent culture in the Smokies. Casada's gift for storytelling pairs with his
training as a historian to produce a highly readable memoir of mountain life in
East Tennessee and Western North Carolina"—Provided by publisher.
Identifiers: LCCN 2020032145 | ISBN 9781621906094 (paperback) |
ISBN 9781621906100 (kindle edition) | ISBN 9781621906117 (adobe pdf)
Subjects: LCSH: Casada, Jim—Childhood and youth. | Casada, Jim—Family. |
Great Smoky Mountains (N.C. and Tenn.)—Biography. | Mountain life—Great Smoky
Mountains (N.C. and Tenn.) | Bryson City (N.C.)—Biography. | Casada family.
Classification: LCC F443.G7 C37 2020 | DDC 976.8/89—dc23
LC record available at https://lccn.loc.gov/2020032145

In fond memory of my parents, paternal grandparents, aunts and uncles, honorary aunts and uncles, grade school and high school teachers, the lords of Loafers Glory, and all those resident in a small Appalachian community who took me to raise. In varying degrees and fashions, I owe them a great deal. This collection of memories and musings on folkways in a truly special part of America is an attempt, inadequate though it undoubtedly is, to express my gratitude to these staunch sons and daughters of the Smokies. Collectively they gave me a wonderful boyhood.

Contents

Illustrations

Four Generations of the Casada Family

Cades Cove Church Reunion, 1951

Downtown Bryson City in the 1930s

The Jim Shelton Family Dwarfed by a Giant Chesnut Tree in Tremont, circa 1920s

Decoration Day at Elkmont, circa 1920s

A Baptism at Smokemont

Chesnuts along Heintooga Road

The Chimney Tops in the Morning Mist

A Cold Day on Nantahala

Fall along a Smokies Stream

Fontana Lake Nestled among the Smokies in Summertime

The Author's Garden

Rain Clouds Dipping below Shuckstack Mountain

Ramp Patch

Spring Blooms

Storm Clouds Laying on Twentymile Ridge

The Author Fly Fishing in Bone Valley Creek

The Author Fishing Deep Creek

Preface

Few things in life are more inviting than a request to share a tale. A sporting mentor invariably laid hold of a corner of my soul at the outset of our periodic meetings when he inquired about my latest woodland meanderings: "Tell me about it." Or as Pat Conroy, a powerful writer who rightly recognized that links to the earth form the essence of our being, put it: "The most powerful words in English are 'tell me a story.'"

I'm descended from a long line of storytellers. This book is in many senses an extension of their efforts in the rich Smokies tradition of telling tales. You'll meet my paternal grandfather, Joseph Hillbury Casada, frequently in the pages that follow. He loved nothing better than taking a comfortable seat in his poor man's throne, a well-worn rocking chair, and launching into some account from his past. I adored this humble yet surprisingly complex man, seized on every soft-spoken word he uttered as precious, and blessedly spent a significant portion of my boyhood in his company.

If we are captives of our youth, as I firmly believe, then the cage of my boyhood was a gilded one to which Grandpa Joe held the key. As these words are being written I can glance over my right shoulder at the sturdy rocking chair that served him so well for so long. In monetary terms it has little value, but it's a touchstone to the past. In my mind's eye it may well be the most precious thing I own.

My father told stories with verve and obvious delight, especially in the final decade of his life after Momma's death. He had the knack and loved sharing memories.

Memory makes a fine mistress, for she is warm, winsome, rendered malleable by the passage of time, and at least for me, of surpassing beauty. Most of this book traces back to the years between 1948, when I entered the first grade, and 1960, when I graduated from high school, although my connection with the Smokies has been a constant over all my days. The region is and ever will remain the home of my heart. Because of that passionate love affair, along with the span of time involved, my looking glass into the past may at some points have a bit of a roseate hue. Likewise, as

Grandpa Joe instinctively knew and invariably practiced, it's a mighty poor piece of cloth that can use no embroidery.

Such considerations being duly acknowledged, this book is an earnest and honest effort at capturing one man's concept of a time when not only the Smokies but most of Appalachia were caught in the throes of a multigenerational change. It would, with increasing force, see the region lose much of its distinctive identity. That distinctiveness deserves to be remembered, respected, and in some cases revered. That's my goal for this book. If I manage to tickle a memory or two with older readers and intrigue younger ones while capturing something of what made the Smokies so special, my mission to provide insight into the fading folkways of a special place will have met with success.

Acknowledgments

As the dedication suggests, in large measure this book is an outgrowth of youthful experiences and interaction with individuals who filled my formative years. Although virtually all of them, other than a few classmates, now reside in what I hope is a mountainous portion of another realm, and together they provided the raw material from which these pieces have been crafted. The only real exception to this exercise in calling back yesteryear is the chapter devoted to a dear friend, Tipper Pressley. More than anyone I know, she strives to keep the heritage of the high country alive. I include her as an exemplar of what to me is a sacred trust, celebration and preservation of the culture of Appalachia.

Appreciable portions of the material have appeared previously, albeit almost always in somewhat different form, in print. The editors who have graced me with the gift of placing my words in print deserve recognition. Naming them runs the real risk of overlooking someone, so they are not listed individually. Suffice it to say they have my gratitude for helping a son of the Smokies bring his recollections into print. If you are an editor who recognizes something in these pages, you've been a beacon along my literary path.

The selections below come from multiple sources, among them newspaper columns, magazine articles, electronic publications, book excerpts, and new material. Although a number appear for the first time, at some point during my four decades as a freelance writer I have at least touched on virtually all the general subject matter. Many pieces, especially those dealing with months of the year, had their origins as newspaper columns. This was primarily in the *Smoky Mountain Times*, a weekly serving my hometown, Bryson City, North Carolina, but material is also drawn from the *Herald* (Rock Hill, South Carolina), the *News & Record* (Greensboro, NC), and the *Spartanburg Herald-Journal*.

Similarly, earlier versions of some selections, particularly the longer ones, were features in state, regional, or national magazines including *Smoky Mountain Living, Carolina Mountain Life, Blue Ridge Outdoors, Blue Ridge Country, Wildlife in North Carolina, South Carolina Wildlife,* and *Tennessee*

7

Wildlife. There are also brief excerpts from my book *Fly Fishing in the Great Smoky Mountains National Park: An Insider's Guide to a Pursuit of Passion.*

As an acknowledged technological troglodyte, someone so backward that my primary phone linkage is still a land line, I still rely heavily on a Rolodex for contact information, I detest the word "blog" (it is a four-letter word completely lacking in romance), and I own a cell phone but probably don't turn it on more than five times a month. Nonetheless, earlier versions of some of this material have appeared in electronic form on "Sporting Classics Daily" and Tipper Pressley's wonderful daily paean to all things Appalachian, "Blind Pig & the Acorn." Also, for close to two decades I've written a monthly e-newsletter (www.jimcasadaoutdoors.com). Over those years much of the subject matter covered here has found expression in it.

In addition to editors, a number of individuals have provided input or encouraged me to produce this work. My brother, Don, who cherishes our highland homeland as much as I do and is blessed to own and live in the house where we grew up, offered valuable suggestions on topics he felt merited coverage. My sister, Annette, is far closer to me in age than Don (she's two years younger, he's ten) and accordingly has greater familiarity with some of the more personal aspects of the stories. Wendy Meyers, a resident of Swain County and a dedicated student of the area's past, has been helpful on various fronts. Ken Wise, a font of flowing wisdom on almost all things associated with the Smokies along with being a highly productive scholar, generously shared his knowledge and provided insight on several subjects. He also read a couple of the chapters and strongly encouraged me to plow ahead toward completion of the book. Periodically readers of my assorted scribblings have urged me to bring some of them into book form. This is my effort to do so. I thank everyone who has ever read my work, tendered words of encouragement, or taken the time to contact me. Writing is an outpouring from the soul, but without readers it means little.

Finally, the folks at the University of Tennessee Press have tolerated my idiosyncracies, dealt graciously with my carping, and drawn on their collective professionalism to make this book a reality. I'm indebted to them.

A SMOKY MOUNTAIN BOYHOOD

Part 1

HIGH COUNTRY HOLIDAY TALES
AND TRADITIONS

Folks in the Smokies have always loved a good time. That came in part from a need to escape the drudgery and back-breaking labor associated with daily life and in part from inescapable realities of blood lines. Most were mixed Scots-Irish, and that heritage always won out, never mind the distance represented by the width of the Atlantic Ocean or a lapse of time dating back generations. From a barn raisin' to a quiltin' party, from an old-fashioned hoedown to indulgence in too much tanglefoot, highlanders will find an outlet for excess energy, mirth, and sadly, sometimes for meanness.

Most of the holidays covered below involved happiness and sometimes hilarity in the yesteryears I have known, while others were somber or even sacred in nature. But even the most serious, such as Decoration Day or revivals, afforded undeniable transports of delight. To eat dinner on the grounds on such occasions is to arrive at the portals of culinary paradise, and if you've never heard beautifully blended voices make hills and hollers ring with a joyful noise from grand old gospel songs, your exposure to music is incomplete.

Observant readers will likely notice some significant omissions in this section of the book, among them Easter, Independence Day, Labor Day, and Halloween. This oversight is conscious and represents nothing more

than that those times of celebration have had less impact on me personally. Certainly I recall things associated with Easter, from egg hunts and
egg fights (hitting hard-boiled eggs against one another to see which one
cracked) to the real reason for that particular holiday with sunrise services
and other special religious activities. For the others, I have faint memories
of firecrackers and cherry bombs on July 4, even fainter recollections of
trick-or-treat activity at Halloween, and recall nothing at all in connection with Labor Day. They just weren't on my radar screen to the same
degree as other holidays and special events. That may not have been the
case throughout the Smokies, for what follows is an intensely personal reflection of what I knew and experienced.

Chapter 1

NEW YEAR'S DAY

When I was a boy, Momma always made a point of having a suitable repast to start off the New Year. We normally ate our main meal of the day at noon. It was known as dinner, not lunch, with supper being the evening meal. Every January 1, however, that routine underwent a temporary change. That day we had our big meal in the evening as opposed to the normal leftovers (or on special occasions waffles or pancakes with scrambled eggs and bacon). Although I'm not sure of the explanation for that change, it likely revolved around the fact that a typical New Year's Day would find Daddy, a couple of his adult buddies, and a passel of youthful understudies in the form of me and some pals, out hunting rabbits. I'm sure that the same situation continued to prevail when my younger brother, Don, was old enough to hunt and I was grown and long gone from home.

When it came to culinary matters, Momma set considerable store on ringing in the new year in proper fashion. Her thoughts on a fitting menu were simple, straightforward, and unvarying. It had to include greens to promote economic success during the coming year, with the idea that the cool-weather vegetables represented the color of money. Normally her bowl of greens would be a mixture of mustard and turnips, often with small bits of turnip root included.

Her manner of cooking vegetables almost always involved a goodly infusion of streaked meat, something today's healthy food nazis would consider a sin of the first magnitude. Whether you call it streaked meat, side meat, fatback, streak o' lean, salt pork, or some other term, this salt and cholesterol–laden ingredient has long been a staple in mountain cookery. Normally Momma sliced three or four pieces of streaked meat with the skin intact and put them right in the pot of greens. After being brought to a rolling boil, greens would then simmer until tender. As this process took place, there was a marvelous marriage between the greens and streaked meat that imparted not only delicious flavor but just the right amount of saltiness.

Accompanied by a sizeable chunk of cornbread, a big bowl of greens could have been a meal in and of itself, especially if some additional slices of streaked meat had been fried to a crisp crunchiness. These were tailor-made for insertion into a piece of cornbread, although Grandpa Joe preferred another approach. First he blessed the food, invariably ending with a heartfelt "You'uns see what's before you. Eat hearty." He then studiously obeyed his prayerful advice, taking pot liquor from greens and pouring it into a big bowl before crumbling in cornbread and dining in pure delight. In my mind's eye I still see him taking the first big bite and saying, "Now that's some fine eating."

At New Year's, though, Momma never stopped with just greens and cornbread. She would also have a big bowl of black-eyed peas, and like the greens, they were seasoned with streaked meat. The peas were supposed to be a symbol of good luck, and Momma also referred to them as representing pennies.

The final dish in Mom's quartet of "must have" edibles was backbones and ribs. While hog jowl is commonly mentioned in connection with New Year's dining, she went "higher on the hog." Incidentally, in today's world it's almost impossible to purchase backbones and ribs at grocery stores, and when I recently asked a local butcher about getting this particular cut of pork, he looked at me as if I'd lost my mind.

Current methods of processing a pig vary markedly from those I knew as a kid. Whatever the explanation, and I've been unable to discover any historical background or widespread tradition connected with this dish, our meat of the day was always backbones and ribs. Maybe Momma cooked it because Daddy dearly loved the hog meat and marrow sucked from the soft bones where ribs connected to the spine.

Quite possibly there would be other dishes forming part of the New Year's meal as well. Momma always had a goal, invariably achieved, of canning two hundred quarts of apples each year, and more days than not from late fall until spring we would have cooked apples on the table. There would also likely be leftover desserts from Christmas feasting, and a personal favorite of mine was to take a hefty slice of her applesauce cake and cover it with a goodly helping of stewed apples. That got rid of any possibility of the cake being a bit dry and made for a wonderful flavor combination.

We didn't participate in other traditional New Year's activities at our house. I don't recall ever staying up late enough to see out the old year. After all, we'd be getting up early on January 1 to head out rabbit hunting. However, shooting guns at midnight (long before fireworks became popular) was a common practice in the area, as the older tradition of "anvil shooting" or "anvil jumping" (using black powder placed in the concave base of an anvil and lighting it to send the anvil sailing in the air) had already gone out of style. So too had the opening of windows and doors at midnight to usher out any bad luck or bad airs, and the shooting supposedly helped scare away haints.

I do remember some mention of first-footing connected with Hogmanay (a Scottish term for December 31). The concept was that the first visitor who crossed the threshold of a house as the old year ended and the new one began would determine the nature of what happened in the ensuing twelve months. Hopefully the first-footer would be a boy or a man (usually in our home it was, in the form of someone who would be part of the New Year's Day hunt arriving at daylight), because that meant good luck. On the other hand, a female being the first to cross the threshold was considered an ill omen. I reckon that perspective would be considered sexist (or worse) today, but that's the way old-time mountain folks looked at matters.

Whatever their views of Hogmanay and New Year's or however they celebrated them, everyone concurred in hopes it would bring good cheer, good fortune, and a bright outlook on life. It formed a sensible approach to new beginnings, and as a youngster I could always count on one great blessing: awareness that the year ahead would unfold in the embrace of my beloved Smokies.

Chapter 2

DECORATION DAY DOIN'S

One of the most cherished of all high country traditions is the annual ritual known as Decoration Day or, in many cases, just Decoration. It combines piety, reverent remembrances of deceased family members, thorough cleaning of burying grounds, music that leans decisively in the direction of old-timey hymns such as "Rock of Ages" and "Amazing Grace," and some of the finest eating a body could want when the hour arrives for "dinner on the grounds." It is in a sense Memorial Day, albeit with a high country flair that makes Decoration Day distinctive.

Limited almost exclusively to the southern Appalachians and Ozarks, the Decoration Day tradition is particularly strong in the rural highland regions of North Carolina. So much is this the case that a noted folklore expert, Alan Jabbour, who for many years served as director of the Library of Congress's American Folklife Center, and his wife, Karen, have written a carefully researched book on the subject, *Decoration Day in the Mountains: Traditions of Cemetery Decoration in the Southern Appalachians.* While the book's coverage does not gee-haw completely with my own experiences and recollections of the event, the differences are mostly minor in nature. They speak more to the fact that almost every cemetery where the tradition endures has some special type of celebration or approach to Decoration Day than to any errors on the part of the authors.

The basic premises associated with Decoration Day include the following:

(1) Preserving linkage to the past, especially among families and tight-knit communities, by setting aside one day each year, almost always a Sunday, for the event. The preliminary work of sprucing up cemeteries by cleaning the grounds, raking or mounding graves, straightening or cleaning tombstones, filling in sunken graves, and the like usually occurs the previous day. The actual "decoration" (placing flowers on graves) takes place on Sunday.

(2) Paying respect to familial links by making the event a celebration replete with food, prayer, and song. Sometimes a church homecoming and Decoration Day are combined, and the same holds true for family reunions.

(3) Offering tribute to those who have gone before with fond recollections in the form of shared oral traditions, vintage photographs, and, increasingly in the last two or three decades, exchanges of genealogical information. These activities combine to provide interested parties with not only a somber yet joyous time but also greater familiarity with their family roots. Many gatherings will feature a gifted storyteller or two, and their offerings can evoke anything from solemn reflection to raucous laughter.

Sometimes, especially in the case of small rural churches, organization of the special day is undertaken by the pastor, deacons, or other church leaders. In other instances an extended family, group of families sharing a cemetery, or possibly an entire isolated community will be involved in planning the event. Often cemeteries where the Decoration Day tradition still holds sway provide year-round visual evidence of the function. This comes in the form of picnic tables (anything from simple sawhorse-and-plywood arrangements to elaborate wooden or concrete tables covered by a tin roof) located on an open, flat area adjacent to the cemetery. Similarly, there may well be a small shed where caretaking tools can be stored.

Timing for Decoration Day varies, although it normally takes place sometime in late spring or early summer. More often than not it is on Memorial Day (which always comes on the last Monday in May) or quite close to it on the calendar, but the two are not the same. Decoration Day was a widespread practice before the concept of Memorial Day came into being, and its primary purpose is to honor all those who are buried in a given cemetery. By way of contrast, Memorial Day involves decorating gravesites of deceased military personnel. It is sometimes colloquially known as Northern Decoration Day, an allusion to the practice having developed in the aftermath of the Civil War in connection with Union soldiers who died in the South. A few cemeteries actually hold more than one decoration event a year, usually in the spring and again in the fall, but this practice seems to be in rapid decline. For that matter, it is probably true that as we become an ever more urbanized society, the basic practice of Decoration Day as it has been known in the high country of the southern Appalachians is also on the wane.

Contemporary Decoration Days sometimes, though not always, involve placing small flags at the resting places of veterans, but more traditional tributes include live flowers (often wildflowers picked near the cemetery), handcrafted crepe paper flowers, lovingly knitted or crocheted flowers, or in modern times plastic ones readily available not only from florists but also from big box and craft stores. These are placed atop or alongside all graves in the cemetery.

Along with flowers (the literal "decorations"), other items emblematic of reverential memory might include removal of all vegetation from the grave mound, use of white stones or gravel to mark a site, or placement of tokens associated with an individual's life (for example, fishing lures at the grave of an avid angler or spent shells at that of a dedicated hunter). Then there is the long-standing tradition of planting flowers (daffodils, iris, grape hyacinth, rambling roses, spirea, day lilies, and yellowbells are old mountain favorites) beside the grave or marking it with ornamental evergreens such as boxwoods, arbor vitae, or yucca.

I personally find Decoration Day one of the most appealing of all high country traditions, even as I fear it will vanish before time's remorseless ravages in decades to come. The annual event offers a prime example of the importance of a favorite adage of historians: "You can't know where you are going if you don't know where you've been." Graveyards remind us of where we have been because they are the resting place of our families, a tangible link to our roots, and a testament to our abiding strength as mountain folks. They let us know, in the words of Thornton Wilder,

"There is a land of the living and a land of the dead and the bridge is love, the only survival, the only meaning." Those cemeteries, and their care, are our lasting link of love between these two lands . It is a linchpin of surpassing importance.

As was so often the case, Ben Franklin captured the very essence of the matter when he wrote: "Show me your cemeteries and I will tell you what kind of people you have." If one believed Horace Kephart and his treatment of mountain cemeteries in *Our Southern Highlanders,* we are a miserable failure as a people and a culture. Yet it must be remembered that Kephart's book was in many senses an extended exercise in stereotyping, written not so much to reflect reality but to sell preconceived notions of highland life to Northern readers. Especially in the revised and expanded edition of 1922, he wandered far from the truth in many areas, but nowhere was he farther astray, nowhere was his depiction of mountain people more shameful, than in his descriptions of graveyards: "The saddest spectacle in the mountains is the tiny burial-ground, without a headstone or headboard in it, all overgrown with weeds, and perhaps unfenced, with cattle grazing over the low mounds or sunken graves." That is patently untrue, as is his suggestion that mountain folk in general show "a remarkable lack of reverence for the dead."

Decoration Day offers a striking, richly praiseworthy statement to the contrary. So, for that matter, do individual markers and cemeteries across the Smokies, inside the Great Smoky Mountains National Park (GSMNP) and out. One would hope that future generations will continue to show just how wrong Kephart was. After all, this matter of honoring our forebears, one with roots reaching deep into the Appalachian past, is among our finest traditions. May it ever be so.

Chapter 3

MOTHER'S DAY

Mom has been gone some two decades now, yet seldom does a day pass when I'm not reminded of her. Usually it is some small, seemingly insignificant occurrence that brings back poignant memories of a woman whose outlook on life seemed to be one of surpassing sweetness and serenity. She was seldom frustrated, and the sole time I ever heard her use a four-letter word was in the immediate aftermath of having given her thumb a mighty whack with a hammer. Even then, she was so mortified at the "damn" that escaped her lips, it seemed that shame instantaneously replaced pain.

Years ago I shared a newspaper tribute to her with both my siblings, and each of them responded with their own recollections. My brother, Don, who shares my tendency to think of things from the perspective of closeness to the earth, reckoned that on Mother's Day he might wear a single white flower from wild strawberries in tribute to the woman and the scrumptious wonders she could work with wild (or tame) strawberries, a homemade pound cake so moist it glistened, and whipped cream. Of course his thinking along this line combined fond culinary memories with the old mountain tradition of wearing a rose (red if one's mother is living; white if she is deceased) on Mother's Day. He also harkened back to early childhood days listening to her sing in church and shared Alan Jackson's rendition of Mom's favorite hymn, the hauntingly beautiful "In the Garden."

My sister, Annette, for her part, rightly recalled just how loving and easygoing Mom was, never mind three sometimes tempestuous children and a husband who could, as is the wont of males in the Casada family in general, be difficult in terms of hardheadedness, almost cussed independence, and a deep-rooted "I'll do it my way" outlook on life. An excerpt from Annette's thoughts goes right to the essence of Momma's personality and perspective.

> When I think of Mom, the phrase "she loved them anyway" always stirs my brain. This phrase definitely held true with the love she held for Dad and us as we were not always an easy bunch to love with our independent, stubborn, and judgmental ways. More importantly, I think the phrase is representative of the way she viewed the world as she always seemed to find that little nugget of specialness in everyone. I have no idea what helped her develop into the positive, warm, loving adult she was, but somehow Momma was just about as pure of spirit as a human can be.

From my perspective, I think of Momma most often in terms of food. She was a splendid cook, and I never eat certain dishes, with fried chicken being at the top of the list, without her coming to mind. Another recurrent recollection is the manner in which she not only tolerated but actively encouraged my passion for the outdoors. Never mind how many times I came home muddy, soaking wet, or smelling of rank stink baits used for catfish, it was somehow all right. Occasions without number I befouled her pristine clean kitchen sink with guts from small game or feathers from upland birds, yet she always took matters in stride and smiled as she promised (and always delivered) a feast from earth's wild bounty. She greeted a gallon of blackberries, a mess of wild strawberries, or a creel of trout like manna from Heaven, and the wonders she wrought with wild game make me wish we had had deer in those youthful days.

Momma's younger years were tough. She lost her mother while an infant, was raised by relatives who, while solid, decent folks, weren't overly endowed with warmth and joy, and moved incessantly from one place to another throughout her childhood and adolescence. Rootlessness, along with endless packing and unpacking, eventually took a toll on her psyche. When she and my father married and bought a home not long before the

Japanese bombed Pearl Harbor, she told Daddy, "I never want to move again." For a period of well over fifty years, her wish was reality. The home they bought for $2,500 (putting $250 down and reducing the mortgage whenever possible, in addition to monthly payments of $25) was Mom's refuge until almost the end of her earthly days.

I have always envied her outlook on life. She found joy in the simplest things, remained eternally upbeat, showed kindness in some way every day, looked upon work as a blessing rather than a burden, and retained a bit of the childhood innocence she never had the opportunity to enjoy fully in her youth. One indication of the latter aspect of her perspective was the fact that none of her children, and later her grandchildren, derived more delight from the Christmas season and special occasions than Mom. When she opened a present, got a surprise, blew out the candles on a birthday cake, or enjoyed something as simple as an ice cream cone, there was invariably a priceless brightness in her eyes and beaming smile on her face.

Of all my warm and wonderful recollections of Mom, though, arguably the fondest ones focus on her role in my development as a sportsman. To my knowledge Momma never hunted, and although she loved to fish she would have been the first to acknowledge she was an inept angler. On the other hand she relished the end results of a successful day afield after small game or a productive fishing trip, and thoughts of the culinary wonders she could work on rabbits, squirrels, quail, or trout still lay a craving on me.

She was a marvelous cook and a living, loving example of the old moun- tain adage "Make do with what you've got." Mom scoffed at the concept of catch-and-release fishing. "You catch them," she would say, "and I'll release them—straight to hot grease." To her, the idea of catching a fish only to return it to the water was absolutely ludicrous. A standard exchange between us was a joke connected with my countless forays after trout. As I headed out the door I'd ask, "Do you want me to keep a mess?" To her that was a question that bordered on idiocy. "You're going fishing, aren't you? And aren't trout mighty fine on the table? Why in the world wouldn't you bring a mess home?"

Momma's tolerance level for a sportsman husband and two similarly in- clined sons was both admirable and incredibly high. She took early risings, muddy boots, tattered and torn clothing, squirrels, rabbits, quail, and trout cleaned in her kitchen sink, incessant talk of the outdoors, the occasional responsibility for feeding our hunting dogs, and much more in stride.

On a strictly personal level, she was an endless source of support and active encouragement of my boyhood hunting and fishing adventures. When Lady Luck saw fit to cast a beam of good fortune on my solitary efforts afield or astream, Mom would brag about my bulging creel or weighty game bag in a fashion that filled a youngster with inexpressible pride. Moreover, when relatives or friends stopped by for a visit, she would often make comments such as "You should have seen that fine mess of trout Jim caught yesterday." To an adolescent such praise brought pleasure that left my spirits buoyed for the rest of the day.

On countless occasions Momma drove me to a nearby trout stream or squirrel woods while Daddy ate his lunch alone. He had a thirty-minute break from work for the midday meal, and since we only had one car, the range of her chauffeuring service was limited to distances that could be covered in no more than ten to twelve minutes. Sometimes she would also meet me at day's end, although more often than not I walked home in the gloaming.

While it never occurred to me as a youngster, one particular example of Mom's love spoke volumes about trust, tolerance, and just how different that world of the 1950s was from the one we live in today. From the time I was eleven or twelve years of age, my parents allowed me to hunt and fish on my own or in company with friends of a similar age. Some of those outings involved several nights of camping in the remote backcountry of the Smokies, and most of the fishing meant wading in rushing high country streams. There had to have been some anxiety, especially when I got home a bit later than usual, but there was also recognition of the need for youthful freedom and understanding that adolescents, while requiring guidance, also had to find their own way.

Long after I was grown and gone from home Mom continued to be interested in my sporting activities. There was never a visit and seldom a phone call when she didn't ask about whether I'd been hunting or fishing and what sort of luck I'd experienced. Those weren't idle inquiries. She genuinely cared, and right up to her death I could do her no finer favor, bring her no greater pleasure, than to show up with a limit of wild trout cleaned and ready for the frying pan.

Doubtless many of you had mothers who blessed you in similar fashion. If so, on Mother's Day, the one day of the year specifically devoted to the marvels and mystique of motherhood, you can join me in looking back with loving longing to the magic a mother brought to a mountain lad's life.

Chapter 4

FATHER'S DAY

Traditionally Father's Day has not garnered a great deal of attention in the Smokies or anywhere in the southern Appalachians. With the notable exception of Tipper Pressley's Blind Pig & the Acorn blog, which has featured multiple entries on the subject over the years, I don't recall ever reading much about this holiday. Sydney Saylor Farr, in *My Appalachia: A Memoir,* makes passing mention of it, but it's more in the form of a family birth connected to the day than as a time for particular celebration. This should not in any way suggest a lack of respect for fathers. After all, I sometimes heard the term "grand sire" used when I was a boy, and the man of the house—at least in my home and in those of my youthful friends—was considered someone of surpassing importance.

For me, though, Father's Day offers an incomparable opportunity to indulge in the pleasures of nostalgia. It enables me to go longingly back to days of childhood, resurrect special moments spent with Daddy, and wonder how well I've succeeded in passing some of the magic of those experiences to my offspring.

For many of my generation, reflections of their fathers come through a distorting mirror. That's because those men belonged to the aptly named "Greatest Generation." Far too many went off to war and never came home to young children who barely remembered them or didn't know them at all. Even more men who saw duty in World War II returned from that conflict touched, tormented, and in some cases forever changed. Post-traumatic stress disorder may be of relatively recent vintage when it comes to the verbiage, but there's nothing new about psychological and other impacts of warfare on soldiers.

My father, although of the proper age, did not see service in World War II. He was employed at a plant, Carolina Wood Turning Company, which was normally dedicated to furniture production. During the war, though, the company utilized all its machinery and the labor of its workforce to production of two wooden products that America's leading military minds considered essential to the war effort: ammunition racks and flare bodies. Apparently the latter of these two items was extraordinarily difficult to produce with the required degree of precision, and the plant where Daddy worked somehow had figured out the process when others couldn't. As a result Daddy, along with a whole bunch of his fellow workers, was considered a greater asset in production on the home front than as just another soldier on the Western Front.

While he worked long, hard hours, I now know that I was fortunate in having a father who was always home, always spent the night under the same roof I did, and who found time whenever possible to serve as a hunting and fishing mentor. He shaped my life on many fronts, with assiduous devotion to academic achievement and becoming an upstanding citizen being well to the forefront. But from the standpoint of enduring meaning and lifelong passion, little mattered more than what he did in terms of making me a sportsman.

The leisure hours of my boyhood growing up in the heart of North Carolina's Great Smokies was, to use a description Daddy employed with pure delight late in his life, a "marvelously misspent" one. Whenever he had a suitable audience he would assume a bemused look and suggest, "It's just not right for a boy of mine to grow up hunting and fishing, tell lies about his experiences in print, and actually get paid to go all over the place while doing so." He wasn't, for a moment, suggesting that I was in any sense an especially wayward youngster or one particularly given to misbehavior. Rather, he was reflecting on the fact that I spent every possible free moment hunting and fishing and that when it came to work, my primary goal invariably involved earning enough money to buy a few trout flies or a handful of shotgun shells.

As for continuation of boyhood ways, I rather suspect he was a bit jealous of the fact that I hunted and fished all over the United States and in several foreign countries. Although I never thought to ask, I'm pretty sure the totality of his sporting experiences never extended outside the high country of North Carolina and Tennessee. He never hunted deer, had only a single experience with wild turkeys, spent little if any time on largemouth bass, and was a sportsman of limited horizons. But he intimately understood squirrel hunting and the manner in which it grooms a woodsman, was an expert in training beagles for rabbit hunting, and was a first-rate wingshot whenever quail or grouse took to the air.

He loved fly fishing for mountain trout. For him fly fishing meant a dry fly. He viewed nymphing with disdain and streamer fishing as something not far removed from piscatorial heresy. Daddy was a purist, unlike the lowly sinner he sired, but that's really beside the point. He blessed me with a bonanza no bank account could have provided. The solitude of sparkling trout streams, something he loved from the depths of his innermost being, was shared from the time I was big enough to tag along.

In that regard his patience surely rivaled that of the Bible's Job. Far before I was really ready for it, he passed along to me a hand-me-down South Bend fly rod made of Tonkin cane. He had that opportunity thanks to the men he supervised at Carolina Wood Turning Company presenting him with a new one. Once a year or so I use it as a reminder of those days he let me tag along on his after-work forays to Deep Creek (he spent the most meaningful days of his own youth growing up on Juney Whank Branch, one of its feeders, in pre-GSMNP days) or the nearby Nantahala River.

Thanks to the fact there was no way I could wade powerful and fast-moving waters, for the first few years of my angling apprenticeship Daddy had to keep me in sight at all times. Such trips curtailed his opportunities to a considerable degree. Yet he readily answered a stream of questions from me that flowed about as rapidly as the creek he was fishing, occasionally let me slip a net underneath a trout he had hooked, taught me a basic knowledge of knots, and in time tolerated my periodic raids on flies in his vest. Doubtless when, at the age of nine, I finally managed to hook and land a small rainbow trout, he breathed a sigh of relief while inwardly thinking, "At long last, he caught one."

As has already been noted, within three years of that momentous experience he joined Mom in a mutual pact that allowed me to venture afield or astream on my own. That gift of trust wasn't blind faith or neglect. It was just mountain common sense allowing me to make mistakes, mature, and spread my wings as I made the long, difficult transition to adulthood. It was without question one of the greatest gifts my parents gave me.

Although we never made a huge deal of Father's Day in our family, after the passage of a full six decades, one event associated with it clings to me with the tenacity of beggar-lice and is about as welcome as a bunch of cockleburs. Beginning at the age of ten or eleven, my burning ambition was to outrun Daddy in a 100-yard race. For some reason we usually held those competitions on Father's Day or the Saturday immediately preceding it.

While he was well into his forties by that time, Daddy had been a fine athlete, continued playing high-level fast-pitch softball a decade after most men put their gloves in a closet, and was lean and lithe as a Smokies sapling. On the other hand, I was small and matured late, weighing only 105 pounds and standing 5'5" at the end of my junior year in high school. Those interacting considerations translated into the harsh reality of Daddy being able to outrun me in every race we ever had. When the time finally arrived when I thought this would be my grand day, a triumphant victory, he also outsmarted me in singular fashion.

That came at the age of seventeen. I had finally reached a point where it was likely I would be able to win our annual race, and as was all too often the case in my youth, I let my mouth run way ahead of good sense. As Father's Day approached I rather impertinently informed Daddy that I was going to leave him in the dust in our upcoming race. Unexpectedly and to my utter dismay, Daddy chose that time to retire from the foot-racing scene, summarily announcing: "I'm getting too old for such foolishness." Although I didn't fully realize as much at the time, that of course translated to the reality of him suspecting I might actually be able to outpace him. Our racing days had come to an end, although periodically right to the end of his 101 earthly years he would grin and say, "You never outran me."

During the same period of adolescence, though, there was one area of sporting activity where my abilities surpassed him. That was in fly fishing for trout. While we didn't exactly compete on angling outings, at day's end there was always comparison of the fish in our respective creels. About the same time Daddy decided to cease our running competitions, I had reached a level of angling ability where my catch was consistently better than his.

He would look at our respective limits of trout, shake his head as if in disbelief, and offer comments such as "You are the luckiest fisherman

I know." In one sense he was certainly right. The gift he gave through molding and making me a fly fisherman was bounty beyond compare.

Daddy wasn't much given to praise of any kind, but when, late in his life, I wrote and published *Fly Fishing in the Great Smoky Mountains National Park: An Insider's Guide to a Pursuit of Passion,* the work gave him a great deal of delight. It was dedicated to him and my brother, and Daddy always kept his copy close at hand. On multiple occasions when someone was visiting, he would find a reason to point it out and, holding it in his hand, say, "Now there's a book I really like." Ever sparing with praise, he was in effect offering me his highest accolades.

When it came to hunting, my father's mentoring was flawless. He introduced me to the basic skills associated with being a good woodsman—patience, persistence, the ability to read signs, sound marksmanship, and stealth—through squirrel hunting. When my legs were long enough to at least come close to keeping up, he began to allow me to tag along on rabbit hunts.

These were group affairs, usually involving a few adults, a pack of beagles, and, as I moved into my teenage years, my buddies. Never once did all those honorary uncles and teachers who were Dad's hunting partners treat me with anything but the utmost kindness and respect. There was no foul language and no drinking—just plenty of camaraderie, careful guidance on matters such as gun safety and respect for the land, and a whole lot of grand times.

We ate what we killed or caught, and lessons in proper utilization of game and fish, not to mention the "privilege" of cleaning the same, were an ongoing part of my outdoors education. Every outing, no matter its nature, was something to be eagerly anticipated, and big events, such as camping trips or holiday hunts, found me almost obsessed.

Daddy was the one who planted those seeds of excitement and then carefully cultivated them as I progressed toward maturity. He made the outdoors an integral and endlessly joyful part of my life. In that regard he shared thoughts that the great sporting scribe Archibald Rutledge offered in a timeless story entitled "Why I Taught My Boys to Be Hunters." Rutledge was of the fixed "conviction that to be a sportsman is a mighty long step in the direction of being a man." He also firmly believed "that if more fathers were woodsmen, and would teach their sons to be likewise, most of the so-called father-and-son problems would vanish."

Dad would have agreed wholeheartedly, and he practiced in person what Rutledge preached in print. A consummate woodsman, he loomed large in helping me not only in becoming a man but in imbuing me with inner resources that have always served me well. He made me keenly mindful, as everyone who cherishes America's grand sporting tradition should be, of a duty, almost a sacred trust, to honor that heritage and pass it on unsullied to generations to come. It was a gift of love and one that comes to mind with considerable regularity and always on Father's Day. Every fish I've ever caught, every backpacking trip taken in the high country, and every step trodden along hardwood ridges in search of wary bushytails is a part of his legacy.

Chapter 5

FAMILY REUNIONS

I was a young adult before Casadas began having gatherings they actually called reunions, but every summer from my earliest recollections of boyhood onward featured an informal assemblage involving the immediate family— my paternal grandparents, living aunts and uncles, and first cousins. One of my aunts, Jessie, the initial member of the family to obtain a college degree, lived in Chicago. For me, and probably to a considerable degree even for the adults, that seemed an impossibly remote distance from the mountains.

Her life had been steeped in sorrow after a commercial plane crash took her husband's life and left Aunt Jessie and an infant daughter, Carolyn, bereft. Being in a faraway big city, one which must have in some ways seemed as alien to a woman raised on a small mountain farm lying back of beyond as the Smokies would have been to a lifelong resident of Manhattan, had to be gut-wrenching on a daily basis. Each summer the strings tying Aunt Jessie's heart to the place of her roots pulled her back to the highlands that once had been her homeland. For two or three glorious weeks she and Carolyn would exchange the bustling world of Studs Terkel and Carl Sandburg (who chose to spend his final years in the North Carolina mountains) for simpler, slower ways of the Smokies. The image of Aunt

Jessie indelibly implanted in my mind is of a woman with a serene smile so ethereal it never quite managed to mask her abiding sorrow.

Their annual sojourn provided the perfect occasion for a family gathering, and at some point during Aunt Jessie and Carolyn's visit Aunt Annie and Uncle Fred would drive up from their Georgia home for a long weekend. All other surviving members of the immediate family lived locally except Aunt Jura, something of an outlier in an otherwise close, devoted collection of siblings. Aunt Jura was a haughty woman with a life shrouded in mystery. Her first marriage ended in divorce while a second was apparently a short-lived disaster. Grandma and Grandpa, with considerable help from Aunt Jura's siblings, actually assumed much of the responsibility for raising her two children. Her presence at these summer gatherings of the clan was unpredictable until she retired from some type of government service in Washington, DC. But everyone else in the family—Aunt Emma and Uncle Frank, Uncle Hall and Aunt Hildred, Momma and Daddy, and assorted cousins—would get together for a time of renewal with those who had left the Smokies. It was not until many years later that there would be a more formalized Casada family reunion, with the ancestral link being descendants of Grandpa Joe's father, William Ambrose Casada.

Other than fellowship and sharing of fond memories, the focal point of these early family assemblies was food. As was also the case at Thanksgiving and Christmas, Grandma Minnie played the lead role in this elaborate culinary drama, but the feasts that I remember with great fondness had multiple stars. All the womenfolk pitched in, helping in the kitchen, cooking their own specialties, keeping rambunctious children and their fathers from getting from underfoot, and generally laying the groundwork for a sumptuous repast.

Of course the men, at least those living locally, played bit roles. All raised large gardens and took justifiable pride in what their plots produced. Most if not all vegetable dishes would be things they had grown, and the meat du jour was always yard bird. Those chickens, and it took several fryers to satisfy the horde's hunger, would come straight from the lot not 100 yards from where we ate. Each spring Grandpa's children bought chicks for him to raise. Some were destined to become laying hens, but many more went from free-range status to the frying pan on special occasions such as this one. The women may have prepared the food, but the men provided it. That was the Smokies way.

Eventually those gatherings of the immediate family gave way to an annual event involving my paternal great-grandfather, William Ambrose Casada. The first was hosted at the home of my Uncle Hall and Aunt Hildred, and in ensuing years reunions were held at various locations across far southwestern North Carolina. That was where most of William's children ended up as they continued the southward trek, like so many others, down the ancient spine of the Appalachians. Today almost all of the third generation descended from him are deceased, and I may well be the senior member of the fourth generation bearing the name Casada. Whatever the case, with deaths of the third generation at an ever-increasing pace at the end of the last century and in the first decade of this one, and notwithstanding intense interest on the part of a few dedicated genealogists, interest in family links stretching back to the nineteenth century has gradually declined.

Quite the opposite is true with the descendants of Grandpa Joe. With a couple of exceptions, his grandchildren, great-grandchildren, and great-great-grandchildren have retained a keen interest in a past that remains tangible, at least for the oldest of us. My brother, Don, continues to unearth family links at an astounding pace, and over time a clear pattern has emerged. Through one or the other of our parents and their families, we are distant cousins to an amazing number of folks living in and around the Smokies. I strongly suspect there is nothing unusual about that pattern.

Most of the immediate family, that is to say my brother and sister, the former's children and grandchildren, and all but one first cousin who is likely still alive but seems untraceable, not only stay in touch but are reasonably close. We're dispersed across the country—from Michigan to Florida, from North Carolina to California, with Illinois, Georgia, and Tennessee thrown into the mix. Thanks to the ease of phone calls, e-mail, and for others who possess appreciably more savvy on the technological front than this hopeless troglodyte even Skype, texting, iPhones, and Facebook enter the picture. We communicate with some frequency. I personally regret the near-total loss of the wonderful world of letter writing, but I reckon I'll just have to "man up" and accept change no matter how much I detest it.

Thanks to that ongoing closeness, the simple act of "staying in touch," I was privileged to be a part of one of the more deeply moving experiences of my life. After years of wandering in the dark wilderness of dementia at the end of a life well lived, in 2004 Aunt Jessie died in her adopted homeland of Illinois. In the years following her demise, her daughter Carolyn indicated a strong desire to return once more to her mother's geographical roots and a reunion with the region that had been an integral part of her childhood summers.

She was especially interested in bushwhacking to the place where her mother had been born in 1915, a hardscrabble farm high up on Juney Whank Branch in the GSMNP. My brother and I knew the site, which lies a country mile and then some from the nearest trail access, quite well. Both of us hiked there numerous times in the company of our father during his retirement years and, once he became too feeble, continued to do so periodically on our own. Carolyn had heard our stories of the remote homestead along with tales told by her mother and various aunts and uncles who recalled childhood days of a Smokies life, the kind of existence that was commonplace for those whom Horace Kephart shamefully degraded as "branch water people" of the early 1900s.

Those tales embraced more than a fair share of terror and tragedy. Not long after Aunt Jessie's birth, one of her siblings, Hattie, died. Poisonous snakes were a constant threat in warm weather. Among the serpent stories was one of a copperhead dropping from rafters into a kitchen dishpan and another where Grandma Minnie returned to the house and found a snake between her and children she had left playing on the floor. In the first instance Grandma addressed the situation with a stick of firewood while a well-placed whack with a hoe ended the second threat. Encounters with copperheads and rattlesnakes, not to mention nonvenomous snakes, were commonplace in the fields and woods surrounding the house.

Life was incredibly hard, but there were plenty of bright moments for infant Jessie and her family. Births of a pair of siblings would soon follow, and she had older brothers and sisters to play with and care for her. For at least one of those siblings, my father, his boyhood days high up in the Juney Whank hollow ranked among the most meaningful ones of his life. Time and again in his later years Daddy, whose mind remained razor sharp right up to his death at the age of 101, would look back with fond longing to Juney Whank Branch and commonplace yet compelling events of his youth—sneaking drinks of cold buttermilk from the spring house, the exploits of a dog named Old Sprat who was pure poison on snakes after a bite from one almost killed him, building dams in the branch and hectic flight when one of those youthful engineering projects flooded a yellow jacket nest, yelling down the ridge to friends making the long walk to school, lunches consisting of items such as cornbread and cane syrup or cold sweet potatoes carried to school in a tin bucket, the routine chores of a farming life, and much more.

Recollections of that type formed a fond backdrop when, in the early spring of 2014, a decade after Aunt Jessie's death and just shy of a century since her birth, ten of us gathered to visit the place where she drew her first breath and where Daddy experienced the rites of passage that once formed integral parts of a mountain boyhood. All of Carolyn's family—her husband, daughter, and son along with the latter's girlfriend—were there together with my brother, his wife, and their oldest son, a local woman who is deeply interested in the region's history, and me. We set off up Juney Whank Falls under grim, gray clouds in a misting March rain that soon had us all soaked. As Don and I pointed out various types of plants and commented on surviving evidence of the long ago human presence, I thought to myself, "The skies are weeping in memory of Aunt Jessie."

By the time we reached the old Casada home place, once a bustling farm with neighbors above and below on the little branch, it was time for a break, and I rather suspect our Illinois guests were more than a bit foot weary and fatigued. We rested on logs near an old stone wall alongside japonica bushes and yellowbells, staunch survivors of flowering beauty attesting to long ago love of things that caught the eye. For me, at least, the emotions linked to our conversation about days of yore, reviving a sense of oneness with that particular piece of land and a bygone family era, were palpable and quietly pleasing. Little did I know they were but a peaceful prelude to a crescendo of sensations.

My brother had spotted a lone bloodroot bloom, doubtless encouraged to flaunt its snowy whiteness early thanks to being situated on a south-facing bank that gathered all the warmth that spring sun can offer, and pointed it out to Carolyn. She walked over to that lovely harbinger of abundant wildflower wonder, the first hint of what lay in store during greening-up days to come, and knelt reverentially. While on her knees she took off her daypack, rummaged inside, and removed a small cardboard box adorned with a ribbon of blue. It carried her mother's ashes.

At that point perhaps it's best to let Carolyn pick up the story with a piece she wrote about the experience on her blog, which carries the title "Ms. Crankypants." As a sidelight, that's about as inaccurate a description as I can imagine. Carolyn epitomizes many of her mother's finest characteristics—soft-spoken, easily given to smiling, instantly likeable, and generally light years away from so much as a hint of crankiness.

Referring to the simple box and the understated ribbon with which it was wrapped, she wrote: "Anything more ornate would not have fit at all." She then commented on the manner in which my father, who had the unlikely given name of Commodore, often remarked about how widespread bloodroot was at the old home place. Then her commentary drew to its catch-in-the-throat conclusion. "I drew a circle around that flower with her ashes and told her that I'd brought a little bit of her back home."

Afterwards, subdued by the power and poignancy of the moment, we ate our sandwiches. They were washed down with sweet, icy cold draughts from the fine spring that had once been the anchor point for the Casada family. It furnished their drinking water, kept perishables such as milk and butter cool, and served for household uses such as cooking and washing.

It seemed to me a perfect reunion, one in which Aunt Jessie's remains returned to the place of her birth through the grace and goodness of her daughter. Carolyn was a child she so cherished and whom she raised with a depth of love and an ample ration of stubborn mountain pride. She dealt with life's sometimes cruel vicissitudes, residence in a land that at times surely seemed alien, and the surpassing sorrow of a lost spouse in stellar fashion. With her earthly journey at an end her daughter did her proud. She brought Aunt Jessie home to the Smokies of her roots, a place where the bloodroot blooms.

There was a postscript to this excursion, one which completed the circle with bittersweet benisons. As we wound our way back down tumbling Juney Whank Branch, near a spectacular waterfall marking its final plunge before being embraced by Deep Creek, the skies opened up. Although I said nothing to my fellow wayfarers and have not done so until this day, the heavy rain meant only one thing to me. The heavens had transitioned from soft weeping to a downpour of tears as their daughter came home for good.

At some point in those Juney Whank hours mixing jubilation and sorrow, Carolyn harkened back to those carefree summer days she spent at the home where our grandparents resided during the later years of their lives. By great good fortune I knew the nice couple who had bought and refurbished the house and made a phone call asking if it might be possible for a cousin who retained fond memories of times spent there more than a half century ago to make a brief visit. They readily agreed, and it was a blessing to tag along as Carolyn, step by step, room by room, traveled back to an important part of her childhood world. Her face glowed with happiness, reflecting a woman at peace with herself. She had attached a linchpin to her past that brought strength, surcease from lingering sorrow, and visible serenity. Her reunion with the Smokies, like that of her mother, had reached completeness.

Chapter 6

HOMECOMING

In one sense family reunions were homecomings, at least for those folks who had moved away from the mountains. Almost invariably such moves were stressful, but jobs that paid well and the security of predictable paychecks outweighed the hold of the highlands. What came to be known as the "Hillbilly Highway" (U.S. Route 23 North), immortalized by Dwight Yoakam in song, ran right through the Smokies. It took sons and daughters of the region to the automobile and other factories of the upper Midwest, and everyone will recall friends, classmates, or family members who traveled that one-way road to a distinctly different life. Others left to pursue military careers, attend college, or seek government jobs. Yet wherever their search for a better life took them, a part of them remained in the mountains. One of the strongest, most readily discernible characteristics of those born and raised in the high country is that throughout their lives, the ancient hills sent them a clarion call—"Come back, come back home."

While some seldom returned in person during their working years, their minds ceaselessly harkened back to the old home place. Then, with children grown and retirement at hand, a surprising number would find themselves once more in the Smokies. That has been an obvious theme in my own high school class reunions. These returns constituted a permanent kind of homecoming, one where the magnetism of the mountains eventually had exerted sway and had its way. Yet dreams of happily returning to one's homeland to finish out the golden years did little to satisfy the deep love of place in that gulf of time between youthful departure and eventually coming home. There was something instilled in Smokies souls from birth, a deeply ingrained need that could only be assuaged by being home. Too often there were heart-wrenching homecomings, those occasions without number of those who left in search of an elusive, often mystical "better life" making a final trip home to be buried in a family cemetery or one adjacent to the church of their youth.

Thankfully, in my experience and the region's lexicon, the word "homecoming" has always been most frequently associated with churches in a distinctly more winsome context. Homecomings to me always meant a time to celebrate one's raising, a testament to enduring Godliness, and recognition of the closely intertwined nature of faith and family.

Homecomings were usually, although not always, held in the summer. That was traditional vacation time. The weather lent itself to dinner on the grounds, side visits with family and old friends, cleaning cemeteries, and more. Sometimes there would even be a weeklong revival associated with homecoming. Such events seemed most frequently associated with small rural churches. Drive on winding country roads anywhere in the Smokies and you will pass numerous small churches with a cemetery to the side or behind the building. More often than not there will be a nearby area with a pavilion covered by a tin roof, perhaps some swings or other playground equipment for children, and either permanent picnic tables or a place for such tables to be placed. Those form the backdrops for traditional mountain homecomings.

My firsthand experiences with homecomings are limited to a special anniversary celebration at the Presbyterian church in Bryson City (this was a one-time event, and to my knowledge, that congregation has never had annual gatherings) along with those from early childhood. For the first few years of my functional memory, every summer found my family traveling to nearby Clay County for a homecoming connected with Momma's family. I have three distinct memories of those events. The first involved what seemed to a small boy an interminably long church service where the primary sources of interest for me were dirt daubers and wasps flying about in the rafters along with the syncopated fluttering of fans wielded by ladies seated in nearby pews. Still, those innocent distractions evidently kept my squirming to a manageable level, because I never underwent the humiliation (which some youngsters did) of being carried unceremoniously from the church. Usually when that happened, sounds of the particular offender would soon be heard through open windows as parental retribution in the form of a solid spanking was meted out.

My second recollection is far more pleasant. It involved long rows of cloth-covered tables. They were loaded with an orderly assembly of food for the gathered multitudes. Separate tables would be devoted, in strict order, to pickles, relishes, and what hi-falutin' society might style hors d'oeuvres (probably not one in ten of those in attendance would have recognized that description); fresh fruits and vegetables such as sliced cucumbers and tomatoes, the colorful appeal of slices of watermelon and cantaloupe, and possibly even an offering or two of store-bought stuff not found in the gardens of those in attendance; a panoply of cooked vegetables with dishes utilizing potatoes, squash, or green beans being predominant; the meat section with fried chicken taking pride of place but also offering country ham, beef stew, and chicken and dumplings; a bunch of bread with cathead biscuits in the ascendant; and finally, a selection of enough cakes, cookies, cobblers, and pies to sate even the most insatiable sweet tooth.

If the previous paragraph hasn't made it abundantly obvious that culinary aspects of homecoming loomed large in my mind, then I haven't gotten my point across. These were occasions when that wonderful word from mountain talk, "founder," came into play in significant fashion. Although this greedy-gut youngster always seemed capable of stuffing himself to the gills, amazingly there were never any repercussions beyond possible hints of a tummy ache on the way home. Momma rightly had little sympathy with such maladies, and she also had a ready restorative. She'd remind me of previous warnings not to overeat (green apples came readily to mind), then offer rumblings to the effect that a good "dose of soda" or a big spoon of milk of magnesia might be just the ticket. Such reminders had remarkable curative effects.

My final memory of those early gatherings involves a temporarily lost pair of shoes. After the preacher's long-winded reminder to everyone to get right with the Lord and after I had partaken of the bounty offered by a regiment of superb mountain cooks, my sister and I adjourned to a little branch running nearby for a spot of play. I could no more resist the allure of flowing water than I could turn down a slice of Grandma Minnie's stack cake, and in no time at all shoes and socks had been shed, Sunday-go-to-meeting britches had been rolled up, and a-wading I went.

Apparently when Momma discovered me splashing happily about, she was so irritated with the fact that I had done a splendid job of dirtying my best clothes and so busy hunting for a switch that she didn't notice my lack of footwear. We were actually in the car and on the road home before that particular matter came to light, and the repercussions to my rear (a repeat dose, no less) and my psyche were severe enough to remain with me from that day forward. Fortunately, a reversal of tracks, with Daddy mad as a wet hornet, revealed the shoes right where I had left them.

Chapter 7

REVIVALS

During my youth, revivals figured prominently in local churches. Coming in many forms and differing somewhat according to the denomination, they formed strong threads running through the fabric of mountain life. Those of the Baptist faith, the most widespread and probably the most contentious of the denominations with which I had appreciable familiarity, were passing fond of revivals. So were small, charismatic religions that dotted rural regions like spots on a geographical Dalmatian. But virtually all organized churches annually had some type of special outreach—maybe guest speakers, evening programs for adults at the same time as vacation Bible schools, or special prayer meetings. These weren't always called revivals, but their tone and intent followed certain common practices.

Summertime was the season for revivals. The weather lent itself to use of locations often linked to these special religious services—tent meetings, brush arbor gatherings, and the like. Also, for the faiths that practiced full immersion, souls saved during the warm months could forthwith be baptized. Many churches, especially those conveniently situated by a creek or river, had so-called baptizing holes where such ceremonies were conducted. Other congregations, lacking proximity to streams, operated in some type of cooperative agreement with churches that were blessed with ready access to water. Often a single long, gently sloping, suitably deep, and readily available baptismal pool would be utilized by a number of churches.

Several such locations that still witness baptisms from time to time are intimately familiar to me. One is located quite close to the famed Calhoun House on lower Hazel Creek while another, named the Reeves Hole after the family who once owned land there, is at Deep Creek Missionary Baptist Church. A few years back, when youthful converts were baptized in the former stream, the experience was made even more poignant by the manner in which committed allegiance to their roots joined hands with a statement and ceremony of faith.

Perhaps two personal notes connected with revivals and baptizing might be permitted at this point. One is the fact that many pools associated with baptism also are choice spots for the attention of trout fishermen. Over the course of my life as a fly fisherman, I have enjoyed literally scores of moments featuring tight lines and fine times in pools known as baptizing places. Second, one such site, the aforementioned Reeves Hole, was the place where I was baptized, never mind that most of my youth was spent in the bosom of the Presbyterian church and my undergraduate education took place at a Presbyterian-affiliated institution. That switch in denominations came as a result of controversy in the Baptist church that my parents had attended, a schism that was but one of literally dozens of examples where local congregations split over some theological issue or deeply held differences between members of the congregation. Often, rather than transferring to a new denomination or another congregation of the same faith, disaffected members would just form a new church.

Music was invariably a significant feature of revivals, with guest singers, quartets, or instrumentalists providing a draw that mountain folks, with their deeply ingrained love of all things musical, found irresistible. How I loved grand old gospel songs such as "Amazing Grace," "Shall We Gather at the River," and "Just as I Am," which were revival standards. But my favorites were a study in contrast—the quiet, contemplative lyrics of "In the Garden" (sung at my parents' funeral services) and the rousing, strident words and tune of "Battle Hymn of the Republic."

Although I was clearly, to use a dandy mountain description, left under the washtub when it came time to dole out musical talent, that in no way diminished my love of music. Whether it was associated with a revival, a square dance/clogging gathering at a local "stomping ground," or the grand custom of string pulling and singing at someone's home on Friday

34

nights or Sunday afternoons (Saturday nights were pretty much reserved for dances), I was an eager grinner at picking-and-grinning gatherings. Yet for all the joy such adventures in music provided, and for all that I still revel in listening to musically talented friends when they get together, when it came to stirring my innermost being, nothing ever quite rivaled the music connected with revival time at the little black church in my community.

As has generally been the case throughout the Smokies, the local African American community in Swain County was a small one. At its peak, and that came during my boyhood, it numbered about 150 individuals. Thanks to where my family lived, in one of a small group of white homes sandwiched between two slightly larger enclaves of houses where Swain County's entire black population resided, the church serving them, Morningside Baptist, was within easy walking distance.

A few years back I attended the funeral service of a woman, Beulah Suddreth, who was a pillar of that church throughout her adult years. The singing, eulogies, and general atmosphere of the service seemed to carry me back to youth on the same angel wings that transported Beulah heavenward. During the going home ceremony I described her in terms of being "as fine a woman as I've ever known" with heartfelt conviction. It was a deeply moving service, one in which racial divides were for a time completely forgotten. Realization of that fact dawned when voices from the group of mourners, all but a dozen or so of them black, greeted both my tribute to Beulah and that tendered by my brother with heartfelt utterances of "amen" or "tell it brother, tell the truth." I have no idea whether the thought occurred to any of the other mourners who were present, but to me the whole atmosphere formed telling testament to the spirit of the woman being memorialized and the manner in which her love embraced folks with total disregard for their skin pigmentation.

That deeply moving experience in turn transported me back more than a half century to a place, close outside a church window open to the cool evening air after a hot summer day, where I was a surreptitious participant in an old-fashioned Negro revival. From my hiding place I could listen to the singing, occasional shouts of religious passion, and the scary sermons of ministers who made fire and brimstone all too real for an impressionable youngster. I heard the seamless rhythm of black voices lifted in praise, was carried along in the sweeping grandeur of sweet notes and timeless hymns of praise, and once more knew the elemental, emotionally packed fervor of African Americans at worship. The whole experience stirred my soul, and while I spoke from the heart in praising Beulah and all she had meant to our family, I somehow felt singularly inadequate before the combined power of those gathered to memorialize her and my mental images of a black revival from six decades earlier where she would have been one of those in attendance.

That was the kind of power and emotion I associate with revivals from my youth. They were filled with fervor, but anyone who ponders their wider meanings soon realizes that such gatherings represented faith combined with fellowship, a break from the ardors of summer labor, and an opportunity to give expression to staunchly held beliefs. Revivals still form a part of the mountain scene, as do faith-based gatherings such as the annual Singing in the Smokies events hosted by the Inspirations. Inexorably though, facing the tides of time and supposed triumphs of technology has changed the old-fashioned revivals I knew as a youngster. I'll leave it to someone far wiser than me to decide whether that change has been for the better, but for me the mere word "revival" will always evoke echoes of ringing voices, fans stirring the air, and sweat rolling down the brow of a preacher who had really gotten down to the serious business of preaching the gospel.

Chapter 8

THANKSGIVING

Most high country families, and certainly those whose roots run deep in the Smokies soil, have substantial food traditions associated with the Thanksgiving holiday. They may have other cherished practices linked to the day as well—a game of flag football, a rabbit hunt on the traditional opening day of the cottontail season, a hike to an old home place where ancestors lived prior to the creation of the GSMNP, or something similar. Whatever the case, it is a day not only for giving thanks but for reflection and warm remembrance.

For me, it is a day when nostalgia reigns supreme. Much of my thankfulness involves looking back to youth and early days of manhood while recalling family folkways associated with Thanksgiving. Many, although by no means all, of those cherished memories focus on our annual celebratory feast. They encompass not only menu items but also the means by which they were procured, methods of preparation, and the manner in which they were identified with the holiday.

Meats featured for mountain Thanksgivings offer a logical starting place when it comes to the foodstuffs that have always meant so much to me. Typically, at least up until the time I reached the age of twelve or so and Grandpa Joe stopped raising hogs, we enjoyed not one but two meat options. Hog killin' time normally occurred a week to ten days before Thanksgiving, although it was dependent on the weather (ideally a cold snap, with temperatures at dawn dipping below freezing, and better still, those conditions coming on a weekend). As a result, there might be fried tenderloin for breakfast. Served along with cathead biscuits, sawmill gravy, eggs, grits, and an impressive selection of sweeteners including sourwood honey, molasses, jelly, jam, and a commercial corn syrup known as Dixie Dew, there was fodder aplenty to start the day. If perchance hog killin' time that particular year had taken place earlier in the month, canned sausage or pink, moist, and indescribably delicious slices of home-cured country ham left from the previous fall would take the place of tenderloin. If that spread of Lucullan dimensions somehow didn't suffice, you could always count on Grandma Minnie having prepared a big bunch of fried apple pies. It made for a lavish and scrumptious breakfast.

On Thanksgiving the family ate only two meals—a hearty breakfast and the family feast in the afternoon. If one got peckish in the middle of the day, a state which was pretty much perpetual for greedy-gut teenagers such as yours truly, there was always a cold biscuit, some leftover cornbread, or fried pies. Along with a glass of milk they provided interim sustenance aplenty.

Although store-bought turkey replaced chicken once my paternal grandparents had become too old and feeble to raise their own meat, for many years the centerpiece on the festive holiday table was baked chicken. One chicken wouldn't suffice, thanks to an extended family of grandparents, aunts, uncles, and cousins assembling for a time of togetherness. Instead, there would be several chickens, guaranteeing not only plenty for everyone at Thanksgiving but the makings of soup, sandwiches, or chicken and dumplings in the days to come.

The manner in which Grandpa Joe procured the free-range chickens fascinated me, and I reveled in joining him in that process. He kept a goodly batch of laying hens throughout the year, and each spring, in addition to the chicks hatched by those hens, he expanded the flock with three or four dozen peeps. These were obtained at the local Farmers' Federation. These newcomers gradually disappeared over the course of the summer and early fall. Pullets, as young and tender frying-size chickens were known, provided the standard makin's for Sunday dinner. Our immediate family, and it was true of Grandma and Grandpa as well, adhered rigidly to lyrics from an old Bobby Bare tune with "chicken every Sunday, Lord, chicken every Sunday."

Fryers were dispatched the same way all chickens for the table were handled in that time and place—either by wringing their necks or chopping off their heads. Simply stated, there was no room for lollipop sentimentalism when it came to living close to the good earth. You understood the cycle of life and the necessity of death, and the latter was handled in a straightforward, no-nonsense manner.

The way chickens destined for Sunday fare or the Thanksgiving table met with the executioner (Grandpa) fascinated me. I understood where meat came from in a manner which probably nine out of ten of today's youngsters don't. I may not have been exactly bloodthirsty, but suggesting I took no interest in the dispatching of hogs, chickens, or, for that matter, wild game would be a decided misrepresentation of reality.

Grandpa staunchly maintained that lifting a hen or two from the roost at night, or worse still, chasing them all over the chicken lot in daylight hours until one was cornered, constituted bad business. "Ain't no one with a lick of sense going to get yard birds for the table that way," he would say. In his view the uproar associated with such practices put hens off their laying cycle, not to mention involving the expenditure of way too much human energy. Accordingly, Grandpa "fished" for his chickens, no matter whether they were summertime fryers or Thanksgiving baking hens.

He accomplished this utilizing an exceptionally long cane pole of the same sort he used while fishing. It rested atop two nails on an outer wall of the chicken house except when put to its intended purpose. The only real difference between his "chicken fishing" cane and the ones he used in the river to catch knottyheads and catfish was its length. It stretched out the better part of twenty feet. Attached to the small end of the pole was a short strand of the black nylon line of the kind commonly used with casting outfits, and tied to the line was a medium-sized fish hook.

Grandpa's use of this tool was both simple and effective. He first scattered a handful of scratch feed or bread crumbs in an open area of the chicken lot, then backed off, leaving the hens busily pecking away. At that juncture he then presented the hook, baited with a small bit of bread, to the chickens. This presentation was as precise and artful as a fly fishermen casting to a rising trout. That was because he always, at least when dealing with mature hens, had specific chickens in mind—old biddies that had been remiss in their egg-laying duties.

Once a hen swallowed the hook, she would be pulled in, squawking and flopping in indignant protest, as Grandpa progressed hand over hand from the butt of the pole to the end holding the chicken. He then sum-marily dispatched the hen by wringing her neck. If additional ones were required, as was the case for Thanksgiving and other large family gather-ings, they would be caught by repeating the process. Then it was time to remove entrails, carefully setting aside the giblets for use with gravy and dressing, dunk the carcasses in scalding hot water, and pluck the birds. With the birds duly plucked and singed with a lighted twist of newspaper, they were turned over to Grandma Minnie. She would work her kitchen wizardry with the dressed birds, and the mere thought of getting into the middle of one of those baked hens, where miniature yolks of eggs in the making provided a special treat on Thanksgiving Day, still sets my salivary glands in overdrive.

Along with Thanksgiving's baked hens, there would be splendid arrays of vegetable side dishes including relishes and other provender. Standard fare include an aunt's ambrosia; brimming bowls of leatherbritches and October beans cooked with streaked meat; stewed greens with small cubes of turnips blended in; creamed corn; casseroles featuring sweet potatoes, green beans, and squash; mashed or scalloped potatoes; cranberry relish; a variety of pickles made from cucumbers, beets, watermelon rind, okra, and peaches; chowchow (for the leatherbritches and October beans); and hominy. Other than the baked chicken, though, two dishes stand out in my mind as truly emblematic of a mountain Thanksgiving.

One was the dressing that served as the standard accompaniment for the chicken and giblet gravy. It was prepared with cornbread made from stone-ground meal, but the key to its distinctiveness involved incorporation of plenty of chopped chestnuts. Alas, these weren't the American chestnuts my father and grandfather had known but Chinese chestnuts that grew on our place. To me the sweet, starchy nuts tasted delicious, but Grandpa would often say, with about as much emotion as this hickory-tough old man ever displayed, "They are good, but they just ain't the same."

A half century has come and gone since those halcyon days of youthful Thanksgivings, but I still gather Chinese chestnuts from my own trees and save them for dressing. For most it might seem a minor or even meaningless gesture, but to me it represents continuation of a deeply meaningful family tradition. Dressing featuring chestnuts is a memory to cling to all my days.

The other item that had special appeal, then and now, was stack cake. It offered one example of many in which Grandma Minnie's kitchen skills came to the forefront. She always made her stack cakes using six or seven thin layers of cake interspersed with applesauce (or, on rare occasions, blackberry jam) prepared from fruit she had dried in late summer or early fall. The cake would be prepared three or four days in advance, and by the time Thanksgiving rolled around, sauce between the layers had soaked into the cake to produce a marriage of indescribably delicious taste. No matter how much I ate before the family moved from the main meal to dessert, there was always room left for a hefty slice of stack cake. Partly for diplomatic reasons but mostly because in those days my innards seemed capable of expansion in a fashion reminiscent of a timber rattler consuming what seemed impossibly large prey, for good measure a smaller slice of Mom's pumpkin chiffon pie would rest alongside my stack cake.

All of the above-named dishes, amplified by orderly ranks of biscuits, hot cornbread, rolls, and maybe some type of sliced tea cake ready at hand on a sideboard, would be on glorious display come Thanksgiving Day. Year after year the women folks worked their collective wonders and brought everything together to a fragrant, delectable finish. The bounty atop the big old dining room table and laden sideboards at my paternal grandparents' home was a joy to behold. When the time was at hand and all was in readiness, the entire family would gather around the food, linking hands in a sense of thankfulness and togetherness. Then in a voice so soft you had to strain to hear him, Grandpa Joe would bless the feast. He would allude to the harvest, express appreciation for health and another good crop year, and always conclude by encouraging everyone to eat their fill.

Rest assured I adhered to his closing suggestion with a degree of gustatory delight that must have been a source of amazement to my elders. Looking back, though, it is not only the wonderful food memories of those simpler days and simpler ways of long ago Novembers that warm my heart and fill me with thanksgiving. I now know that this was but one aspect of a Smoky Mountain boyhood filled with treasures beyond measure.

Chapter 9

OLD-TIME NATURAL CHRISTMAS

In today's world, obtaining the family Christmas tree involves nothing more than a stop at a store, viewing trees stacked side-by-side in a vacant lot, or retrieving an artificial tree from the attic. Real "adventure" in obtaining the family tree involves going to a Christmas tree farm and wandering amongst growing trees until one is spotted that strikes the fancy. Mind you, the Christmas tree industry has been a real economic boon for some mountain folks, but it marks a dramatic change from what was once common practice. During my boyhood virtually everyone cut their own tree, and often it involved an outing in which the entire family participated.

Our family search for the ideal tree, always a pine, began at Thanksgiving with the opening of the rabbit hunting season. My father and I would give every tree of the right size and promising shape a visual "once over," and those with considerable potential would be filed away in our minds as "possibles" come tree-cutting time. When the big day arrived, a Sunday afternoon about ten days to two weeks before Christmas, the whole family would pile in the car and head out to cut a tree. For us kids there was a sense of great excitement, and Momma, who enjoyed anything and everything connected with Christmas with all the eagerness, anticipation, and joy of an eight-year-old, fell right into the spirit of things.

Yet tree cutting was but one part of a wide-ranging Christmas decorating process, virtually all of which involved using materials from nature.
Taking this approach offered three distinct advantages. Decorations from
nature were lovely, cost nothing, and procuring and preparing them produced wonderful moments of family togetherness. I look back on those
bygone Yuletides with a great deal of longing. Perhaps indulgence in some
natural Christmas nostalgia will evoke similar fond memories for others or
inspire a contemporary approach to the season. With that in mind, here's a
whole host of suggestions for holiday decorating joy straight out of Smokies
days of yesteryear.

Mistletoe was a must, and it loomed large indeed in Mom's overall
decorating scheme. That in turn proved a boon for me, because I loved the
entire process involved in obtaining quantities of it sufficient to satisfy her
needs. In some places mistletoe grows low and can be gathered with ease.
Take a winter canoe trip down a low country river in either of the Caro-
linas and you'll see big bunches of the leathery green parasite, loaded with
waxy white berries, adorning one tree after another. It will be at a height
where you can ease a canoe under it and pick enough for a major outbreak
of kissing fever in no time at all.

In the high country of the Great Smokies, on the other hand, mistletoe
seems to be comparatively scarce, and invariably when you find an oak,
maple, or maybe a honey locust bedecked with a few clumps, they will be
way up in the top of the tree. However, far from being a cause for dismay
during my boyhood, that remoteness, scarcity, and inaccessibility presented
precisely the sort of challenge a teenager welcomed.

Basically, there were three ways to procure mistletoe. Occasionally it
was possible, provided one had sufficient agility and a virtual absence of
fear (or common sense) to climb a tree to obtain mistletoe. Such challenges,
especially the delicious hint of climbing danger, something which always
appeals to a teenage boy, made that approach to obtaining mistletoe more
interesting. A second method, more commonly employed for the simple
reason that finding a climbable mistletoe-bearing tree occurred infrequently,
was to throw rocks or sticks at the clumps of greenery. Sticks with some
heft and size to them were preferred for the simple reason they were far
more likely to produce satisfactory results than merely chunking donnicks.
They required too much accuracy, whereas a stick of some size cut a fairly
big swath as it flew through the air.

My favorite tactic, however, involved shooting the mistletoe out. A tightly choked shotgun would sometimes do the trick, although if the mistletoe was very high in a tree, even the most closely patterned shot strings would spread out enough to result in tatters of mistletoe rather than sizeable clumps. Moreover, should you be lucky enough to shoot out a fairly nice-sized piece, chances were it would have pellet holes all through the leaves.

On the other hand, a .22 rifle in the right hands was perfect. It required expert marksmanship to cut away a bunch of mistletoe right where it joined a tree limb, but that challenge was no small part of the fun. The "sport" became even more delightful if three or four boys were involved, each trying to outdo the other in demonstrating their shooting prowess.

My decidedly modest armory, which consisted of a single-barrel Savage Model 220A shotgun, a well-worn Daisy Red Ryder BB gun, and a slingshot, didn't run to the luxury of a .22 rimfire. However, a good buddy did own one, and he was quite happy for all of us to take turns shooting it so long as each of us sprung for our own ammunition. Since .22 long rifle loads cost only a penny each in those days (less if you bought a box of 100 or if several boys pooled resources to purchase a "brick" of 500), even mountain boys who were anything but flush could afford enough cartridges to have real fun.

Our normal mistletoe-gathering days came on a Sunday afternoon a week or two before Christmas. You couldn't hunt on Sunday and by that point in December one or more of our mothers would have mentioned needing some of this prime Yuletide decorating material. That was all the excuse we needed to head for the woods. Those of us—James Lee Sossamon, Frank Fry, Jackie Corbin, Bill Rolen, Bruce Parris, and others—who regularly formed the youthful portion of the rabbit-hunting brigade led by my father and Claude Gossett had already been keeping a keen eye out for mistletoe in much the same fashion as Daddy always sought an ideal Virginia pine for our family tree. Accordingly, we always knew where plenty of mistletoe was available.

When several of us got together, relying not only on James Lee's .22 but likely using his Jeep for transportation, it made for an afternoon of great fun. We would take shot about, tease one another about misses, brag about hits, and indulge in all sorts of verbal foolishness connected with thoughts of getting whatever girl happened to be the apple of our respective eyes at the time under some mistletoe.

I remember precious little in the way of positive developments in the latter context, but I do fondly recall Momma's pleasure and her special knack for making me feel good when I came home bearing mistletoe. She would make over the fresh greenery as if it were almost equivalent to gifts of the Magi, decorate it with red ribbon, and hang it at two or three likely places in the house. For a mountain boy of the 1950s it was an innocent, intriguing, and flat-out joyful experience.

Along with a plentitude of mistletoe, Mom always wanted a few two- or three-foot long clippings from a honey locust tree. She disarmed the plentiful thorns by tipping each of them with a colorful gum drop, thereby making an unusual, attractive decoration. If a few of the gum drops mysteriously vanished thanks to the depredations of youngsters with a sweet tooth, Mom quietly replaced them and, in keeping with the spirit of the season, never uttered a word about missing candy.

Wreathes and table centerpieces made from natural materials such as hazelnuts still in the husk; cones from hemlocks, white pines, and other types of evergreens; sweet gum balls; sycamore balls; milkweed pods; old wasp nests; small bird nests, and the like were standard decorative features of Christmas. So were wreaths made from grape vines and then interlaced with evergreens or sprigs of holly. The sycamore and sweet gum balls could also be dipped in a flour and water mixture and then dried to give them the appearance of miniature snowballs. They could also be painted silver or gold. These carefully crafted items gave Momma a great deal of pleasure, always drew favorable comments from visitors, and added appreciably to the overall festiveness of our house at holiday time.

Another approach to similar decorations focused exclusively on nuts— hazelnuts, black walnuts, hickory nuts, acorns, butternuts, and chinquapins. For visual variation, Mom always included some hickory nuts and acorns still in partially opened hulls.

Galax leaves were popular for wreathes, table decorations, wall hangings, and mantle adornment. During winter months, galax leaves turn wonderful hues of red, purple, maroon, and magenta along with their basic green. Leaves also have a noticeable sheen and keep well for a couple of weeks. Galax is so attractive that at one time hardy mountain folks, always looking for a way to earn a bit of cash money, would gather it for wreaths or to form in great clusters to sell to city folks. Just as those who gather ginseng were locally known as "sangers," those who pursued this seasonal work were styled "gallackers."

Holly is one of a handful of trees, with persimmon being another one, that comes in male and female forms. With its bright red berries, she-holly was always an important part of decorating for Christmas. It was fashioned into door hangings, used as edging around doors and windows, spread atop mantles, featured in decoration with candles, and more. Looking for a berry-laden tree was a standard sidelight to the search for a perfect Christmas tree in our family outing.

Cedar was another widely used evergreen, and cutting cedar branches, ideally adorned with plenty of the tree's small blue-green berries, to use with holly, pyracanthia, nandenia, bittersweet, or other berry-laden plants was another means of turning to nature at Christmas. Daddy would have no part of a cedar tree for use as our family tree. Although cedars often have ideal shapes, he maintained that dealing with them, given the way they stuck and pricked the skin, just wasn't worth the trouble. On the other hand, he readily acknowledged that using cedar for other decorative purposes brought a pleasing aroma to the house.

Running cedar (also known as ground cedar and by other names) likewise found its decorative place. This ground cover, found widely throughout the mountains, was easily gathered. It almost always occurred in large patches. Sometimes they covered a half acre or more.

Making garlands of popcorn for the family tree using popcorn we had grown, shucked, shelled, and popped was a favorite seasonal ritual. It provided double fun because some of the popper kernels would be salted and buttered. Thus you could snack while stringing popped kernels using a needle and strong sewing thread. Usually a large quantity of corn would be popped, and some would be blended with molasses to make popcorn balls. This was a marvelously messy process, and never did finger licking seem more enjoyable.

Sometimes inedible parts of game animals were fashioned into centerpieces for the festive holiday table. For example, deer sheds blended with greenery worked quite nicely in this regard, and a pair of wild turkey fans placed end-to-end made a nice oval atop which you could place she-holly or other berry-bearing greenery. Wall hangings featuring small deer sheds, turkey feathers, whitetail tails, grouse feathers, honey locust pods, and the like were also possible.

The foregoing offers but a sampling of items we used (not the deer- and turkey-related items, since both were extremely scarce in the Smokies of the mid-twentieth century, something which is today no longer the case) for holiday decoration. To the list could be added the limbs from white pines and hemlock which always figured prominently in the season, although thinking of the fate of the hemlock brings sadness to a season of gladness. One has to wonder if it is fated to go the way of the lordly American chestnut, which in its own right was an integral part of Christmas a century ago.

In yesteryear, as these approaches to decorating suggest, mountain folks turned straight to nature's rich bounty for much of their Christmas preparation. The end result was simple beauty and a seasonal connection with the outdoors and the good earth. That link was an integral part of mountain life throughout the year, and it was only logical and appropriate that it be incorporated into the celebration of Christmas.

Chapter 10

MOMMA AND THE SPIRIT
OF CHRISTMAS

If the spirit of Christmas embraces things such as love of family, togetherness, warm feelings, goodness, excitement, and faith, then Momma was the quintessence of that spirit. Many adjectives seem appropriate when describing her love of life in general as well as the Yuletide season in particular, but to me none is more fitting that the word "merry." She always had a sparkle in her eyes, breathless excitement for even the most ordinary of undertakings, and a constant joie de vivre. She was merriment personified.

Born in Clay County, she spent much of her youth far from her highland homeland. Her mother died when she was just beyond infancy, and her father apparently decided it would be best if relatives raised Momma. Her adoptive parents moved frequently, and it was always my impression that the resulting instability affected her a great deal. Certainly once she was back in the Smokies she never wanted to leave, and I heard her comment to that effect on many occasions: "There's no place like these mountains."

Although she never said much about it, and certainly the care and devotion she lavished on her adoptive parents in their later years would have led one to think otherwise, clearly warmth and love were scarce commodities in her childhood. Likewise, she never had much in the way of Christmas gifts as a youngster. This was evident in two ways—the frequency with which she mentioned an elderly man who had befriended her and given her a quilt at a point when her adoptive family was living in California and the pure delight Momma took in everything associated with Christmas right up until her death.

She loved the rituals of preparing for the season, especially decorating with materials from nature. Gifted with considerable crafting skills, at one time or another during her adulthood she made Cherokee-style baskets, knitted, crocheted, enjoyed macramé and appliqué, grew and rooted all sorts of indoor plants, prepared lovely flower arrangements, was a superb seamstress, and had a real knack for decorating. Never was the latter ability on fuller display than at Christmas. It might also be noted that Momma was exceptionally frugal, a combined product of upbringing and necessity, and all these hobbies saved money.

Momma was always involved in anything and everything connected to Christmas at Bryson City Presbyterian Church—filling pokes with stuff for young kids, working behind the scenes in connection with pageants, and volunteering in any way she could. Similarly, some of my earliest Christmas memories revolve around charitable endeavors in which she would do her part and then some to make sure there was some joy in the season for those who were less fortunate. Later on, although anything but a political creature, she didn't have much truck with food stamps and government support. But like many hardworking mountain folks Momma believed in helping those who were down and out. She always worked with her children to craft handmade Yuletide gifts for their teachers, rightly feeling that the personal effort had more meaning.

Then there was Christmas-related cooking, and as an endlessly hungry boy who still holds his own as a trencherman, that was of immense importance to me. Momma was a splendid cook, and one of our family's real losses was her compulsion, when Parkinson's disease afflicted her late in life, to throw away a great many things. Among the items lost to that well-intentioned but misguided mania to organize were hundreds of discarded recipes.

Fortunately though, she had already passed many of her favorite recipes on to my wife and other family members. Among those that survived were chestnut and cornbread dressing, orange slice cake, applesauce and black walnut cake, pumpkin chiffon pie, her special approach to preparing squirrel, cracklin' cornbread, Russian tea, popcorn balls made with molasses, fried pies, stack cake (handed down from Grandma Minnie), and candy.

However, if I had to pick out one dish in which her culinary skills shone brightest, it would not necessarily be associated with Yuletide.

She could fry chicken better than anyone I've ever known, and that included Grandma Minnie, who was an absolute wizard in the kitchen. I know how Momma did it. Each piece was dipped in egg and well coated with flour, then slow fried, followed by a session of sitting in a cast iron skillet in an oven on low heat. This was standard dinner fare on Sunday, and by the time we got home from church that big skillet full of chicken would have achieved crunchy, moist, and tender perfection. All of her children know the process and remember it well, but duplicating the end product to a degree that matched her fried chicken has always eluded us.

Momma took quiet pride in her cooking skills, and she loved to see her family and friends eat. Throughout my boyhood, she truly fed the multitudes in terms of setting the table for our friends. We never had a lot of money, but you could rest assured the Casada table was set with a precious plenty. There was never any issue with an extra place or two. It's a testament to Momma's generosity and hospitable nature that my friends ate with us far more than I ever ate with their families. We were at times almost a communal kitchen for neighborhood kids.

Speaking of kids, no starry-eyed youngster, no "Christmas will never come" mind-set, or the firmest of believers in Santa Claus has ever derived more sheer joy from receiving gifts than Momma. As much as she gave of herself, and she was tireless, totally unselfish in that regard, she loved to open presents. Curious as a cat or eager young child, for days before December 25 finally arrived she would pick up gifts bearing her name from under the tree, heft and maybe shake them a bit, and wonder out loud: "Now what that could be?" Similarly, I can hear her, decades later, saying with a mixture of disbelief and excitement when handed a gift: "Another one for me!" She was careful in opening presents, because after all, wrapping and ribbons could be recycled in the "waste not, want not" approach to everything which was her mantra. Still, it was easy to tell she would have loved to rip the paper asunder like a youngster.

Year after year, once all the presents had been opened, she would offer thoughts to the effect of "I can't believe how lucky I am," "I'm so thankful," and "This has to be the best Christmas ever." She may not have had much of anything that was "the best" as a child, but far from looking back with regret or bitterness, she brought an attitude of optimism, excitement, and simple goodness to the season of Christmas.

She enjoyed a good joke. There were always gag gifts in our family, and at times Momma would laugh until tears rolled when Daddy received something such as underwear adorned with images of Mickey Mouse or a Sammy Davis Jr. audio tape (Daddy absolutely detested the popular singer). Her laughter was infectious, and even though she was the butt of jokes more than a fair share of the time, it never troubled her.

A classic case came when on the Christmas, late in Momma's life, when my brother and sister-in-law gave her a box of dried beans labeled "Hillbilly Bubble Bath." As was her wont, Momma had shaken the nicely wrapped package a number of times prior to Christmas Day. The beans rattled around quite noisily, but she couldn't for the life of her come up with a thought as to what the decorative wrapping might hide. Such was her intense curiosity that she gently implored: "Can I open this box first?" When she did and the gag gift was exposed for all to see, there was a moment when, as her family convulsed in laughter, she didn't realize just what had happened. When the piece of mischief did dawn on Momma, her response was "Oh, shoot!" That was about as close to an oath as she ever came.

As a clan, Casadas have never been exactly gifted when it comes to diplomacy. All of us are wont to speak our piece in decidedly direct fashion, and if Momma hadn't been a moderating influence, goodness knows where her offspring might be. Daddy could be highly opinionated, and his father, Grandpa Joe, was the essence of mountain stubborn and "quare." Momma, on the other hand, always seemed to have just the right thought, action, or word when a soothing, smoothing touch was needed. She possessed a seemingly endless supply of dimes when a child did some extra work around the house, was always a soft touch when it came to providing a snack or special dish, and was game to try almost anything one of her children asked her to do. But of all the countless times she offered just the right gesture, a few words of praise, or maybe a little pat on the shoulder, the moment I remember most came at holiday time when the whole family was seated at the table.

My younger brother Don was probably sixteen or seventeen years of age, and all of us, including my wife of only a year or two, sat down to one of Momma's meals. Midway through the feast and from totally out of the blue, Don suddenly brought up a most unexpected subject. "I've come to a conclusion," he pronounced. "I was born by accident." It was undeniably true, since he came along a half generation after my sister and me, but no one had ever so much as dared hint at the matter. Silence reigned supreme for a seeming eternity in what has to rank as the finest example of a pregnant pause I have ever experienced. Then Momma offered the perfect response. "Yes, but you were the most wonderful accident I could ever imagine."

That way of thinking was at the core of Momma's being. She was completely unselfish, genuinely moved anytime something was done for her, loving in the sort of fashion that grows in meaning over time and given reflection, and the embodiment of everything associated with the true spirit of Christmas. No one loved the season more or brought more to it in terms of warmth and a giving heart. I was blessed by having her make Christmas truly special for me for almost six decades, and maybe offering some index to her innate sense of understanding what was meaningful to her children, grandchildren, great-grandchildren, and daughters-in-law forms a fitting way to conclude this rather lengthy excursion into Yuletides of yesteryear.

Many Christmases after her death we enjoyed a cake—most likely one from a recipe she provided—atop a Fostoria stand she gave to Ann (my wife). Also, at some point during the season I make a point of rereading some book she gave me, indicating her recognition of a budding bibliophile. She chose my first book, Zane Grey's *Spirit of the Border,* when I was nine years old. It still holds a place of pride on my bookshelves. My daughter will wear jewelry Momma passed down, my sister will recall them wrapping gifts together or sewing something for some family members, and I know my brother and his wife think of her every year when they fashion a cross using materials from the wilds of the Smokies. It is a practice of reverence and respect for the bounty of the land Momma would have adored.

Most of all, though, and it often happens at the oddest of moments and for reasons that transcend my ability to explain, I'll think of her. Doing so will bring temporary sadness, but it will soon give way to gladness and a smile. That's the way she would have wanted it, because Anna Lou Moore Casada was a woman and a mother who walked life's path as a shining embodiment of the spirit of Christmas.

Chapter 11

CHRISTMAS HEARTBREAK

In December 1916, hard times held the high country of the Smokies in a stranglehold. The *Lusitania* rested at the bottom of the Atlantic, our traditional allies in Europe were stalemated on the Western Front, and visionaries realized America's entry into World War I was in the offing. But the small boy living on the headwaters of Juney Whank Branch in a remote fastness of the Appalachians was blissfully unaware of ominous international affairs. Nor did he fully appreciate the near-desperate financial straits of his large family.

His father, while a willing worker, found jobs providing cash money elusive and transitory. Cutting acid wood, gathering chestnuts by the bushel for sale, digging ginseng roots, gallacking, and an occasional spate of hiring out were about the only types of endeavors where money changed hands. Almost everything else was on a barter system.

Such matters were beyond the lad's ken, but with Christmas approaching he did have a consuming desire for a single gift. Throughout spring, summer, and fall his father had periodically let him use what mountain men considered the ultimate tool—a pocket knife. His apprenticeship with the knife involved practical matters such as cutting up seed potatoes for planting and whittling wooden pegs to hold barn doors in place, but there had also been pure pleasures such as shaping a dogwood fork into a dandy slingshot and, with a bit of help, crafting a gee-haw whammy diddle.

To the boy's great delight, his father had also commented, more than once, "First thing you know you'll be ready for a knife." With those words and experiences firmly implanted in his youthful mind, he repeatedly expressed a single wish for a Christmas gift—a pocket knife. While his parents warned him money was tight and his expectations were unrealistic, those cautionary words were unheard.

He had worked hard, and though he knew from previous Yuletides not to expect too much, the boy thought surely a pocket knife was manageable. Come daylight on December 25, the boy, along with his numerous siblings, rushed to the fireplace area of their simple log home to check stockings their mother had lovingly knitted. Each stocking contained a single orange, mittens, or headwear she had made, a couple of apples, chestnuts and hazelnuts, and some hard candy.

The starry-eyed boy immediately noticed, right at the bottom of his stocking, a tell-tale bulge in the shape of a pocket knife. Eagerly he dug through the fruit, nuts, and candy to reach that item, only to have unbridled excitement give way to abject dismay. It was indeed a pocket knife of sorts—a piece of hard candy shaped and colored to resemble the real thing.

Heartbroken, he rushed from the room so no one would see tears rolling down his cheeks and hear his sobbing. That disappointed little boy was my father. Yet to his lasting credit, a testament to the toughness and resiliency of mountain character, his dismay did not result in lingering bitterness. Instead, he managed to turn that moment of abject sadness into enduring gladness.

First with his sons and subsequently with his grandsons, whenever Christmas rolled around Daddy made sure a knife of some type—first a quality pocket knife with two or three blades, then later fixed-blade hunting knives—appeared under the tree. He continued this practice for virtually all of his 101 earthly years, and one of the highlights of December family gatherings was hearing him relive that sad yet shaping moment from his youth.

"I never want my offspring to be without a good knife," he would say. "It's a companion that will serve you well in some way, every day, for all your years." Whenever one of us pulled out a pocket knife he had given us, Daddy's eyes lit up with sheer joy. He took immense pride in the Eagle

Scout rank attained by each of his grandsons and was delighted they had Boy Scout knives to complement those he gave them.

At his funeral service, we all carried knives he had given to us or that came from his own sizeable collection. Afterward, we bushwhacked to his boyhood home place on Juney Whank Branch, now well off trail and deep in the bosom of the GSMNP. There we shared memories, recalled his love of this formative place that figured so prominently in his boyhood, and toasted his memory with pure, sweet water from the spring that once served his family.

As I did so, I grasped a tangible link to the man—a knife embodying his spirit and memory. I suspect others did the same.

Part 2

SEASONS OF THE SMOKIES

One of the crowning glories of the Smokies revolves around its four distinctive seasons. Each has its special characteristics, appeal, and wonder. Of course there are negatives as well. Anyone who has suffered through a late February bout of cabin fever when day after day brings gray skies and cold rain understands the dourness that can creep into those of Scots-Irish descent. Their forebears came from a far northern land where winters were grim and light was thin. Likewise, those who have endured sweltering temperatures and high humidity during August's dog days readily understand why early Smokies settlers built their humble abodes in locations that afforded gentle breezes and shade from the stifling sun of summer. Yet seasonal irritants such as these soon pass, and when compared with the bluebird skies of Indian Summer or the loveliness of a still, chill winter day when rime ice coats the tops of distant peaks and it seems you can see forever, they seem almost meaningless. For every day that is dismal, each season in the Smokies offers days without number that make it a delight to be alive, surrounded by ancient hills and embraced by welcoming hollows.

Chapter 12

A LAND OF DELIGHTFUL VARIETY

Spring

Spring comes to the Smokies in fits and starts. White splashes of flowering service trees adorning an otherwise barren landscape serve as the first harbingers of earth's rebirth, and the knowing observer might want to mark them for a later visit. Serviceberries, with their mild flesh and seeds carrying a hint of the taste of almonds, can be a welcome delicacy come June. Soon signs of earth's reawakening appear everywhere. The white of dogwoods vies with the vivid lavender of redbuds for attention in the forest, and myriad wildflowers adorn the understory. Among them are wild iris, jack-in-the-pulpit, bluets, wake robins, violets, and the dozen or so species of trillium found in the region.

As the days gradually lengthen and the sun's beams slowly strengthen, April soon gives way to May, and there's no word that better describes that month than magical. It vies with October for the Smokies' finest month of the year. Perhaps that comes in part from the perspective of a lifelong fly fisherman, but anyone intimately familiar with mountains will likely concur to a considerable degree.

May, a month often described as "merry," brings frequent showers to the Smokies. These normally lack the intensity and heavenly pyrotechnics of summer rains, and to be a wandering wayfarer on some backwoods trail as gentle spring rain falls is to be a player in a special time and place. Gardens begin to thrive, and their bounty makes the brow-wiping labor of hoeing out weeds and plowing seemingly endless rows well worthwhile.

Summer

Gradually spring yields to summer, although in the Smokies you can never quite define, other than by the calendar, exactly when the transition takes place. Down at lower elevations, for example, wild strawberries, those scrumptious little red jewels that sometimes adorn old fields and trail edges, definitely belong to spring. On the other hand, at trailheads along the highest ridgelines leading down into headwaters, you will find the delectable morsels ripening in the heart of summer.

Still, whatever the elevation, summer has readily distinguishable hallmarks. Stream flows lessen, days lengthen, mornings are often overcast until close to noon, and late afternoon thunderstorms crop up with some regularity. The season also brings what, at least to those who cherish solitude, might be described as a people problem. In fairness, flatlanders are to no small degree the region's economic life blood, but there can be too much, way too much, of a good thing. If you have any doubts about this, try making your way through tube-toting hordes parading up and down lower Deep Creek on a July day, try to find an unoccupied Park backcountry campsite on a weekend, or gaze on the bumper-to-bumper flotillas of canoes, kayaks, and rafts on the Nantahala River.

Yet the dog days of August and early September, with the song of a thousand katydids reminding those who bother to heed the message that cooler weather lies not far off, carry promise of an end to the tourist invasion and relief from heat-induced torpor. Even on the most stifling of days there's pleasure to be found while roaming in the gloaming or daydreaming at dawn, two months hence, when leaves will be turning and skies such a brilliant blue they almost hurt one's eyes.

Fall

As a boy, some of my favorite reading focused on Robert Ruark's timeless tales of experiences along the North Carolina coast with his grandfather, whom he styled the "Old Man." These enduring stories first published in *Field and Stream* and later anthologized in *The Old Man and the Boy; The Old Man's Boy Grows Older;* and a collection I was privileged to edit and compile, *The Lost Classics of Robert Ruark*, rank among the finest material ever produced by an American sporting scribe. Even though the setting for them was at the other end of the Old North State, hundreds of miles from my highland homeland, there was much in the tales of a timeless partnership between a youngster and his mentor with which I readily identified. In particular, I shared a certain degree of the Old Man's disdain for what he called "Willies Off the Pickle Boat" and what longtime mountain locals sometimes style outlanders, sports, or less kindly, Floridiots.

It's not that xenophobia necessarily runs rampant in the Smokies. After all, tourists represent a vital and growing economic force, and even in my youth they showed up in such numbers that locals often took them into their homes during the week of July 4. Still, it's nice to take a break between Labor Day and color change with its accompanying hordes of "leaf peepers." Cluttered roads suddenly become uncrowded, school's back in session, backcountry trails are little traveled, and the pace of life is a bit slower. For me, that change to normalcy and the accompanying diminution of the human presence have always heralded the arrival of autumn. So it remains. To be sure, there are countless other harbingers as well—an invigorating briskness to the morning air, sumac bushes wearing shawls of scarlet, Indian paint brush and wild asters flaunting their flowers, occasional sightings of droves of wild turkeys, hungry trout, Joe Pye weed and ironweed in purple splendor, and the fulfillment of harvest time.

In some senses this is my favorite time of year. Nights are cool enough to make a sweater welcome for nighttime strolls and a decent sleeping bag a comfort in a backcountry campsite. On clear nights, particularly if a strong cool front has moved through in the past day or two, walking or even sleeping under the stars becomes a sensual experience. In the latter case, filled with a hearty evening meal that likely involved everything that isn't good for you and tasted absolutely wonderful when cooked over an open fire, you find yourself deliciously tired and full of good spirits. Sleep comes readily, although as consciousness fades you realize that these fall days are a closing time of sweetness before winter lays its icy hand on the land.

Winter

Winter in the Smokies can be problematic, ranging from bitter cold with rhododendron leaves curled up like Cuban cigars to sunny days with temperatures edging above the 50-degree mark that just beg for a jaunt outside. Weather can change with remarkable rapidity with clear skies at first light soon giving way to those festooned with mackerel scales and mare's tails. To the knowing eye, they herald driven snow flying crossways by night. That unpredictability can be irritating or invigorating, with everything depending on individual perspective.

Grandpa Joe tended to be philosophical about the vagaries of winter. If it was cold enough for needle ice to decorate plowed ground, for north-facing slopes to freeze hard, and for icicles to earmark every spring seep, he simply declared, "It's a good time for a body to be close to a fire." Let it warm up a bit, though, and he would be "out and about," as he liked to put it—maybe checking on the chickens, performing some winter chore such as pruning grape vines or apple trees, hunting squirrels, or setting out rabbit gums.

His approach to winter was a sound, sane one. Rather than grousing and griping, he'd tell tales. Instead of bemoaning the aches of age and arthritis that he occasionally described as "the miseries," he'd fix a batch of pepper tea (a strange, fiery brew prepared by parching dried hot pepper pods, then steeping them just as you would regular tea) and declare that it would keep disease and winter woes at bay. He savored fine mountain food at all seasons, but somehow winter, with the comfort of soups and stews, corn pones, and cabbage fixed a half dozen different ways, brought out the best in him. In short, Grandpa was an optimist when it came to his personal life, although he had a far less positive outlook on the world in general, and he was convinced winter was a time for contemplation. Give him a warm fire and a rocking chair, a Sears & Roebuck catalog, or an audience in the form of an adoring grandson, and he was as satisfied as a bear snoozing in its comfortable den.

"Winter," he would opine, "gives you time to meditate and meander," and that's precisely what he did in mind and body. He rested and reminisced, but he also planned and made projections for the future. He was in the winter of his years, but his spirits were those of spring. That's not a bad perspective for all of us, no matter our age.

Chapter 13

WEATHER WISDOM

Spring in the Smokies sports many faces or, as Grandpa Joe put it: "A fellow can't trust spring. It tends to be mighty fittified." A spell of balmy days with temperatures rising into the seventies in the afternoon will give way to cold rain, biting winds, and sometimes even frost or, at higher elevations, a skiff of snow. I still have chilly memories of a day in early May at the Bryson Place on Deep Creek, back when the GSMNP fishing season opened on the first weekend of that month rather than running throughout the year. Daybreak greeted our camping party with ice atop the water bucket.

The frost-free date, even at lower elevations, doesn't come until the end of April and there's always the possibility of a killing frost in early May. Old-timers in the mountains recognized the vagaries of spring weather and had highly descriptive terms connected with them. The ones with which I am most familiar and have heard most often are all linked to winter: Catbird Winter (sometimes referred to as Catbird Squall), Dogwood Winter, and Blackberry Winter.

These terms come from the first-rate observational skills of those who went before us. Weather figured far more prominently in the high country of yesteryear than it does today, thanks to the dramatically different lifestyles of our forebears. They lived in close harmony with the land and depended on it for existence. Accordingly, the ability to read signs, recognize weather patterns, and move in rhythm with the good earth was vital to their existence.

All the types of winter actually refer to cold spells after greening-up time is well under way. According to Grandpa Joe, who had a real knack for predicting the weather by reading signs, observing cloud patterns, and watching animal behavior, Catbird Squall coincided with the first springtime appearance of the fussy and highly vocal gray bird (their primary call sounds like the mewing of a cat, hence the name). After migrating to the Deep South or beyond in the winter, catbirds return to the mountains for mating in April. Whenever Grandpa sighted the first one he would comment: "Look for a cold spell in the next week or so, because now that the catbirds are here we're in for a spell of Catbird Winter."

In truth, Catbird Winter always seemed to me to come more or less simultaneously with Dogwood Winter, since the avian migrants normally arrived about the time dogwoods were in full flower. Grandpa, however, would have none of that, insisting that there were two distinct cold snaps. Whatever the case, predictably, year after year, there would be some chilly weather, often accompanied by a light frost (and sometimes a heavy one), when dogwood blooms were at their peak.

Blackberry Winter is the most frequently mentioned of the three springtime periods of cold as well as being the latest. Often it seems that winter has its final fling, a last chilly goodbye before the full magic of May spreads its warm, soothing spell on the high country. It falls when blackberries reach the reawakening stage and their blooms begin to show white. I know that once blackberries had bloomed in association with two or three days of cold, Grandpa always felt comfortable in setting out tomatoes and other plants susceptible to frost. "I've known it to frost once or twice in my life after Blackberry Winter," he would say, "but a body can feel pretty comfortable putting out tender stuff once that cold snap has come and gone."

There's even an old song with the words "Go away, go away, Blackberry Winter" in the chorus. Of course I have always thought the line should be "Blow away, blow away, Blackberry Winter," because invariably strong winds that typically accompany a strong cold front were associated with that final chilly spell of spring.

There are additional colloquial terms for periods of unseasonable cold in the spring, including Locust Winter and Redbud Winter. All seem peculiar to the South and particularly to the Appalachians, but other sections of the country have delightful descriptions as well. Perhaps my favorite, one I've heard several times over the years while turkey hunting in Missouri or Iowa, is Long Handles Winter. That's a term folks there use to suggest that once that particular cold spell has passed, it is time to put the trusty old union suit away until it is once more needed in late fall.

Like so many other aspects of traditional Smokies culture, these special aspects of spring seem increasingly to belong to a world we have lost. As we become more urbanized, more dependent on hyped-up television meteorologists than personal observations for our weather predictions, and do far less gardening and farming, our sense of connection with the earth's seasonal rhythms lessens. Maybe that's why Grandpa Joe, who never drove a car and who viewed any and all things modern with skepticism, was often given to comments such as "I don't hold much with this here progress folks are always talking about."

Grandpa Joe was a great one for heeding what he simply styled "signs." He faithfully adhered to the signs for all his planting and harvesting and was sufficiently superstitious to see all sorts of ominous portents anytime something unusual happened. He reckoned blue jays were minions of Satan, saying that when these fussy, aggressive birds raised a ruckus, they were speaking on behalf of or reporting to the Devil. Always a bit paranoid and closely attuned to things he considered evil, Grandpa suggested that when it rained while the sun was shining, witches were dancing and cavorting. He wouldn't have any part of drinking a Coke, and he once justified that approach by putting a small piece of streaked meat in a coffee cup and then pouring Coca-Cola over it. A half hour later we went back to check his "speriment." The fat portion of the meat had literally vanished. "A man would be a fool to drink anything which eats away streaked meat," he commented. For a young boy it was difficult to argue with that logic.

Grandpa was reluctant to a fault when it came to launching a project on Saturday he couldn't finish the same day, figuring that anything that required so much time it had to be continued on the Sabbath could and should wait until Monday. While Grandpa didn't carry a pinch of salt in the left pocket of his overalls for good luck, at least to my knowledge, I knew others of his generation who did. He was not, however, averse to toting a shiny buckeye to ward off the ravages of rheumatism. I sometimes carry one myself, figuring it can't hurt and might well help.

Mountain folks I knew as a youngster harbored countless other quirks of behavior related to superstitions and signs, but nothing garnered closer attention or was considered of greater importance than "reading the signs" as they related to weather. Like countless others of his ilk, simple folks living off the land, Grandpa was more closely attuned to the world about him than most of us are today. Lacking slick-talking weather prognosticators with all sorts of gimmickry to illustrate and support their forecasts, hardy mountain folks made their own judgments about what the future held in store weatherwise. I won't suggest the signs were infallible, but those who followed them had learned through long experience and close observation.

After all, the ability to read and heed signs was vital when it came to matters as varied as when to put crops in the ground, split fence rails, or work up firewood, not to mention having a firm grasp on winter needs such as adequate hay for the family milk cow or sufficient wood and kindling for fires through the months of cold. In certain situations, such knowledge could literally be a matter of life and death. A fine example is the story of how Bone Valley Creek, a feeder stream of Hazel Creek deep in the heart of the GSMNP, got its name. A herd of cattle moved into the stream's upper reaches in order to take advantage of lush grazing offered by the greening-up time of early spring were caught in a powerful storm that produced deep snows. The entire herd froze to death, and for years afterward their bones littered the valley. Hence the name of the stream and the long, deep valley embracing it. One has to wonder whether the herders had paid attention to the old adage "If there is no snow in January, snow will come in March or April. "

As an aside, two of Bone Valley Creek's feeders are the Desolation and Defeat Branches. The place-names for this haunting though lovely place lying next door to nowhere are unquestionably suggestive.

Because of the potential dangers they posed, cold and snow form dominant themes in traditional mountain weather lore. Old-timers would look heavenward at layered rows of gray, scudding clouds on a bitter day and refer to them as snow clouds. Several times during my boyhood I was out rabbit hunting when a bluebird sky in early morning rapidly yielded to such clouds. Whenever this happened, one of the older members of the party would make a comment to the effect that "clouding up when there's frost and sparkling sun means rough weather before the day is done." Another common bit of doggerel associated with this type of weather was the couplet "Mackerel skies and mare's tails make wise seamen set short sails." Of course the Smokies are a long way from the sea, but the concept of bad weather was the point.

An even more reliable sign of snow and bitter weather came with animal behavior. Somehow animals, both domestic and wild, have an innate sense of sudden, dramatic changes in the weather. On the same rabbit hunts that produced the abovementioned weather pronouncements from senior members of the party, something occurred in the middle of the day that was highly unusual. Well into the hunt and long after cottontails had ceased the nocturnal feeding which is standard for them during the winter, our pack of beagles would strike a hot trail, one that left no doubt that a rabbit had recently passed that way. That was strange behavior for cottontails, since during winter they normally hold close to their "beds" or "hides" until dusk. Grandpa and Daddy both explained the behavior by saying: "They know a snow is on the way." Sure enough, every time this happened, it was snowing by late afternoon.

Countless other examples of forecasting snow or bitter cold, whether in a short, specific time frame or for an entire winter, come to mind. One old, oft-used couplet suggested that with "snow lingering on the ground, it's waiting for more to come around."

A cross-legged snow, one which saw wind-tossed flakes falling in different directions and crossing each other in the sky, foretold another snow in the next day or two. Similarly, listening to an open fire was considered a fine way of forecasting winter weather. When logs made a swishing noise resembling the sounds produced by walking through soft snow, it augured frozen precipitation in the near future. A flock of chickens also could do a first-rate job of forecasting. In the same kind of situations that saw rabbits moving at an unusual time, chickens would go to roost far before dusk. Sun dogs, a curious luminescence around the sun, were also deemed an indicator of approaching hard weather.

Any mountain resident worth his salt knew that you could judge temperatures by observing rhododendron leaves without any need to consult a thermometer. The tighter the leaves curled and the more they drooped, the colder the weather. The leaves wouldn't begin to unfurl until a warming spell was in the offing. Each year in today's world, come fall, Johnny-jump-up newspaper prognosticators and self-ordained prophets make a great amount of to-do about caterpillars and how their coloration and the width of their bands foretell what lies ahead. One couplet connected with them maintains that "when caterpillars' coats are mostly black, winter won't cut you any slack." Yet in my experience there are more reliable indexes to what winter holds. Grandpa Joe swore by the thickness of corn shucks, and I've found this to be a consistently accurate gauge. "Shucks on corn extra thick; look for cold winter coming quick." The same holds true for onions. "Onion skins very thin, mild winter coming in. Onion skins thick and tough, coming winter cold and rough." Similarly, if squirrels seem inordinately busy in gathering and burying nuts, or if they build noticeably larger nests than normal, expect bitter weather and lots of it. Bears denning earlier than their standard practice inexorably led to a similar conclusion: "Bears early to den, look for a chill winter wind."

Although I've never actually taken the trouble to perform such a countdown, old-timers staunchly maintained that the first mountain snow will come six weeks after the last thunderstorm in September. Along with summer and fall observations related to what winter might hold, the season itself offered various short-term indexes to impending weather. Among widely held mountain beliefs were that weather for each of the twelve days between Christmas and January 6, known as the Ruling Days, offered insight on how months of the coming year would be. Likewise, if the sun was shining on Candlemas Day (February 2, today more commonly known as Groundhog Day), you could expect much more snow and ice ere winter ended. The snowiest day of the year was supposedly Dorothea's Day (February 6). You still hear snow described as "poor man's fertilizer," suggestions that "April snow is as good as cow manure," and the belief that "much snow means much hay," while a traditional couplet connected with snow and what it meant for the coming year on the farm maintained that "when there's lots of snow, a fruitful crop will often grow. " There's considerable truth in these statements connected with the benefits that snow held for agriculture. Snow soaks gradually into the ground in sharp contrast to the runoff from heavy rain, and it also picks up trace elements in the air and deposits them on earth to nourish the soil.

As their liberal use already implies, a great many of the old "sayings" are rhythmic couplets. Remembering information was made easier by use of rhyme. Here's a fairly extensive sampling of what I've heard or read over the years.

When the wind's in the south,
It has snow in its mouth.
   ★★★
When the ground and grass are dry at morning light,
Expect snow before the night.
   ★★★

70

When heavy frost is on the grass,
Snow seldom comes to pass.
★★★

The higher the clouds, the finer the weather,
No clouds at all, that's even better.
★★★

Clear, cold moon,
Frost coming soon.
★★★

Smoke goes west, good weather's past;
Smoke goes east, bad weather's next.
★★★

When an old man's joints ache,
Cold, rainy weather is at stake.
★★★

Birds active and flying low,
Beware of a coming snow.
★★★

When clouds hang heavy on the hills,
Expect coming rain and chills.
★★★

A ring circling round the moon,
Means rain or snow coming soon.
★★★

When the moon carries a halo,
It's a sure sign of coming snow.
★★★

Rabbits moving on a winter day,
A heavy snow is on the way.
★★★

When dimmer stars disappear,
Rain or snow is quite near.
★★★

When clouds move against the wind,
Rain or snow is around the bend.
★★★

When it is hard to kindle a fire,
That's a sign of weather dire.
★★★

If Candlemas be fair and clear,
There'll be two winters in the year.
★★★

A winter filled with sounds of thunder,
Sends a message of summer hunger.
    ★★★
Trees holding their leaves extra long,
Look for winter to be extra strong.
    ★★★
When hornets build their nests extra high,
Look for snow nearing your thigh.

Our mountain ancestors, of necessity, paid careful attention to the world of nature in which they lived and which in turn gave them life. Today, thanks to generations of worship at the altar of that often false god known as progress, we have lost much of our linkage with the natural world. That's saddening, but somehow thoughts on observations of weather folklore as practiced by our forefathers are gladdening.

Before leaving the near-irresistible subject of weather lore, given my lifelong love for fishing and the undeniable fact that weather affects one's success in the sport, mention of that aspect of old-time prognostication seems merited. Both Grandpa Joe and Daddy always asserted that weather dramatically impacted fishing, and Daddy swore by the Solunar Tables prepared by John Alden Knight. Deep down I have to agree, but I've always held the optimistic view that anytime you can go fishing is a good time. Take whatever perspective you wish, but Izaak Walton, the author and naturalist who wrote the enduring classic *The Compleat Angler* summed it up quite nicely.

If the wind's in the north, the skillful fisherman goes not forth;
If the wind's in the east, it's good for neither man nor beast;
If the wind's in the south, it blows the fly in the fish's mouth;
When the wind is in the west, then fishing's the very best.

Chapter 14

SMOKY MOUNTAIN RAIN

No single topic is more likely to open a conversation than weather, and rain is invariably discussed. It's almost as if everyone subconsciously follows the pattern of a grand local character from my boyhood named Arthur Blanton. Arthur was a harmless, eccentric fellow, usually described with something along the line of "he's not quite all there," which would be taboo today. Yet he was self-sufficient and happily made his way through life in his own peculiar fashion.

A key aspect of that life was a daily routine that found him wandering around the streets of Bryson City toting a capacious tow sack. In it he carried soft drink bottles picked up from ditches or given to him by folks who wanted to help Arthur a bit. When he had accumulated a suitable number of bottles, he would carry them to local grocery stores or distributors of what he called "belly washers" for redemption. They brought two or three cents each, a refund of the deposit paid on the original bottle. Arthur also gathered pieces of wire that he strung from tree to tree around his humble abode in a mystifying maze. Warm and outgoing, he always wanted to talk a bit with everyone he encountered. Although anything but articulate, he had rightly come to the conclusion that weather formed an ideal conversational gambit. Accordingly, whenever you encountered Arthur, he would smile and opine: "A little shower of rain wouldn't hurt nothing."

Winter or summer, no matter what the situation, his offer of that weather-related pronouncement on the current state of affairs was totally predictable. Old Arthur may have epitomized the expressive mountain word "quare," but in his preoccupation with weather in general and rain in particular he couldn't have been more normal.

The Smokies get an abundance of rain, and experts characterize much of the area as a temperate rain forest. Along with a plentitude of rainfall come quaint and sometimes highly descriptive local expressions connected with precipitation. A personal favorite describing an extended rainy spell is "it came a young Noah." Then there are varied and delightful depictions of sudden, heavy rains—"it fell a flood," "it came a frog strangler," or "we had a stump floater." There's also a crude description for particularly heavy precipitation: "It rained like a cow pissing on a flat river rock."

A good friend and longtime fishing buddy of mine from over Graham County way, Marty Maxwell, has an agreeable way of describing the manner in which sudden storms can develop: "It can come up a storm out of a hornet's nest on Big Snowbird Creek." Ronnie Milsap, a native of the same county, was squarely on target with lyrics from one of his classic hits, "Smoky Mountain Rain It Keeps on Falling."

My favorite aspect of rain in the Smokies, or for that matter anywhere, links to the sound of it falling steadily on a tin roof. I was blessed to grow up in a house with such a roof, and there's no sweeter lullaby, no sound so soothing, as the patter of rain falling on tin. If somehow that sound could be replicated in a fashion that lasted all night and since there are "go to sleep" machines that play soothing sounds of ocean waves, mountain creeks, and the like, presumably it could be easily accomplished, I think you would have the perfect antidote for insomnia.

Another blessing connected with Smokies rain, especially in locations offering distant views, is being able to observe summer storms or see scattered showers develop. Times without number as a boy I watched from the porch of our home as rain and lightning played along the main ridgeline at the head of Kirklands Creek, up around Frye Mountain, and on out towards Alarka. The same held true for storms developing to the north around Sharp Top and on the headwaters of Deep Creek and the main ridgeline of the Smokies. Often those distant rains fell when our garden needed a soaking shower, but as a rule they did not reach the bottomlands around town. The most common direction for summer rains falling in Bryson City saw them move in from the southwest, coming up the Tuckaseigee River. Pretty much anywhere in the Smokies where you have a vista providing views for appreciable distance, it's possible to enjoy this sort of phenomenon.

Along with the joy of watching such rains embrace distant ridgelines there's the pleasure, should they draw close enough, of listening to the march of advancing rainfall moments before it engulfs you. When lightning figures in the equation, as it does more often than not during Smokies summers, taking shelter is advisable. Still, like some mad man raging at the elements, there were times in my boyhood when, drenched in sweat from hoeing corn or hot because of a long walk home after a trout-fishing trip, I relished standing out in a sudden summer shower filled with elemental joy while getting soaked to the bone.

For children, and those of more advanced age whose hearts remained young, summer rains offered pleasures beyond a good soaking. Farmers and gardeners welcomed their life-giving moisture, but brief rains also furnished all sorts of opportunities to play. To walk barefooted through a mud puddle, with the softened soil squishing between one's toes, was to know a pleasure no modern, store-bought toy or resort trip can fully duplicate. To smell the heady aroma of dry summer soil when the first drops of a rain dampened it was to savor nature's perfume at its finest. To squish through soaked grass in bare feet was pure delight, and the same held true when a big summer rain got the creeks up and provided great tubing conditions.

The latter, normally occurring only a couple of times a summer, were what Grandpa Joe called "settin' in" rains. By that he meant it had "set in" to rain all day. These tended to be soft, steady rains falling from leaden, unchanging skies. As earth absorbed all the moisture it could hold, streams would rise and, for someone like me who was obsessed by fishing for trout, offer brief but exceptional angling opportunities. This was especially true for brown trout, which love low light conditions, and lots of insects being washed into the stream sho' nuff puts them on the prod.

For brown trout rain presented a rare opportunity to gorge, and in a broader sense all plant and animal life in the Smokies is blessed by an abundance of moisture. The results include lush vegetation, opportunities (at least back when most everyone raised a garden) to produce bountiful crops, and a geographical setting which provides the greatest biodiversity found anywhere in the Northern Hemisphere. The Smokies are a portal of paradise nurtured by rain.

Chapter 15

MUSINGS ON THE MONTHS

For a goodly portion of two decades I've written a monthly e-newsletter that a few thousand people receive and presumably read. A standard feature of the newsletter has been characterizations of each passing month as it unfolds in the Smokies, and much of the stimulus for those word pictures comes from a life devoted to reading.

I've been a serious reader all my life, thanks to a variety of factors such as the undoubted blessing of being raised in a home without a boob tube, growing up next door to the woman who founded the local library (Marianna Black), being gifted by parents who realized the world of wonders opened before you with books, and maybe just a natural inclination to enjoy the printed word. If you asked me to name my favorite writers, it would be mighty difficult to limit their ranks to even as few as a dozen.

I rode the purple sage and lived the spirit of the border with Zane Grey as a boy; thrilled to each new Old Man and the Boy tale by Robert Ruark, who would be my choice as our greatest outdoor writer, in the pages of *Field and Stream* magazine; admired Theodore Roosevelt and the way he lived the strenuous life; and enjoyed the hunting tales of southern scribes such as Archibald Rutledge, Charlie Elliott, Havilah Babcock, and Nash Buckingham. Yet were I asked to name my favorite writer when it comes to a blend of wordsmithing and carrying my soul back home, there would be no hesitation, no pondering as to the comparative merits of various authors. Simply put, John Parris ranks at the top of my list of those who have chronicled high country days and ways.

The contents of all his books came from columns he produced for the *Asheville Citizen-Times*: *My Mountains, My People; Mountain Bred; Roaming the Mountains; These Storied Mountains;* and *Mountain Cooking*. Parris was a man who cherished the folklore and lifestyles of his native heath, and he had a rare knack for capturing these subjects in moving fashion. His standard stylistic approach was to use a month or some other subject and then employ it repeatedly while capturing tidbits of information. Over a period of more than forty years he wrote three pieces a week for the *Asheville Citizen-Times,* and occasionally Parris would launch into a lyrical description of a month, a season, or perhaps some particular activity with a litany of sentences that, more often than not, began with the words "It is."

Although they are longer, more detailed, and reflective of my observations rather than those of Parris, the odes to the months that follow adopt his style to an appreciable degree. They are offered as a tribute to a giant of mountain letters and in unabashed recognition that his was a stylistic twist that worked wonderfully well. As Parris instinctively realized, there's something about these ancient hills and hollows we call the Smokies that will lay hold of a body and never let go. I know that, as likely is equally true for every reader who has spent much time in this part of the world. Here's my extended paean to the Smokies, their wonderful diversity, and incidentally to the memory of John Parris. I hope that it is in some small measure worthy of his legacy, because I greatly admire his writing. Many of the pieces make full use of his "It is" methodology. When, late in his career, he favorably mentioned a published effort of mine, I was prouder than a bantam hen with a newly hatched batch of chicks.

Much of the month-by-month material focuses on outdoor activities and the folkways of food. Both loomed large in my youth, a time when not only youngsters but folks of all ages spent far more time outside than they do today. As a result, they also had a great deal of interest in weather phenomena. That's a subject covered in some detail in an earlier chapter, but where sayings or bits of weather wisdom refer to a specific month, they are included below.

January's Enduring Joys

For me, January will always be more a month for reflection than resolutions, and as my years grow longer and my hair becomes thinner and whiter, living in the past becomes increasingly pleasant. During my boyhood, January was a time of year when Grandpa Joe would ease close to the fire in the living room (we'd never heard of a "den" except as a place bears holed up when the weather turned bitter). He would get settled comfortably in his rocking chair and, if the weather was inclement, pay a bit of grudging verbal tribute to "Uncle Arthur" (arthritis) or the "miseries." The latter word embraced a whole litany of ailments—chest colds, rheumatism, arthritis, general cases of the mollygrubs, or just not feeling particularly pert. Since he most frequently talked about miseries when it was cold, with either a chilling rain or snow falling, I suspect that most of his trouble centered on arthritis.

Overall though, Grandpa wasn't much of one for complaining. He was tough as a hickory hoe handle and about as inured to pain as any human you are likely to encounter. Even when he shattered his hip while out squirrel hunting and had to slide and crawl through snow just to get to the road, he refused any kind of pain relief in the aftermath of orthopedic surgery. Folks at Swain County Hospital found this so remarkable they commented: "That is sure one tough old man."

While Grandpa was far removed from hypochondria, he was powerfully given to philosophizing. So fiercely independent he couldn't and wouldn't work for another man, he took orders from no one but Grandma Minnie (and did that reluctantly and irregularly). He distrusted any and all government authority, an approach that seems increasingly wise to me with each passing year, had more than a streak of paranoia, and when someone disagreed with him was regularly given to a pithy pronouncement: "You'll learn!"

As his attentive one-person audience, sometime understudy, and regular sidekick, none of these examples of being what mountain folks sometimes describe as quare bothered me a bit. We got along just fine whatever the season, but one of my favorite times of the year to be with Grandpa Joe was January. There wasn't much work to be done other than occasionally tending the fire or feeding the chickens and hogs. As a result I could sit in comfort and listen to hour upon hour of gripping stories.

Grandpa's voice was barely above a whisper, and I had long thought that was just his peculiarity until recently coming across a recording of

Granville Calhoun. Made when that grand old sage of Hazel Creek was 90 years of age (he lived to 103), it provides remarkable listening. In the recorded interview Calhoun sounds a great deal like Grandpa did, and his voice is soft as chamois. Yet straining to hear and understand what he said is worth every bit of the required effort. Other than a slight difference in accent, when listening to Calhoun I could have been back in the 1950s sitting alongside Grandpa.

As old men are wont to do, and I find myself increasingly guilty on this score, Grandpa talked primarily about things he had experienced over the course of his life, with a distinct and no doubt intentional focus on January. Here is a compendium of some of the joys he recalled. I have no way of knowing how truthful they were. I can merely note that although Grandpa certainly knew how to embellish, he also was a stickler for factual accuracy. Wherever the boundary between fact and fiction lay in his tales, it really doesn't matter after the passage of more than half a century.

He talked of killing a "painter" (panther) when he was a young man, and described the scream of a cougar so accurately it sent chills down my spine. "It was like the cry of a woman dying," was the way he put it.

He recounted glory days of the American chestnut, when mast was so plentiful that his family, along with every other one earning a hardscrabble living in the high country, gathered great quantities of the nuts in the fall to sell and eat through the winter. "A bait of roasted chestnuts on a cold winter day," he would say, "made for some mighty fine eating."

Food figured prominently in other parts of his monologue as well. Grandpa could speak of simple mountain vittles in a fashion that invariably had me all primed to eat when Grandma called us for dinner or supper. Of course the fact that she was a splendid cook and that I was permanently peckish didn't hurt.

I loved his oft-recounted tale of a massive snowfall of some three feet. It was of the soft, fluffy kind and so deep rabbits couldn't run. He and his brother caught a whole sack full of cottontails in that snow.

Speaking of rabbits, often during those joyful January days Grandpa and I constructed rabbit gums. Merely thinking of those devices leads me to wonder whether anyone makes and uses these simple, effective traps anymore.

Grandpa was greatly given to whittling, and often as he talked he worked on a piece of wood. He might be shaping the beginnings of a flutter mill or fashioning a Jacob's ladder, but one of his favorite projects was shaping and notching, ever so carefully, a dogwood fork. Dogwood is a dense, extremely hard wood (so much so that old-timers often used a section of it as a wedge when splitting firewood), and that meant the whittling process was a slow, tedious one. Yet patience and persistence were bywords for Grandpa—he never, ever hurried—and steady whittling, possibly with a bit of attention from a whetstone if his knife's performance didn't suit his exacting standards, perfectly suited his demeanor when in a tale-telling mode. Once he had the dogwood fork shaped to satisfaction, all the piece of wood required was to be outfitted with some inner tube rubber, stout twine, and a rectangular piece of leather. The end result was a fine slingshot.

Eventually Grandpa would tire of talking, perhaps with a nap in mind, and at that point he'd gently shoo me out of the house. "Cold January days," he would say, "are a time for young boys to plunder about and maybe see if they can find a squirrel or jump a rabbit. They are also a time for old folks like me to hang close to a warm fire with a cup of Rooshian (Russian) tea."

Those naps hadn't always been his practice, but an event from a January day when he was well into his seventies, briefly alluded to above, needs to be shared as a sort of wrap-up to this month as well as an explanation of his suggestion that it was the duty of the young to take care of outdoor rambling in the dead of winter.

Grandpa Joe had always loved to squirrel hunt, and it was something he pursued with a passion that never dimmed despite the toll of advancing years and aching joints. When he shared hunting stories, sooner or later Grandpa would harken back to the time when the American chestnut reigned supreme in mountain forests and when squirrels were incredibly abundant. I guess you could say he was looking back to the "good old days" in his own way. Even though bushytails numbers weren't what they had once been by the time we were staunch partners separated by a generation, he still hunted them with a will. Time and again I heard him say "a mess of squirrel flanked by a platter of cathead biscuits, a bunch of baked sweet potatoes, and some of your Grandma's squirrel gravy" was about as near to culinary heaven as a body was likely to get.

It was on an early January day, bitterly cold and with a skiff of freshly fallen snow on the ground, that the urge for such a meal seized Grandpa's fancy. He set out from the house with his trusty little .22, never mind the temperatures in the twenties or the snow. Alas, the trip went bad in a big way. Grandpa slipped and fell, perhaps a half mile from the nearest road, and shattered his hip. Somehow he managed to slide and crawl through the snow until he got to old U. S. Highway 19 above Bryson City. He yelled and waved for help as one car after another passed by, but since he was high atop a bank where the road had cut through a ridge, no one noticed him. Finally, realizing something had to be done, Grandpa gritted his teeth, turned on his side to his uninjured hip, and slid down the steep bank to the roadside. From there he was transported to the hospital.

Somehow this tough old man survived the ordeal, and folks at the hospital told my father they had never treated anyone with a higher tolerance for pain. Once he came out of anesthesia used to repair his hip, Grandpa refused any and all pain medication. Eventually he was able to walk again and get about quite well, although it took a bit of a mean trick—my sister and I hiding a crutch on which he had become overly dependent—for him to realize he was pretty well back to his pre-accident status. Predictably, given a stubborn mind-set which those who know me well will readily realize was passed down to at least one of his grandchildren, come the following autumn he once again took to the squirrel woods. Indeed, late fall and winter bushytails jaunts were a part of his life until two or three years before his death, but he never again went out in the snow.

Januaries of my boyhood that found me spending considerable time with Grandpa were filled with wonder and joy. Looking back on those experiences reminds me, in a warm the cockles of the heart fashion, that in many ways I was mighty privileged as a youngster. I had a dad who took me hunting, a mom who gladly cooked any game I brought home, and a grandfather who was just a boy trapped in an old man's body. On top of that, Grandpa Joe had endless quantities of that most precious of possessions, time, which he freely shared with me.

Lightning in January means snow in April.
If January has no snow, in March expect flakes to blow.

February Figurin'

Grandpa Joe didn't particularly care for the month of February. It tended to bring bitter weather, with more than a fair share of cold rain or snow, and as someone who had, for his entire life, spent most of his waking hours outdoors, that was disgruntling. He held strong opinions about the month and as was his wont on any subject when he was around me never hesitated to express them. "February needs to be short," he would mutter in his barely audible manner, "because if the month was any longer I don't believe a body could stand it."

One thing about Grandpa though; at heart he was an optimist. Mind you, he may have had an overly healthy streak of distrust in mankind in general, and during the years I knew him he had no truck whatsoever with the government, bureaucrats, or organized religion. Still, he always looked ahead to coming spring with eagerness, and by February, no matter how miserable the weather, he would be talking about planting by the signs, getting his garden spots laid off, ordering a bunch of baby chickens through the local Farmers' Federation, and fishing experiences that lay ahead. Those mental exercises dominated our conversation in the dead of winter. He variously described them as "figurin'," "dreamin' and schemin'," or just "looking down the road."

February's good for that. For the gardener, colorful seed catalogs promising more than one ever actually manages to grow have arrived. They lend themselves to sessions of dreaming, whether or not you buy seeds from them (Grandpa bought bulk seed locally), and if you want to save money, get seed suited for the area, and deal with local merchants, that's still a good way to go.

For the sportsman, the month then and now amounted to something of a wipeout. Sure, squirrel, rabbit, and bird seasons were still open, and when I was a boy we hunted hard right through until closing day. However, surviving bushytails tended to be mighty wary by this time of year, and usually we had already pressured all the nearby prime cottontail places hard. In today's world, thanks to changes in equipment and even in seasons, trout fishing is possible. When I was a boy that wasn't the case. Trout season in both GSMNP and state waters was closed until April or early May.

Nor did I enjoy the opportunity, as a youngster, to do something that is a standard part of every February for me today. It's a month for sporting shows and expos. They likely existed in faraway places all those decades ago, but back then a sporting show involved a visit to Doc Woody's tiny sporting goods store or an hour-long gander of wishful thinking browsing the Sears & Roebuck catalog. Grandpa enjoyed the latter activity as well, although to my knowledge he never ordered a single item from that wish book or transacted any business whatsoever through the United States Postal Service. He didn't receive any social security, his children attended to matters such as taxes, and he functioned exclusively in a realm of barter and occasional expenditure of modest amounts of cash money.

While aspects of my current approach to February, at least when it involves matters such as tax preparation or perhaps attendance at a regional or national sporting goods show, is a dramatic departure from youthful days, others remain closely attuned to what the month. Every returning February finds me indulging in my own dreamin' and schemin', scouting for turkeys, making arrangements for a trip or two, planting some early garden items if the soil is dry enough to permit it, and getting ready for more serious garden work lying not far in the future.

Thinking about and doing such things gets me through February, as was the case in the 1950s when Grandpa would start talking about spring fishing. Never mind that his planning involved nothing more than a trip up Deep Creek or maybe just down to Devils Dip in the Tuckaseigee River a short way below his house. That stands in marked contrast to the cross-country and even international travel I've been privileged to enjoy, but the month's sense of building anticipation, with realization that the worst of winter will soon be gone, sustained me then and now. Thanks to a grand old mentor's outlook from long ago, that planning and preparing for the immediate future fun offers an ideal way to dispel any temporary blues associated with cabin fever in the present. When all else failed, I could always heed the advice offered by a couplet associated with the month:

> Curl warm in a corner with a book as a friend,
> And your February blues are soon at an end.

It's a nostrum that has served me well for many a February, just as Grandpa Joe found refuge in reliving past glories and planning future triumphs.

> A warm October means a chilly February.
> If February gives much snow, a fine summer it doth show.
> When February brings snow and ice, look for June to be mighty nice.

March Madness: Winter's Final Fling

> The stormy March has come at last,
> With winds and clouds and changing skies;
> I hear the rushing of the blast
> That through the snowy valley flies.

—William Cullen Bryant, "March"

March is a time of the year in the Smokies that can be, depending on your outlook or maybe just a given day's weather, anywhere from marvelous to miserable. A traditional mountain "singsong" points to that changeability:

> Clouds on the hills that rise toward the sky,
> Signal a day when it will be dry.
> But clouds lowering around the mountain's top,
> Mean rain soon begins to drop.

Such uncertainty possibly explains why old Will Shakespeare, who seemed to know something about everything, warned about the Ides of March. Honesty compels me to acknowledge that I didn't know "Ides" from Adam's off ox until I looked it up (it refers to the fifteenth day of the month in March, May, July, and October and the thirteenth day for the remaining eight months), but I've always understood that March carries with it a certain element of madness, a reason to beware.

Being a sanguine sort at heart, my means of dealing with March and its madness have, over time, leaned heavily toward following Grandpa's example and taking a positive spin. Once the month arrives you can pretty well be comfortable in realization that the miserable state of mind known variously as cabin fever, winter blues, mollygrubs, or fireside frustration won't hang around much longer. As greening-up time eases into the mountains, birds start singing with a will, poke shoots stick their heads through warming soil, branch lettuce begins to sport its seasonal rosettes, and old-timers start thinking about some type of tonic to clean the system. The tonic might take the form of tried-and-true sulfur and molasses, a mess of spring greens, a bait of ramps, or sassafras tea.

A fine mess of poke salad was Grandpa's favorite. Cooked three times with the water being drained the first two, then topped with slices of boiled egg and sprinkled with streaked meat fried to a crisp, it made a tasty dish indeed. It also happened, thanks to an overabundance of Vitamin A, to be a powerful purgative. As Grandpa Joe described in his distinctive fashion, "It will clean you out and set you free, and it's the proper way for a feller to head into spring."

Poke has always held a special place in my heart. I thoroughly enjoy eating the wild vegetable, but what places it particularly high in my esteem is that fact that it provided the first cash money I ever earned. My second grade teacher, Emily Davis, was passing fond of it. Anytime I could fill a number eight poke (paper bag) with tender shoots of poke it would fetch two bits to put in my pocket. For a month or so every spring, until the stalks started growing too rapidly and the taste became rank, Mrs. Emily was the customer of a young boy's dreams.

March brings the first real hints of color to the Smokies after months of a dull palette where black, brown, and grey, along with the leathery green of rhododendron, laurel, evergreen trees, and plants like teaberry have been about all there was to tickle the eyes. You begin to spot white splashes of service trees coming into bloom at lower elevations, and as a knowing youngster I always made a mental note of these, realizing they would provide a tasty snack when berries ripened a couple of months down the road. Pussy willows show the soft sheen of swelling buds and splashes of yellow from spring-blooming witch hazel (it mostly blooms in late November and early December) may be detected. It's a grand time to find old home places, because the tell-tale sight of aptly named yellow bells and those of japonica bushes ranging across the red spectrum from salmon to scarlet, crimson to carmine, send out a clarion call: "Hardy mountain folks once lived here, and they celebrated returning spring with the blooms of these equally hardy plants."

You might find early bloodroot abloom on a south face or hints of gold as double daffodils, often located close by the ruins of long forgotten homes, greet your eye as they swell toward full loveliness. Like day lilies, iris, and several other long surviving flowers of the Smokies, they endure thanks to getting their growing business taken care of before shade from the overhead canopy starves them of light.

Lordly turkey gobblers declare dominion to every creature within earshot, and lesser avians, from quarrelsome crows to trilling cardinals singing "pretty, pretty" at daybreak, reward the astute nature observer. On a warm day the March woods are a veritable Tower of Babel, and anyone who speaks or writes of woodland silence in the spring hasn't been a wayfarer in the Smokies during that season. Sometimes there's so much noise it seems like a hammering cacophony, but what a glorious madness March can be. No wonder the late writer Carson Brewer, a man madly in love with the Smokies, chose *A Wonderment of Mountains* as the title for one of his books.

March snow is as good as manure.
When March has April weather, April will have March weather.

Oh, April

Spring comes to the Smokies in starts and spurts, stumbling and stuttering along as it tries to find the right beat. A spell of balmy days with afternoon temperatures rising into the 70s is suddenly replaced by weather belonging to the depths of winter. Frost is a distinct possibility and late snows aren't out of the question. As was so often the case, that sweet swan of Avon, William Shakespeare, got it just as right for the Smokies as for the sceptered isles of Britain when he wrote of "the uncertain glory of an April day."

The month is a time for getting down to serious business with gardening, and in my youth that meant waiting eagerly until there was a dry spell of a few days which let the soil reach a point where it could be plowed. All garden plowing was done by horses or mules, and the same held true for much of the tilling of larger sections of ground on farms. Relatively few folks had or could afford tractors. Besides, a fair portion of the cultivated ground was too steep and rugged for the use of machinery.

An elderly black man plowed our garden every spring, and I'm almost certain he did the same for Grandpa Joe's patches. I loved to hear him coming up the road, with the clopping of his mules' hooves beating a staccato rhythm on the concrete of the roadway and the equipment (a harrow, plow, drag, and other implements) carried in his rickety wagon clanging and jangling in a most satisfying fashion. Even more delightful was watching him at work. The team of mules obeying his every order, the ground being deeply tilled with precision, and then the whole process being rounded out with a drag harrow which left the surface smooth as a baby's bottom.

April also meant the first trout fishing of the year, some dealing with knottyheads in the nearby Tuckaseigee River, and the season's first camping trip. Add to that the unfolding grandeur of the Smokies' grand diversity of wildflowers and realization that the end of the school year was no longer impossibly distant, and it was a fine time to be alive.

When April features a constant chill,
Come October the barn we'll fill.
A moist April means a clear June.

May's Magic

For a wide variety of reasons, I have always found May magical. Along with October, which would certainly give it a run for the money, it's my favorite month of the year. Poet James Russell Lowell waxed eloquent with his question "What is so rare as a day in June?," but had the Smokies been his homeland and the geographical source of his inspiration, he would assuredly have chosen the month of May. He would even have gotten some internal rhyme in the bargain. Or take the apt description from Shakespeare's *King Henry IV*, "as full of spirit as the month of May." The month's a time of early harvest, of gardens beginning to show real promise, of bedding bream and rising trout, and of spring in all its lushness. The threat of frost is gone, but nights remain comfortable or even a tad chilly, while daytime presents none of the withering heat and humidity to be faced in coming months.

Here, in no particular order of importance, is a sampling of some of May's myriad delights. It's a month that sets my proclivities for indulging in nostalgia into overdrive as I look back on all its days meant to me as a boy. The end of another school year was in sight, and not even the looming threat of semester's end exams could entirely dim the luster of that fast approaching and glad day. The weather had reached a point where it was fairly predictable, and that meant opportunities for weekend camping/fishing trips with the Smokies adorned with all the splendor of returning spring. Beyond that, the month held wonder in its hand in so many ways, and for an adolescent they were wonders to be embraced and enjoyed. Maybe the best way of depicting May, as I have known and loved it, is through resurrecting some of those miracles of green-up in the high country.

May meant ripe wild strawberries that were, in the 1950s, available in great abundance in old farm fields and open areas in the GSMNP that had once been farms. These spaces had not yet reverted to forest and wild strawberries, along with dewberries and blackberries, thrived in them. Wild strawberries were tedious to pick, equally demanding when it came to working them up, fragile, and fresh ones did not keep well. Moreover, they carried a real possibility of a confrontation with a copperhead or rattlesnake. Yet the taste of wild strawberries more than made up for all those shortcomings and danger. Over shortcake, sliced atop a bowl of vanilla ice cream, made into a trifle, in home-churned strawberry ice cream, used for preserves or jelly, topping for cereal, or just eaten by themselves, they offered a small sampling of pure culinary paradise.

May meant fishing for trout, and after the winter doldrums warming water temperatures put them on the prod and brought joy to the heart of a boy who, according to his father decades later, had squandered away half his life "fooling with fish." Camping trips in the back country were a traditional part of the angling experience. The first weekend in May brought the opening of trout season in the GSMNP (today the season never closes), and I don't think I missed an opener from the time I was eleven or twelve years of age until I went off to college. Most backpacking trips involved the headwaters of my "home" stream, Deep Creek, at a place known as Poke Patch. Wading could sometimes be mighty cold, as could sleeping arrangements. I didn't own a sleeping bag so a single Army blanket constituted my bedding. Yet what I'd give for a May night or two at a backcountry campsite, bone-tired, but with a cheery fire, trout frying in the pan, potatoes and onions in a second skillet, and a "kilt" salad of ramps and branch lettuce waiting in the wings. I'll take such a setting and such fare over anything a five-star restaurant with a hoity-toity chef, majestic maître d's, and ever-attentive waiters can offer. Fresh from the stream and properly prepared, trout are a gift from the food gods.

It was a time for enjoying the garden's early produce. Spring onions, radishes, new potatoes, black-seeded Simpson lettuce, spinach, broccoli, and other delights would have "made" by mid-May, and in a most gratifying fashion they signaled that months of incredible bounty were in the offing.

May meant boyhood games of the kind that required no formal organization, no adult supervision, and indeed nothing but a bit of youthful ingenuity and an abundance of energy. Rolly-bat, marbles, slingshot competitions, bike riding, rock skipping at the river, building forts, swinging on big grape vines, "riding" slender pines or poplars, and other carefree activities filled hours without number in my youth.

The month also began the swimming season. I'm not sure I ever swam in a man-made pool until I was grown, and certainly I was able to swim long before I ever paddled in anything other than a creek or river. May was pushing things on the swimming front, but the first dip in icy cold Deep Creek, leaving your lips blue and your body covered with goose bumps in no time at all, was at once an obligation, an annual rite of passage, and a joy.

As an adjunct to swimming May brought a resumption of float tubing. That involved drifting down the creek on an inner tube, back when all tires came with them and when they were made of real rubber, happy as a lark and heedless of all cares. This was usually done after a big rain when the creek was high and the ride was an exciting one not only because of the rapidity with which the creek moved but because the limbs of bushes and low trees overhanging the creek held scores of water snakes. No matter how many times you experienced one of them dropping atop you or just alongside the tube, there was always an element of fright and an involuntary yell. Today tubing is big business on readily accessible GSMNP streams, and I'd as soon walk around Times Square in New York City as to mingle with the flotillas that sometimes seem to cover creeks in the Smokies from bank to bank.

May was a grand month for catching and selling night crawlers. Warm spring showers bring thoughts of procreation to the worm world, and when that happened those giants of the underground, night crawlers, did exactly what their name suggested—they crawled at night. With an evening of joyful effort a spry young fellow equipped with a flashlight, a big bucket with some moss in it, and a quick hand could catch what for a boy amounted to a minor fortune. Night crawlers brought a penny apiece, and earning three or four dollars for a few hours "work" was big money in the 1950s. It wasn't really labor at all but rather a nocturnal delight. Mind you, I'm sure that much stooping, bending, and grabbing would bring a quite different perspective from me today (and overall soreness on the morrow).

It was also a time for catching and selling spring lizards (that's what we called them, though they were actually salamanders) to sell to bait stores. Good ones fetched three cents apiece and the red speckled ones brought a nickel. Much like dealing with night crawlers, this involved quick hands and scrambling in seep branches and springs while turning over rocks. I had a female classmate, Maxine Freeman, whose whole family "hunted" lizards, and the endeavor was actually an important source of income for them. They did it at night using a technique almost like fishing. I now know that it's easier to catch them that way, but my spring lizarding was a daytime pursuit.

Like gathering ramps in the Park and a lot of other activities I took for granted as a boy, this is something that is, in the words Georgia politician Zell Miller used in a book title, "purt nigh gone." There are severe limitations on what types of salamanders are legal and today's youngsters for the most part lack the gumption, not to mention the knowhow, such pursuits require.

A bit of the cash earned from catching night crawlers and spring lizards would be wasted, because no Bryson City boy worth his salt could resist putting a few pennies on the railroad tracks. I'm sure this was illegal, although I'd like to think it wasn't dangerous. All I know for sure is that the trains that ran in Bryson City did a marvelous job of flattening out copper wheat pennies. If you know the phrase, "flat as a flitter," it was certainly applicable in this case.

In the final years of my high schooling, May meant junior-senior proms. While my number one interest throughout adolescence was outdoor activities, it would be wrong to suggest I studiously ignored the fairer sex. I still harbor fond memories of my senior prom and can mentally walk through everything involved from when I first picked up my date (a former "steady" girlfriend who had rightly ceased to be my steady when I got involved in some silly "two-timing"—I doubt the word "steady" or the phrase "two-timing" get much if any usage today) at the home of her aunt and uncle right through to evening's end.

More than anything, the magic of May meant just being a boy. I look back with longing on those carefree days. No planning was necessary when it came to after-school hours or weekends. Alone or with other boys I might decide to go seining for minnows, indulge in an hour or two of knife sharpening and whittling, play some mumblety-peg, laze along the riverbank waiting for a bobber to bounce, pick wild strawberries, take a hike with my slingshot or BB gun in hand in search of adventure, admire wildflowers growing close to home, or spend the day with my grandparents. Simple things brought sublime pleasure, and looking back I realize that I was truly blessed in enjoying a Smoky Mountain boyhood. The title of a book by one of my favorite outdoor writers, Archibald Rutledge's *Those Were the Days,* pretty well sums up my memories of May in yester-youth.

He who doffs his coat on a winter day, will gladly don it in the month of May.

June's Glorious Barefoot Days

Until a couple of years ago, I hadn't seen anyone barefooted, other than toddlers, in a 'coon's age. Then I passed a nicely dressed young woman on the sidewalk who was devoid of any footwear. I did a double take, thought maybe she was a leftover flower child from a half century ago, and then started thinking about the meaning and magic of going barefooted during my Smokies boyhood.

For the period spanning my earliest memories until the point in my early teens when high-top tennis shoes or penny loafers entered the picture, going barefooted was one of the grand pleasures of late spring and summer. Momma had a sort of unofficial "opening day" of the barefoot season that came when school let out, but well before that point, whenever temperatures climbed into the 70s I would be imploring her to let me go without shoes.

I can remember her dire predictions such as "you'll catch your death of a cold" or expressions of the ridiculousness of my desires to the effect of "I declare, I believe you'd go barefooted in the wintertime if we'd let you." Occasionally on a sunny weekend in May Momma, no doubt beaten down by constant requests to shed my shoes and possibly secretly sympathetic with my desires, would give in for a few hours.

Boys, and even to a certain extent girls, had plain disdain for shoes. Going barefooted saved wear and tear on costly apparel and was just sheer fun in the bargain. I can even remember Joe Benny Shuler, the father of University of Tennessee football legend Heath Shuler, coming to the first-ever day of Little League baseball in Swain County shoeless. When someone asked him about his unshod feet, he proudly pronounced "Shulers don't wear shoes in the summertime." Neither did any other boy with much spunk.

May was a month of ups and downs when it came to going barefooted, because at times it was just too cold. Then there would be spells of a few days when it was plenty warm enough to divest myself of the hated footwear as soon as I got home from school. Going barefoot in school was totally taboo, although I can remember asking teachers, more than once, why we couldn't at least get rid of shoes while out on the playground. Oddly enough, I've seen old school pictures from earlier in the century when virtually all the boys and even some of the girls would be free of the burden of shoes.

By June though, all was right in the world when it came to barefooting it. School was out or almost at an end (I recall a couple of years where making up snow days cost students their normal freedom on Saturday and also saw the school year extend a week or two into June). Three months of blissful freedom were at hand. Mind you, along with just being a carefree boy there were chores as well. They included an endless and losing battle against Bermuda grass on the hillside below our house, with my weapon being a pitchfork to dig up that vegetative spawn of the Devil bit by bit. I detested that particular duty but other ones, such as mowing the lawn with an old reel-type push mower I still own, helping Daddy in the garden, picking blackberries to sell for the whopping sum of a two bits a gallon, and spending time at my grandparents formed more pleasant parts of the picture. I also picked up welcome spending money by caddying at the local golf course. No one had heard of a golf cart then and only a tightwad of the most miserly sort carried his own clubs.

While a goodly portion of the time I spent with my paternal grandparents involved work, I never really thought of it in that way. While I certainly performed chores there, they invariably involved helping out Grandpa Joe in some way or other. I suspect that at times I was more of a hindrance than an aide, but he gladly tolerated my presence and had a way of making everything so interesting I never really looked at it as labor. Besides, he didn't have any Bermuda grass in his lawn.

I wore shoes—rugged brogans colloquially known as clod hoppers— for the chores. After all, reel mowers and bare feet weren't a suitable mix, and the same held true when it came to wielding a pitch fork, swing blade, or mowing scythe. Most of the rest of the time though, I traipsed around without footwear. By mid-June I would have built up a callus layer of armament on my feet worthy of an armadillo, although comparatively tender insteps remained vulnerable. Mind you, there were stubbed toes aplenty, and bare feet were an open invitation for nasty cuts from glass or a bad encounter with a honey locust thorn. I still have painful memories on stepping on a locust thorn and driving it all the way to the bone in arch of my foot. My screams must have been something to behold, because our next door neighbor, Marianna Black, came over in a huff and told Mom in no uncertain terms she shouldn't be whipping me so hard.

How I wish I could recall the expression on the face of this wonderful, good-hearted but sometimes slightly intrusive lady when Mom showed her the thorn she had just extracted from my foot with a pair of pliers. I suspect it was one of the few times Mrs. Black was, at least temporarily, at a loss for words. She recovered quickly though and helped Mom complete the repair job.

Tender insteps and occasional hazards aside, the bottoms of my feet, and for that matter those of any youngster worth his salt, were tough as leather. They may not have been fireproof but one "watch this" test of toughness was to use your heel to crush a carelessly dropped cigarette butt that was still glowing. Another one was to walk on concrete or asphalt during the heat of the day. There were other minor obstacles to be overcome, and I don't think a summer ever passed without them presenting me with a painful problem at some point. The two I remember most were stubbed toes and making a bit of a mislick of some kind while riding a bicycle barefooted. In the latter regard, it's one thing to catch the bottom of a pair of jeans in a bike chain; bare flesh tangling with the chain is a different proposition entirely.

To my youthful way of thinking going barefooted equated to freedom. I was a Huck Finn of the high country or a Robinson Crusoe of the ridgelines. The feel of cool mud between one's toes was nothing short of wonderful. I knew all about the pleasures of mud packs before ever hearing of facials for ladies, and I didn't have to visit a high-dollar spa for such treatment. Similarly, walking through freshly plowed ground, wiggling your toes in the fertile soil, gave a sense of connection to the good earth that exceeded anything you experienced when wearing shoes.

Other joys of being barefooted included wading in branches without any thought of getting your shoes wet (and a subsequent tongue lashing or worse from parents), going night crawler hunting after an evening rain and feeling the wet grass and worm castings beneath your feet, or pushing around in rocks at the edge of a creek just to see if you could turn up some ideal slingshot ammunition. Youngsters, at least up until adolescence, simply didn't want to be troubled with footwear. After all, there's something almost magical about wandering through dewy grass in the early hours of morning or walking around after a late evening shower.

Today my feet are so tender that a 40-yard walk to the mailbox would find me hopping off the concrete or treading ever so carefully. In those glorious old barefoot days though, it was sheer magic to go unshod, and I have to feel a bit sorry for any reader, no matter what age, who didn't enjoy this special privilege of youth.

There were no signs such as those reading "no shoes, no shirt, no service" commonly seen today. I wouldn't have dared enter Bennett's or Conley's drugstore without a shirt on, but being on the premises of one of these wonderful emporiums dispensing ice cream, fountain drinks, milkshakes, and comic books while lacking shoes was no problem. Indeed, it was commonplace.

I even remember attending federal court sessions, an unusual but interesting source of entertainment, with bare feet. If you got a talented, stem-winding lawyer of the old school with an inclination for dispensing folksy wisdom or who just happened to be moved to the heights of oratorical eloquence, or even some n'er-do-well defendant who decided to argue the merits of his turning a corn crop into easily stored and dispensed liquid form, there was real fun to be had by those in the court audience. I never saw a judge cast a second glance at bare feet, although one did have the bailiff remove me and a bunch of my friends when we dared enter his courtroom wearing Bermuda shorts.

I fear that the magic of going barefooted as a matter of course has pretty much gone the way of one-speed bicycles, boys playing war, and cowboy movies on Saturday afternoons at the local theatre. But I'm guessing that there are still goodly numbers of those from my generation who recall a time of shoeless feet and carefree days with nostalgic yearning. Maybe the random recollections that follow will add further fond mental treks back to June days.

June was the first squash and zucchini of the season, initially as welcome as they would become worrisome in a few weeks thanks to their amazing productivity.

It was blackberries beginning to show red and, with that color change, conveying the welcome message that pickin' time was a-coming soon. Better still, if you knew where to find them, dewberries and wild raspberries were already ripe.

June meant early corn tasseling as it bore promise of the indescribable delight of a couple of roasting ears slathered with real butter and bursting with golden sweetness.

It was bees busily going about their business with locust and sourwood blooms on the menu.

June was an old man wearing a straw hat and patiently hoeing corn, down one row and back the next one, row after row, until at long last he was truly in the short rows.

It was the incomparable taste of water from a mountain spring, so cold it set one's teeth on edge.

It was home-churned ice cream atop a fresh-baked cobbler, the perfect end to a filling meal.

June was young boys riding bikes to go to a "secret" fishing hole.

It was those self-same boys running a trot line, managing a throw line, setting limb lines, or jug fishing for catfish.

It was rocking chairs on the porch in the gloaming, stringing and break-ing the first green beans of the year while enjoying simple conversation with family or friends.

It was making music in an impromptu pickin' and grinnin' session or shaking a leg in an old-fashioned hoe down.

June was an old man and a young boy enjoying a special time together while just plundering about.

It was birds singing in the cool of morning, young rabbits frisking around the edge of fields, crows fussing for no other reason than that they seemed to enjoy being raucous, and the eerie eight-note call of a barred owl in the twilight.

It was hikes to waterfalls, trips to the old swimming hole, tube rides down tumbling creeks, and general revelry in streams of the Smokies.

It was somber remembrance in visits to remote graveyards along Fontana's north shore or elsewhere in the Park, with loving looks back to a world we have lost and thoughts of those who prepared the way for us.

June is now bittersweet recollection, at least for those of my age, of a time when it didn't take much to entertain a youngster and when family gatherings were times of true celebration.

June was and remains a month of countless faces and moods without end, but in the high country it has always been a time, most of all, to enjoy abundant blessings. Poet Robert Burns knew that the month held joys aplenty, as he reminds us with the lines "Oh, my luve's like a red, red rose, That's newly sprung in June."

July: In the Good Ol' Summertime

I genuinely believe that today's youngsters are being deprived. There is simply no way that computers and a panoply of other devices involving technology beyond my ken can substitute for the joys of playing outside, spending the night with a friend, camping, fishing, helping raise a garden, or any of countless other activities which produce closeness to the good earth.

In the sweetness of long ago summers the month of July was a time of unending joy. Heat had begun to lay holt of the land, but it seemed late afternoons, more often than not, brought a brief thunderstorm and cooling shower to set everything right and make for perfect sleeping with the windows open. An insect chorus in full voice provided a lovely lullaby, and if it was a tad too hot, you could always flip your pillow to the cool side.

Still, July heat was a palpable thing, at times so much so it wilted the spirit and gave rise to all sorts of heat-related sayings. Here are some of them, shared because colloquialisms of this sort give spirit and meaning to our language, and mountain talk has always been rich in this regard. Smokies folks have a gift for imagery, and the examples below attest to that.

Hotter than a two-dollar pistol.

Hotter than the hinges of Hades.

Hotter than Beelzebub's belt buckle.

Hotter than Satan's shins.

Hotter than Lucifer's legs.

Hotter than the Fourth of July.

Hotter than melted asphalt.

Hot enough to fry an egg.

So hot trees are paying dogs to do their business on them.

So hot the egg's cooked soon as it leaves the hen.

Hotter than a summer kitchen with a wood-burning stove.

So hot that I saw a rabbit race with the cottontail and the beagles just walking.

Hot or not, July was chock full of things to do, and here, in no particular order of precedence or importance, are some of these things I enjoyed in Julys from long ago.

Eating ground cherries while hoeing in Grandpa's corn patch or gathering a mess of roastin' ears.

Building flutter mills and operating them in branches.

Picking, stringing, and breaking beans to be put up in one quart jar after another and then lovingly stored for winter use.

Running a needle equipped with heavy thread through whole beans (which had been strung) to hang in the summer sun to make leather britches.

Catching lightning bugs and putting them in a jar.

Teasing grampuses (if that is the right plural) out of their underground holes with a broom straw.

Savoring ice cream floats from the drugstore or, for a change, peanuts in a bottled Coke.

Splurging on quarter cherry milkshakes.

Enjoying music making at someone's home on Friday nights.

Square dancing in Cherokee or at what is now the Stompin' Ground in Maggie Valley on Saturday nights.

Visiting the local pool hall (Dad would have had a red-eyed hissy had he known of these visits) where the cool air, click of balls, and male camaraderie overlaid with vague hints of something slightly illicit had magnetic appeal.

Saturday matinees at Gem Theatre, where a dime would get you a cartoon, another installment of a serial, news of the world, and a grand

Western movie. If I happened to be in plush circumstances (that is to say, possessed of a quarter burning my pocket), the movie would be enjoyed in style with a soft drink and candy such as an O. Henry candy bar, a caramel concoction on a stick that would last the entire movies, Sugar Babies, or something similar.

Lazy days along the Tuckaseigee, catching catfish and knottyheads while fishing at Devils Dip or the Reese Hole.

Enjoying the company and pithy wisdom of old Al Dorsey, the ultimate high country river rat.

Observing the delightful eccentricities of true characters of the sort who seem to have become scarce as hen's teeth in today's world.

Searching for glass drink bottles to redeem them.

Joining Grandpa Joe for all sorts of simple pleasures—an ice cold "watermillon" after a day of hoeing and doing other garden work, a hearty dinner featuring Grandma Minnie's cooking and the bounty of summer's garden truck, cutting canes to dry and make into fishing poles, checking out mast in anticipation of the fall squirrel season, and much more.

Riding my bike up Deep Creek to swim, fish, or in my teenage years, to flirt with girls whose families were camping in the GSMNP.

Camping trips at the Bryson Place.

Late afternoon fishing on the Nantahala River.

Night fishing in the Weeks Hole on lower Deep Creek.

Caddying on the local nine-hole golf course, now long lost to development and a recreational park.

Hunting golf balls in the rough on that course and, in my teen years, spending hour after hour atop a tractor mowing the fairways with gang mowers. Other work included dragging the sand "greens" and using the tractor's side blade to trim the rough.

Enjoying the simple pleasures of reading books from the Marianna Black Library. My tastes were eclectic, ranging from the Westerns of Zane Grey to mysteries by the likes of Agatha Christie and Sax Rohmer, from outdoor classics such as the works of Theodore Roosevelt and Robert Ruark to simple adventure stories in the Hardy Boys series.

Savoring the latest issue of *Field and Stream* magazine while waiting in the barber shop for Jim Traywick or Cecil Morgan to trim and shape my flat-top.

Shooting countless BBs from my trusty Red Ryder air gun at targets that ranged from tin cans to blue jays, silver dollars to English sparrows.

Spending the night at the homes of friends or relatives.

Cruising town in the evening with buddies who were fortunate enough to own a vehicle.

Hitchhiking to Cherokee to work and doing the same thing to get back home at day's end.

Living in a time when local physicians still made home calls on occasion.

Playing pick-up baseball games at the makeshift field near our home.

Digging fishing worms in the chicken lot of Aunt Mag, a wonderful old black lady who lived just down the road.

Hearing whistles signaling the start of work, breaks, dinner time, and the close of the work day at Carolina Wood Turning Company.

Playing war. This would be the ultimate in political incorrectness in today's world, but building forts, lining up armies of lead soldiers, using "maypops" or pine cones as make believe hand grenades, occupied endless enjoyable hours.

Making simple tools such as bow-and-arrows, slingshots, or popguns. The search for appropriate materials was, in and of itself, an exercise in joy. Looking for a hickory sapling that might become a bow, a dogwood fork for a slingshot, or an elderberry shoot of the appropriate size for a popgun gave one a perfect excuse to wander through the woods.

Swinging on wild grape vines.

Using a rope tied to a tree limb over Deep Creek to swing out over a swimming hole and then cannonball into the deepest part of the pool.

Looking for early signs of the bounty of fall that would come in a few months—fox grapes, hazelnuts, walnuts, pawpaws, and more.

Listening to old men tell tales beneath the evergreens then located next to the 5- & 10-cent store at the town square. The location had a pair of delightful names. It was known as Loafers Glory in polite circles, but a far more common, pithier one was Dead Pecker Corner.

Watching some of the men gathered there play endless games of checkers.

Anticipating and the observing the annual arrival of a wonderful eccentric simply known as "the goat man" (his real name was Charles McCartney). He traveled with a smelly entourage of goats that pulled a ramshackle wagon stacked high with all sorts of junk.

Enjoying a hamburger at the old Na-Ber's, which still exists but in a new location.

Eating fried apple pies, warmed up and topped with a scoop of vanilla ice cream, at Dent's Café.

Watching old men talk and watch set fishing poles as their lines dangled from the only bridge in town in the Tuckaseigee River. On one memorable occasion Al Dorsey hooked and eventually landed a catfish that weighed close to 50 pounds, and by the time the epic struggle was over it seemed like everyone in town had gathered to watch him do battle with the whiskered giant.

Spending hours skipping rocks, with each stone having been carefully selected for balance and flatness, in the river. Boys competed with great zest to see who could get the most skips.

Playing games of pitch and catch with treasured baseball gloves, taking time out every week or so to rub some mineral oil into the leather to make the glove more supple.

Joining other boys to build a top-secret "clubhouse" in the form of a crude building made of resiny, new-cut pines.

Listening to country music on WCKY, WWL, or WSM. I can still, in my mind, hear the show host on WCKY out of Cincinnati saying "This is your old friend Wayne Raney coming to you through 50,000 watts of pure power."

Almost everyone we knew well grew a garden, took pride in it, and not only ate from it in the summer but did plenty of canning. Mom's canning focused on soup mix (corn, crowder peas, limas, tomatoes, and okra), tomatoes, green beans, and apples. She never really satisfied until the shelves down in the basement were stacked full of quart Mason jars holding the bounty of the garden, Dad's small orchard, and, come fall, hog meat (she canned cracklings, covering them with lard, and also put up other portions of the pig, with the hams being cured by Daddy).

Boys collected baseball cards and used those cards on the spokes of their one-speed bikes (with foot brakes) to create a most satisfying racket.

Baseball heroes included Mickey Mantle, Roger Maris, Willie Stargell (he played minor league ball for a season in nearby Asheville), Stan Musial, and others. At this point in time baseball was THE American professional sport.

For most boys, fishing of some kind was almost a given. It might be fly fishing for trout, river fishing for catfish, or lake fishing for a whole bunch of different species. Whatever the case though, far more boys fished then than seems to be the case today. I still see the occasional youngster along a creek or the banks of the river, whereas in my adolescence if would have been difficult to find a summer day when there weren't half a dozen boys watching their line or waiting for a bobber to bounce.

Summertime in its multi-faceted splendor peaked in July, and even now I look back to it with great longing and a sense of loss. I suspect the same holds true for many others of my years. Those were splendid days in the summer sun and the summer of youth, a carefree time when, like most homes, mine had no television and when parents had no second thoughts about letting a youngster wander fields and woods on his own. It was a time of wonder and most certainly had many features we are gone forever. To be nurtured by nature and blessed with parents who understood that growing up involved freedom to spread wings was life in the Smokies at its best.

> If a cool August follows a hot July,
> Coming winter will be hard and dry.

August: Dog Days in the High Country

The term "dog days" dates back to ancient Rome and comes from the star Sirius, also known as the Dog Star. The hottest months of the year in much of the Northern Hemisphere and certainly the Smokies are July and August. They come when Sirius is in its closest proximity to the sun. I suspect you could ask two dozen mountain old timers about dog days and none of them would refer to Romans, Sirius, astrology, or the like. Similarly, few would be able to give the traditional forty-day period constituting dog days—July 3–August 11. Yet without exception they would be familiar with the term "those old dog days of summer," associating them primarily with August, and would have plenty of thoughts and knowledge of traditional folklore they associated with the term. Smoky Mountain dog days offer sensations and superstitions of many kinds, and ultimately you have to see, smell, and sense them, as opposed to trying to describe their special aura, in order to appreciate them fully. If you have deep roots in these ancient hills, dog days have meaning aplenty for you. They are a time of transition, the cusp between summer and fall, and a time for both fond reflection and looking ahead.

Honesty compels me to admit that August has never been my favorite month. Indeed, if pressed to rank the twelve months of the year in terms of which ones I like least, there would be a close race between August and February. There's plenty to dislike about August. It brings some summer's worst features in the form of withering heat, breath-sucking humidity, attention from bothersome or painful pests such as dog pecker gnats and yellow jackets, every problem imaginable plaguing the garden, fishing generally in the doldrums, and heartfelt longing for cooler weather gnawing at you while sweat drips off your brow.

Then too, there are superstitions stuck away in one's sub-consciousness. I can't claim to be above all such phantasmagoria, but as Grandpa Joe would have put it in his blunt way, "That just ain't so." I'll pick up a penny whether it shows heads or tails, but I've also been known to carry a buckeye in my pocket. During dog days thoughts of snakes striking blindly and being hyperactive thanks to shedding their skins are impossible to shake. The same holds true for worrying about sores and a pronounced tendency towards infection resulting from walking barefooted in dew-laden grass ("getting dew pizening"). I could offer a take-off on Grandpa and say "that ain't so," but deep down there's a bit of niggling doubt about the threats presented by dog days.

Yet as I grow older, contrary to what is the supposed tendency for those advancing years, in many senses I become increasingly optimistic. Some of that optimism focuses on the positive things associated with the month of August. It sees many garden vegetables reach their peak of productivity—okra loves the heat and will produce like there is no tomorrow as long as it is cut regularly, crowder peas seem to go from purple blooms to swollen pods prime for picking in no time at all, there are more luscious tomatoes than a body knows how to handle, and corn has peaked. In addition, the observant wanderer who ventures outdoors has a surfeit for the senses.

August is a morning fog burning away under the withering intensity of a relentless sun.

It's a million watery diamonds sparkling on the web of a writing spider as the sun first breaks through the fog.

Sometimes it's an extended period of rain, seemingly day after day.

It's a time of portents aplenty on what the weather holds in store during the months to come. You can count the number of morning fogs to get a pretty good idea of winter snows.

It's the delightful aroma of kudzu blooms, a reminder that even the most noxious of plants can have its appealing side.

It's fox grapes ripening along branch and creek banks, bearing aromatic promise of some of the finest jelly ever to adorn biscuit bread.

It's the disappearance of the last of the summer's sourwood bloom and with it realization that the tastiest honey known to mankind is stored in combs and ready for harvest. Incidentally, scrumptious as fox grape jelly undeniably is, it has to take second place to sourwood honey when it comes to forming the perfect culinary accompaniment for a biscuit hot from the oven. A big biscuit, split in half while piping hot, with home-churned butter slathered on it and topped by a generous dollop of sourwood honey, has to be about as close to earthly heaven as one can get when it comes to foodstuffs.

Dog days mean Hickory King field corn made and drying on the stalk prior to storage in a crib or barn, fine stuff for fattening hogs, feeding chickens, or making corn meal.

It's packsaddles on corn stalks, a dose of pure pain if you happen to brush up against one of these stinging brethren of Beelzebub.

It's those same corn stalks wreathed and wrapped by vines of October beans, with pods yellowing in the sun and bearing fruitful promise of hearty late fall and winter eating once they have been harvested, winnowed, and stored.

It's peaches drying on muslin cloth atop a tin roof, a prelude to the pure bliss a fried peach pie can bring to a frosty winter morning in months to come.

It's jars of bread-and-butter pickles, side by side with chowchow, resting atop a kitchen table until every last jar is sealed.

It's a muskmelon so ripe that the stem slips from the melon and the "musk" sets one to drooling.

Dog days is okra fried in the pan, milky sweet corn sliced from the cob to form a key ingredient in soup mix, and tomato vines so laden with fruit that they threaten to topple their stakes.

It's mountain half runners being canned by the quart.

It's kraut in a churn bubbling and "making" before being ready to can.

It's the wonderful fragrance of dust being laid by a brief, welcome shower.

It's dust devils dancing across sere fields, carrying milkweed spores on a wild whirlwind of a journey.

Dog days is a twelve-year-old boy with feet tough as a pine knot and skin brown as fresh fallen chinquapin, filled with growing dread of the arrival of another session of school, the end to three months of freedom, and the necessity of returning to the seeming torture of wearing shoes.

It's a stringer of catfish, the product of a day spent waiting for bobbers to bounce or maybe wading shoals where channel cats like to hang out when rivers are low and oxygenated water at a premium.

It's maypops turning yellow in a fallow field or along a pasture's edge, with knowing country folks breaking them open to suck the sweet/sour pulp from around the seeds.

It's swallowtail butterflies and fritillaries dancing in the air around the deep purple flowers of ironweed or the less impressive but still attractive blooms of tall Joe Pye weed plants.

It's hornets' nests grown large, something to be avoided at all costs, telling a tale of what winter holds by their size and height above streams over which they are so often constructed.

Dog days mean dreams of coming fall, when the yellow of turning hickories will send a message to squirrel hunters and when the heat is exchanged for a welcome chill in the morning air.

It's the glorious passage of a cool front when you can smell hints of autumn on gentle breezes. Somehow such moments add spring to one's step and bring a quickening of the soul.

It's a brief respite between the "laying by" of crops in the heart of summer and the "laying in" time of coming fall.

All anxiety about or dislike for August aside, in my youth it was a month of anticipation. You knew that once dog days had come and gone, the bluebird skies of Indian Summer weren't far behind. Then too, even as a kid there was some carefully masked but nonetheless eager anticipation associated with the month. Though no red-blooded boy would dare mention it, there was inner excitement connected with knowledge that the opening of school would bring new teachers, some new students (mayhap a comely lass among them), new challenges, and more. Summer was coming to an end and had begun to pall—it was time to get ready for the arrival of fall.

If the heat of early August comes on strong,
Coming winter will be hard and long.

The Sweet of September

Almost sixty Septembers ago I set out, excited, more than a little bit scared, and wide-eyed with wonder in the way only an innocent mountain lad could be, for college. At the time I had never seen the ocean, never spent more than a few nights away from the house I grew up in, had set foot in only five states, and had almost no experience in dining out or sleeping in a hotel or motel bed. My longest journey from home had been the senior high school trip to Washington D. C. Even though the geographical distance to where I would attend undergraduate school (King College in Bristol, TN) was not a long one, it was a move into a strikingly different world.

I was, at least for a semester, a terribly homesick son of the Smokies. Had I been pressed at the time, I would have been hard put to say what I missed most. Certainly I missed friends and classmates. Likewise my thoughts turned frequently to my family—parents, sister and brother, grandparents, cousins, aunts and uncles. Then there were the simple pleasures of small town life that suddenly had been taken from me as a result of this rite of passage to adulthood—cherry cokes at Bennett's Drug Store, milkshakes at Glen Conley's establishment just across the street, burgers from Na-Ber's, fried pies topped with a scoop of ice cream at Dent's Café, Friday night football, basketball on Tuesday and Friday nights after fall gave way to winter, the sound of the clock striking the hour at the old courthouse, the lonesome whistle at Carolina Wood Turning Company sending signals to workers, anticipation of the coming squirrel and rabbit seasons, the waning days of the trout season (which in those days closed, at least in the GSMNP) in mid-September, and so much more.

Now, looking back from the vantage point of three score years, I think what I missed most were the sensory joys September in the high country provided. The sights, scents, and sounds of the month were soothing and clearly had been permanently seared on my soul. Much has changed since those halcyon days of youth, but to me the sweet of September in the Smokies continues to be those things captured by one's senses. What follows is a glimpse at some of them, although rest assured these ruminations are but a whisper of the wonders provided by this month forming the bridge between summer and fall.

September is the sound of katydids singing as if there is no tomorrow, and to a considerable degree they are right, because there won't be too many tomorrows before frost puts an end to their fragile existence.

It's the heady aroma of plum grannies (also known as Queen Anne's pocket melons or muskmelons) wafting through the evening air in a mountain garden. While these old-timey fruits have relatively little taste, they are beautiful to the eyes and would make a Chanel No. 5-quality perfume if their essence could be captured.

It's Red and Golden Delicious apples ripening on trees and bursting with sweet goodness at the first bite.

It's long strings of leather britches (dried green beans) hanging in the sun to remove the last bit of moisture before storage.

It's hot pepper plants pulled up by the roots and hung upside down to dry and be used for seasoning or pepper tea in the cold days of winter.

It's ground cherries dropping their Chinese lantern–like fruit to the ground in sere fields of corn and a country boy enjoying an impromptu feast as he gathers a handful of these golden delicacies.

It's chinquapins bursting from prickly burrs where this cousin of the American chestnut has grown up in fire scalds. To see one of these shiny nuts, a delicacy that boys sometimes brought to school in their pockets in yesteryear, is to understand immediately the old mountain words of praise for a dark-eyed girl, "she's got chinquapin eyes."

It's buckeyes littering the ground, a seeming nut treat that is actually poisonous but not without its uses, at least in mountain folklore. Carrying one of these irregularly shaped nuts in your pocket is supposed to bring good luck and ward off the pains of arthritis.

It's hazel nuts peeking from husks changing from green to golden brown, and the wise soul will hustle to beat the bushytails to these treats.

It's the banana-like smell of ripening pawpaws, a largely forgotten fruit from nature's rich bounty that happened to be George Washington's favorite dessert when prepared in a custard.

It's persimmons hanging heavy from trees with shiny green leaves beginning to show hints of red and gold. They already sport a bright orange color that can tempt the unknowing to take a taste, but as anyone who has sampled an unripe persimmon knows, this is a case of haste making terrible waste. On the other hand, when they do ripen a persimmon pudding is nectar of the gods.

It's shades of red and purple, maroon and magenta, adorning some of the first plants to show color—dogwoods, sumac, devil's club, pokeberries, and more.

It's pumpkins and cushaws ripe in the field, and acorn and butternut squash in the garden. All promise golden goodness in pies and casseroles come Thanksgiving and Christmas.

It's fall vegetables—turnips, kale, mustard greens, black-seeded Simpson lettuce, and cabbage—showing good growth and promising fine fare to come.

It's the splendor of dahlia blooms flourishing in the cool nights and moderate days, bringing splashes of colorful glory to gardens and flower vases.

It's a boomer cutting on red oak mast high up on a main ridgeline and grey squirrels doing the same at lower elevations.

It's a mountain fisherman savoring the last of the summer's dry fly action using a terrestrial pattern to imitate plentiful grasshoppers, ants, or beetles.

It's big brown trout beginning to show the first hint of the spawning migration to come six weeks down the road, and miniature torpedoes darting for cover when the careless fishermen spooks rainbows in the low waters of the season.

September wheedles and enchants in so many ways, and it holds no peer as a month for longing. There's bittersweetness in the fashion in which it carries us backwards to days of youth, there's eager anticipation of impending fall, and there's a farmer's quiet satisfaction in the passage of another growing season in earth's never-ending cycle. Take any of its many faces—a season of harvest, a time for nostalgic contemplation of things past, or an interlude for dreaming of memories yet to be made— September is a month to mesmerize.

If there's a thunderstorm in late September; expect a snow in late November.
Doves fleeing south before a September storm; look for a winter to be anything but warm.
Doves calling on a September day, means gentle rain is on the way.
When late September brings an early frost, fail to stack firewood and you'll pay the cost.
Snakes in September a-headin' to the den, a sure sign cold's about to set in.

An Ode to October

October is a month of magic. It blends so much of the grandeur of the mountains in a heady brew that one is almost moved to wish for a year of Octobers. If May is the miracle of earth's rebirth, October is the fulfillment of that greening-up time come full circle. Laying by time has come and gone, crops are ready to be harvested, the whole world seems gilded with gold with scattered splashes of other colors merely adding emphasis to its beauty, and the Smokies stand out in all their unrivalled splendor. That's October, and here are some of the features that combine to adorn her lovely face.

October is a hunter's moon, cold gold just clearing the eastern horizon as a farmer leaves his fields at eventide. If you don't feel close to the earth and a bit awestruck under such a moon, I humbly suggest that an urgent appointment with the nearest qualified psychiatrist is in order.

October is a mountain boy, roaming in the gloaming after an afternoon of squirrel hunting, feeling deep in his heart that it is almost possible to touch that hunter's moon just showing on the skyline.

It's a buck in the prime of his years, full of virility and driven by the ages-old impulse to reproduce. He wanders the woods, neck mightily swollen, as he works scrapes, leaves his scent on limbs, and searches for does in estrus.

It's a wizened and wise country farmer, a man who has lived on land that has belonged to his family for generations, pursuing the timeless rituals of the harvest—picking apples from the farm's orchard; filling a corn crib with full ears of dent corn that will fatten hogs and feed chickens that lay eggs tasting far superior to anything ever found on grocery store shelves; gathering pumpkins to make pumpkin leather, bake into pies, feed raw to the hogs, or carefully store in a root cellar for use in the months to come.

It's wrinkles on that patriarch's face, or maybe they are just character lines, telling a tale of a life well lived.

It's October beans drying on standing corn stalks.

It's golden persimmons, wrinkling as they ripen and drop to the ground. If you have sufficient gumption you can beat the critters—deer, 'possums, 'coons, coyotes, and foxes—to this candy from nature. If that results in a persimmon pudding, consider yourself rich beyond any amount that ever appeared on a bank statement.

It's molasses fresh in the can or jar, mere days from pressing but full of promise atop breakfast biscuits for months to come.

It's another season of honey duly taken from hives and stored for satisfaction of even the hungriest of sweet teeth.

It's an aging man and a young boy, one carrying a single-shot .22 and the other an old hammer shotgun, heading to woods marked by that sentinel of autumn, hickory trees clad in cloaks of gold, for a day of squirrel hunting.

October is table fare from the product of such a hunt, fried squirrel with recently dug sweet potatoes flanking one side of the platter and a heaping mess of turnip greens cooked with diced young turnips and streaked meat on the other. Add biscuits and a big gravy boat full to the brim with squirrel gravy and you have a meal of the sort royalty is seldom privileged to sample and savor.

October is apples enjoyed in so many ways—in refreshing cider, apple butter, dried and turned into fried pies, apple sauce, fritters, deep dish pies, a run of brandy, and more.

It's a lot full of hogs, eating red-rooted pig weed, corn fodder, more than a fair ration of shelled Hickory King corn, inferior pumpkins, bruised sweet taters, the last of the year's watermelons, and whatever else the good earth has to offer. Little do the swine know that their world of plenty will soon give way to an Armageddon Day. As the first hard freeze arrives towards month's end or maybe early in November, their salad days are numbered. In my adolescent world hog-killing time was incredibly busy but if you've never eaten fried tenderloin taken from a pig that very day I would submit that yours has been a life of culinary deprivation.

It's the sweet and satisfying smell of newly plowed ground, with everything turned under to rot in the winter before plowing and planting time returns once more with the glories of spring.

It's the heady allure of nature's perfume floating on gentle breezes, a mixture of fall flowers, just a hint of dust, ripe or ripening fruits, a touch of sweet decay, a bit of manure from the barn, and more. If you can't smell autumn, about all I can say is you ain't mountain folk.

October is a sense of quiet satisfaction in knowing that another year of hard work, good crops, and simple fulfillment has come to an end.

It's a broom sedge field turned into a treasure chest of sparkling diamonds as the morning sun glistens with a million beams of brightness after the season's first heavy frost. It's a kid rich in freedom while having no idea he is poor in worldly goods riding sleds made of cardboard in that same field once it has dried in the sun of an Indian Summer afternoon.

It's a flock of turkeys, with the jakes already bigger than their mothers and the hens of the year almost as big, working their way along a pasture edge, flipping cow piles and dining on a buffet of grasshoppers and other insects.

It's a pack of beagles in training for the soon-to-open rabbit season hot on the trail of a cottontail in the cool of evening.

October is walnuts dropping to the ground and providing promise of both hard work in the gathering and cracking and rich rewards in the form of cookies and cakes.

It's added pep in an old man's step on a brisk morning and a sense of urgency in a young boy anxious to be home from school and out in the afternoon squirrel woods.

It's shelves groaning with canned goods, freezers full of garden truck but with space left for plenty of venison, and dried goods hanging beneath barn rafters in mesh bags. It's a pot of leather britches soaking before cooking or maybe one of October beans holding a chunk of streaked meat for flavor simmering on the stove.

It's a well-worn Duxbak jacket hanging on a peg silently begging to be used, and an old dog that recognizes that jacket means good times in the fields and woods.

It's the incomparable aroma of Hoppes' No. 9 and burnt gunpowder.

Most of all, October is a month that blends the fulfillment of spring and hard work of summer on the land as yet another performance of nature's never-ending cycle of death and rebirth, gray grimness and green richness, is completed.

In my judgment that October is a month filled with enduring wonder. I have conscious memories of well over three score Octobers, and the richness of autumn in all her glory eternally stirs the soul and uplifts the spirits in much the same way these storied mountains reach towards the sky.

> If October has heavy frosts and winds blow wild, expect January to be
>   quite mild.
> Rain aplenty in October means winds will blow come December.
> The hunter's moon of October with no sign of frost,
> Means no frost at all until November's full moon.
> If there's no Indian Summer in October or November, look for it to come
>   in December.

November Nostalgia

To me, November always evokes pleasant thoughts—they include fond memories of boyhood rabbit hunts with a bevy of human and canine companions, the culinary joys associated with Thanksgiving, the wonderful weather the Smokies so often provide in this month, spawning speckled trout on the move, and the sort of crispness in the air at daylight that fills youngsters with juice and puts a bit of added spring in an old man's step. But it's also a time, as Scottish poet Robert Burns reminds us, "When chill November's surly blast, Made fields and forests bare."

A few years back a good friend who lives in the Topton, NC named Ken Roper offered me a description I hadn't heard in decades. He said that on a particular November morning he had stepped out on his porch to a "frost so big you could track a rabbit in it." I would submit to you that his description, and it is one I heard often as a youngster, captures the essence of a November morning. I think back on November days, lots of them, when frost melting as the sun's rays hit it turned an overgrown, abandoned pasture or piece of farm land run to broom sedge into a place of wonderment. Before my eyes frost yielded to the sun's inexorable march, and sparkling diamonds literally had their moment in that sun before melting away. To witness such things is to know, beyond any doubt, that there is a supreme presence.

Though in far slower fashion than melting frost, November witnesses leaf fall and a distinct change in the landscape. Those who confine all their walking and wandering to warmer months miss something, because woodlands shorn of their leaves provide a different and delightful perspective. By month's end you don't have to worry about blundering into a rattlesnake or copperhead or making a painful intrusion into a yellow jacket nest. You also have ample occasion to notice things that are all but invisible in spring and summer. Signs of one-time human presence, distant vistas that had been blocked by vegetation, sprightly plants such as galax or partridge berries that pass largely unnoticed, maybe the red seed pods of hearts-a-bursting-with love or jack-in-the-pulpit, and the like form a feast for knowing eyes.

I always kept a keen eye out for walnut trees as a boy, although I must admit that gathering nuts was not the primary reason I sought the tree. Rather, if there was a tree at the edge of a field or along a fence row, something easily spotted when a party of us took to the fields on a rabbit hunt, there was always the possibility of a squirrel or two being nearby. I'd give the limbs a thorough look-see, searching for a tell-tale bulge or something that looked a bit out of place. Occasionally I would be rewarded and a bushytail would add a comforting bit of heft to the game bag of my hand-me-down Duxbak hunting coat.

Thoughts of that old hunting coat, and Duxbak attire in general, strike a distinctly nostalgic chord with me. In the 1950s and 1960s Duxbak was THE choice when it came to field clothing. Camo attire was unheard of, but the stiff, sturdy, enduring nature of Duxbak was another story entirely. To my knowledge today's world of outdoor clothing has nothing approaching it in terms of combining reasonable cost and durability. I know that I would no more have thought of going afield without Duxbak pants, vest or jacket, and cap than I would have skipped a Saturday rabbit hunt to hang out in the local drug store or even visit my girlfriend of the moment. One did, after all, have to have priorities.

Duxbak has gone the way of so many other fine American-made products, but I'm guessing that anyone who reads these words and recognizes the brand is on the upper side of fifty years of age, hunted as a youngster, and remembers the attire with fondness. I knew that on a personal level such was the case, and it was a forlorn Christmas indeed when my gifts didn't include Duxbak clothing of some kind. Such are the thoughts that course through my mind this time of year, for November is a month somehow meant for nostalgia. With the harvest done and winter ahead, it's a time for looking back in longing.

As the month advanced, November was for me as filled with eager anticipation as the days immediately preceding Christmas. It may seem strange to think of a boy getting excited about the opening day of rabbit season, but for me it was a truly special time. The season usually opened the Saturday prior to Thanksgiving and ran through the end of February. By opening day our beagles had been in training for weeks, and if you think a dog can't tell when you are about to go hunting, you haven't spent much time around hunting dogs. As a wonderful black lady who was a good friend of mine put it, in simple yet heartfelt fashion, "they know." When they saw Duxbak clothing the beagles would go into a hind-legs-dancing frenzy, and it would last until such time as a couple of good races (we never shot the first rabbit of the day "on the jump") had them settled down to the business at hand.

When we headed down to the kennel in the pre-dawn chill of that first Saturday, I felt like jumping and cavorting with the beagles. The inner boy in me had been solidly stoked with a breakfast of bacon and eggs, maybe biscuits if Mom had made them the night before (Dad's culinary efforts didn't run to biscuits, and Mom drew the line at personally preparing breakfast at ungodly hours) or otherwise plenty of toast. As an "adornment" for the bread portion of breakfast there were ample choices such as recently made molasses, homemade blackberry jam, or maybe a container of Dixie Dew. The latter was store-bought cane syrup with the finest bit of labeling advertorial I've ever seen: "Covers Dixie like the dew and gives a biscuit a college education." Blend it with some soft butter (the real thing) and sop it up with a biscuit, and you were in culinary high cotton.

There would also be stewed apples from our little orchard, heated and mixed in with a bit of butter. Or, if the dining stars were really aligned in the most propitious of fashions, there would be pork tenderloin. If you haven't eaten fresh pork tenderloin from hogs you raised, butchered, and processed, with a fine helping of milk gravy on the side, I feel a bit sorry for you.

There was always the possibility of tenderloin around the rabbit hunting opener, because hog-killing time at Grandpa's (he raised hogs for the whole family and everyone pitched in on the first Saturday it was cold enough to do the job right and not have to worry about flies, yellow jackets, or spoiled meat) always seems to come around mid-November. That happy coincidence meant there was decent chance of tenderloin to start opening day out in the right way.

After a hearty breakfast and packing an even heartier dinner, we would head out with our beagles, pick up a couple of my buddies, and then link up with Dad's best friend, Claude Gossett, and his pack of dogs. Sometimes, though not always, there would be another adult or two to the party. Protracted discussions and strategic planning worthy of a major military campaign had already been handled in advance, so all that remained was to drive wherever Daddy and Claude had decided to open the season.

Interestingly, and this is a major change from the situation in today's world, we almost never encountered posted signs or were denied permission to hunt. Occasionally someone would place a bit of limitation by saying, "Go ahead and hunt rabbits but don't shoot my birds." Otherwise, posted land or denial of permission to hunt was about as scarce as those "birds" (quail) are in today's world. In terms of access, the "good old days" truly were good.

Big game, most notably the comeback of the whitetail and wild turkey, has changed all of that, although there are other factors as well. For example, a far smaller percentage of the population of Smokies of today has local roots stretching back for generations than was the case in the 1950s and 1960s. Daddy knew a lot of folks and Claude Gossett seemed to know everyone not only in Swain but Jackson and Macon counties as well.

To me then, and now, those were days of indescribable bliss. I didn't need mossy-horned deer to get me excited, and I doubt if a strutting gobbler charges my adrenalin much more now than a good rabbit race did then. Incidentally, that's saying a mouth full, because wild turkeys hold a corner of my hunter's soul.

In those halcyon days of yesteryear, a single-shot shotgun, some simple gear, a pocket full of shells, and countless carefree days afield gave me a start down a glorious sporting road that still stretches out before me. It also kept me out of trouble. I never felt deprived because we didn't have a television, it took a virtual act of Congress for me to get permission from Daddy to "borrow" the sole car our family owned, the phone was on a party line and was pretty much off limits for adolescent chit-chat, and we almost never went out to eat. Yet if you think somehow my youth was devoid of riches, you would be wrong.

The greatest of American outdoor writers, Robert Ruark, may not have set the best of examples in his personal life, but he was squarely on target when he suggested that a youngster who hunted and fished in the fashion I did wasn't much of a candidate to become a juvenile delinquent. I was far too busy having fun, and some of the most joyous and memorable of all my countless times of boyhood wonder came in November. It's a month to evoke nostalgia and be thankful for many reasons beyond the celebration of Thanksgiving.

A warm November portends a bad winter.
November ice so thick it'll bear a duck, coming winter will be snow and
    muck.
Snow early in November, look for a hard and cold December.

December Delights

My love affair with December stretches back to memory's earliest stages, and along with memorable gifts such as my first gun, a treasured hatchet, pocket knives, Duxbak clothing, and the joys of time spent with my extended family, thoughts of food stand well in the forefront of all the things I associate with the Yuletide season. Some evidence of my fixation with foodstuffs is offered by the fact that some years ago, when finishing up editing of an anthology of material by noted author Archibald Rutledge entitled *Carolina Christmas,* I could not resist the temptation offered by his writing to add, with my wife's able assistance, a concluding section on food memories and recipes. After all, Rutledge has the literary power to conjure up hunger pangs even when you've just eaten, and any author capable of that merits some coverage of his favorite seasonal fare.

When he writes about baked sweet potatoes with juice oozing from their skins and filling the air with the aroma of brown sugar, when he describes a haunch of venison flanked by plantation vegetables and roasted to perfection, or when he draws attention to the delectable delights of a pecan pie, I have to watch myself or I'll be drooling. Yet his ability to produce pleasant gustatory reflexes with the mere mention of traditional dishes has another side, for it sets me on my own path of time travel back into a world of December delights and boyhood wonder.

My food memories from boyhood in the Smokies involve plenty of provender to satisfy even the most peculiar of palates, and much of it involves dishes you don't encounter every day. I hope what follows will make you a bit peckish, and if you don't know what that means, as my ninth grade English teacher Thad DeHart would have said, look it up. Perhaps my most powerful memory involves Mom's applesauce cake. Part of that no doubt derives from a passin' powerful sweet tooth and the fact that some way, every day, I think of my dear departed mother. Many of those exercises in turning back time's pages involve food, for along with an abundance of other talents Mom was an accomplished cook who loved to feed others. Rick Bragg may claim, in one of his exquisitely crafted books, that his mother was *The Best Cook in the World*. He's entitled to his opinion, but in my world at least it was a toss-up between Momma and Grandma Minnie.

We had a small apple orchard on our land, and that no doubt explains, at least in part, the manner in which apples figured so prominently in our daily fare. Dad tended the Red Delicious, Stayman, and Golden Delicious trees with great care. That meant annual pruning, careful spraying, and hard if joyous work at harvest time.

Many of the apples would be canned in late September or early October, with Mom's annual goal being 200 quarts of what we simply called fruit (stewed apples). Seldom did a day go by when we didn't have cooked apples or applesauce on the table. Other apples would be dried, providing the key ingredient for a mainstay of hearty winter breakfasts, apple stack cakes, and fried apple pies. The cream of the crop, those apples which were unblemished, was stored in a huge bin and airy baskets in the basement. One of my youthful jobs was to go through these every week or so to cull out rotting apples. Typically I would catch them when they just showed a spot, and Mom would turn these into a cobbler that was delicious and easily prepared.

By December we had already gathered the year's harvest of black walnuts as well, and these too went into a variety of Christmas delicacies.

Applesauce cake was made better for a marriage of the oily, pungent flavor of walnut kernels with the juiciness of apples, the meaty tang of seeded Muscat or yellow raisins, and just the right blend of spices. Walnut kernels also figured prominently in Mom's fudge, and at least three or four times during December she would bake a whopping batch of oatmeal cookies chock full of raisins and walnuts. She had a magic touch with cookies, always making sure not to overcook them. That resulted in moist, chewy morsels that, when still warm and accompanied by a glass of milk, were pure culinary heaven.

Mom always made her applesauce cakes the weekend following Thanksgiving, a time when her sons and husband were busy getting the opening days of another rabbit season off to a rollicking start. Looking back, I suspect she was also glad to have us out from under foot. Whatever the exact motivation for her timing, by the first of December she would have a bevy of perfectly baked applesauce cakes "aging" in a downstairs room we never heated. They got better with each passing week, thanks at least in part to the periodic addition of a dollop of wine or apple cider to keep them moist. Similar to fruit cakes, they benefited from passage of a bit of time before being eaten. A few weeks "resting" allowed the myriad flavors to mix, mingle, and eventually mate in a marriage of perfect taste.

Don't get me wrong though, Christmas food involved more than desserts, and for that matter, the sweets covered here merely scratched the surface. It seemed like Mom was baking something almost every day in the two weeks immediately prior to Christmas, with candy roaster or pumpkin pies, tea cakes, sweet breads, half a dozen kinds of cookies, and the like figuring in the holiday picture.

Meanwhile, with cottontail season being open, we dined once or twice a week on rabbit, along with the occasional feast of quail or grouse. We had already been enjoying squirrel for weeks, but none of us ever tired of game on the family table. I didn't realize it at the time, but it was probably welcome in terms of family economics as well. Other than small game (thanks to being scarce as hen's teeth, deer and wild turkeys were not a part of my youth, either as a hunter or in terms of food), our main meat at this season was pork. There's nothing unusual about that, because until the current generation pork was the primary meat for most mountain folks.

Our pork came from hogs Grandpa raised, and until sometime in my early teens we had an annual family hog killing that occupied a whole day and produced great foodstuffs in a variety of forms. There was canned sausage, stored by making the sausage patties, frying them, stuffing them into quart jars, and covering the meat with newly rendered lard before sealing. It was a central feature of many a breakfast, and quite often our evening meal would feature either biscuits or cracklin' cornbread with sausage gravy. That way a quart jar of sausage went a long way.

At other supper times another pork product would figure prominently in our supper. Dinner was normally our main meal of the day in the summer and on weekends throughout the year. Quite often in spring and summer we would have a cold supper of cornbread and milk, but in fall and winter months this changed a bit. We would still have the same fare, but the cornbread would be a freshly baked pone filled with cracklings. For those of you among my readers unfamiliar with this treat, it was cornbread made from stone-ground meal infused with an ample quantity of cracklings—the crisp tidbits left from rendering pork fat into lard. They carry enough cholesterol to be a cardiologist's nightmare and provide enough flavor to bring tears to a glass eye.

On special occasions we would have country ham (Daddy cured ours), invariably offered in company with either biscuits or grits—maybe both. Another part of the hog reserved for festive meals or company was tenderloin. Although it is never tastier than when eaten fresh the day of a hog killing or the next day, tenderloin was also canned and made for some might fine eating.

When we didn't eat pork, except on Sundays, which were reserved for yard bird, wild game usually graced the table. Fried young squirrel or baked squirrel when dealing with older bushytails, when accompanied by milk gravy, biscuits, sweet taters, and turnip greens that had already been nipped by frost and that included plenty of little pieces of the diced root in the bargain, was a most satisfying meal. Much the same held true for rabbit, and Mom could work wonders with either of these critters.

We only had chicken or turkey, mostly the former, on Sundays and special occasions. These were not "store-bought" birds. Instead, they were free-range chickens raised by Grandpa Joe. I can assure those of you who have never known the pleasure of eating free-range eggs or consuming chicken raised on a diet of which scratch feed was merely a supplement, nothing from Perdue Farms or Tyson even comes close.

Chickens went to their Sunday or holiday dinner final reward in one of three ways. Some were caught and unceremoniously had their necks wrung. Others were caught and went straight to Grandpa Joe's equivalent of a guillotine for barnyard fowl; namely, a razor-sharp ax dealing with a chicken's neck stretched across the section of log where he chopped kindling wood. Or the most common method, and the one that really tickled my fancy, was catching them using a fishing pole, an approach already described in the coverage of Thanksgiving.

A baked hen from Grandpa's lot, cooked to a lovely brown turn in Grandma's oven, was about as good as eating got. She would make gravy using the giblets, adding three or four boiled, chopped up eggs as well, and with a leg or thigh and a brace of biscuits slathered with gravy, I was in pure paradise. The only thing that made it better was being given the privilege of digging into the picked-over carcass to get the little eggs in the making to be found inside. There was a whole line of miniature yolks of diminishing size in the body cavity, and I reckon it's been even longer since I ate those than it has been since I had a chunk of cracklin' cornbread, fresh from an iron spider and adorned with butter made in a hand churn.

Those may seem somewhat strange Christmas recollections to at least some of you, but that was life as I knew it in boyhood. One thing for sure, from an early age there was no mystery about the origin of the food I ate, and I understood the cycle of life in a practical, down-to-earth way that probably not one youngster in a thousand does today.

Our Christmas food came from what we raised, cultivated, fed, harvested, preserved, or killed, and I'm convinced it meant more to us as a result. I might add, in closing, that it was also, thanks to the kitchen magic of Grandma Minnie and my Mom, incredibly delicious. Sure, there were memorable gifts, special moments of various kinds, the joys of caroling and gathering all the greenery and decorations for what was a truly natural Christmas, but looking back nothing enchants me in quite the same way food memories do. Hopefully you have some similar treasures in the storehouse of your mind, and here's some further personal recollections of the season.

December was hoping against hope for a big snow.

It was enjoying snow cream whenever we had a good snowfall.

It was rabbit hunting almost every day once classes let out for the two-week Christmas vacation, and, when the beagles needed a break, heading out for a mixed-bag hunt in the quest for squirrels, maybe a grouse, quail, or a rabbit to shoot on the jump.

December meant checking rabbit gums and traps set for muskrats and mink (I almost never caught the latter) at dawn with the chill of the air, the water, and the trap steel leaving hands almost without feeling.

It was spending lots of time with Grandpa Joe at his home, listening to him weave one tale after another from his own boyhood while we enjoyed the comfort of rocking chairs pulled close to the fire on a bitter evening. He told tales of hard times when his family ate snowbird pie (using birds caught beneath an ingenious trap triggered from indoors by pulling a string that held up a big box—the birds would be lured beneath it with scattered cornbread crumbs). At some point he always turned to chestnuts and squirrel hunting, and that would get him choked up a bit because of his affinity for the noble chestnut and sadness at the blight that destroyed it.

December involved delight in sampling and savoring Grandma Minnie's fine fixin's—stack cake, fried apple and peach pies, pickled peaches, biscuits and biscuit bread, and a great favorite of mine, cracklin' cornbread.

It was enjoying orange candy slices purloined from the waxy, sugar-coated candy used to make a cake.

It was breakfast feasts on sausage prepared at hog-killing time in November. Mom would make rich milk gravy filled with sausage bits, and ladling that over crumbled cornbread was for sure eatin' at its finest.

December was visiting cousins and being part of the everyday farm work. I particularly enjoyed getting corn from the crib at my Uncle Walter's and shelling it by hand to feed chickens.

The month meant availability of enjoying "seeded Muscat" raisins, which came in clusters with the dried raisins still attached the way they were when harvested. They were available only at this time of year.

It was savoring a steaming cup of Russian tea after having been out in the cold.

It was watching Grandpa Joe "sasser" coffee so hot it would burn one's lips, or staring in amazement as he drank pepper tea for his health. The latter was made by roasting hot peppers he had grown, dried, and parched. He steeped them in hot water just like tea was prepared.

It was accompanying Grandpa Joe on a shopping excursion as he valiantly tried to come up with a gift for each of his many grandchildren. He didn't have much money, nor did he have much of a feel for gifts a child would welcome. Still, his good intentions and buoyant spirit of the season more than compensated, and I always had deep appreciation for the pair of hunting socks or maybe a lovingly crafted slingshot he gave me. Today I'm sort of like he was—a terrible shopper with little sense of what to get for others—although I am blessed with a bit more cash money than he was.

December meant wondering whether my gifts would include a book.

From an inexpensive copy of Zane Grey's *Spirit of the Border* and a rebound copy of the first edition of Horace Kephart's *Our Southern Highlanders* to a now well-worn *Bartlett's Familiar Quotations,* books were presents that lasted, and Momma always came through.

It was participating in or enjoying pageants at the church followed by presentation of gifts to children.

Christmas meant watching the Lawrence Welk Show with Stanley Black, the elderly widower who lived next door. He was lonely, we didn't have a television, and it was a time all of us cherished.

December days before Christmas meant church choir carolers singing at the door.

It was the inexpressible delight associated with the arrival of December issues of *Outdoor Life* and *Field and Stream* at the local barber shop. These were always filled with ads that could send a wistful, outdoors-loving boy off in all sorts of directions filled with dreams and vicarious experiences.

One December brought that proud day when, hunting alone except for a canine companion, an aging, past-his-prime beagle by the name of Lead, I brought home three rabbits, two squirrels, and a quail. That hefty game bag seemed to me the equivalent of a son of the Smokies having killed three of Africa's Big Five in a single outing.

It was listening to old folks talk about subjects such as Old Christmas, the Ruling Days, and Yule logs.

It was seeing Grandpa unwrap a suit of clothes with nothing more than a quiet "thank you all," then watching his eyes light up with pleasure as he opened a big box of his favorite Apple Jack dry twist chewing tobacco.

What I remember most though, something that now resides solely in memory, is being with my parents. December will never be quite the same without them, and even when I was in college and beyond, returning to the bosom of the Smokies and the loving embrace of my family was the perfect way to close out another year. They are long gone, but thanks to their love, guidance, and parenting, along with the happy circumstance of being born and growing up in a special part of the world, I'm blessed, and always will be, with a filled storehouse of sparkling things to remember about December.

Snow on Christmas, Easter will be green,
Green on Christmas, Easter will be white.

Bryson City as seen from Sharptop. By Keith Curtis
and courtesy of Bo Curtis.

Bryson City as it was in the author's boyhood. TVA Kodak Collection.
Atlanta National Archives.

Anna Lou and Commodore Casada, 1941. Photo by I. K. Stearns
and courtesy of the Carl Grueninger family.

Anna Lou Casada
with the author,
circa 1944, next to
the cow pasture
which was adjacent
to the family home.

Anna Lou Casada and the author, circa 1944, with the town of Bryson City in the background. This was taken in the yard of the author's boyhood home.

Aunt Jessie Buhmann and baby daughter Carolyn.

Don Casada in 1956.

Memorial hike to disperse Aunt Jessie's ashes.

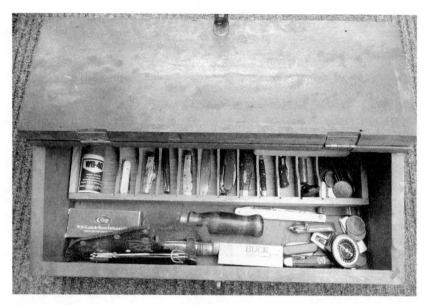

Pocket knife collection. Courtesy of Joshua Casada. Box made by Daddy out of curly poplar. The only metal is in the hinges and clasp.

Al Dorsey seated at Loafers Glory. Courtesy of John Quinnett.

Anna Lou and Commodore
Casada in later years (1995).

Don Casada (foreground), Jim Casada, and Ann Casada at the spring
which served the old Casada home place on Juney Whank Branch.

Casada family gathering, circa 1951.

Uncle Fred McKnight and
Grandma Casada.

Grandma Casada and
the author, circa 1943.

Grandpa Casada and his great-
granddaughter, Linda Spoon.

Aunt Hazel Colville and the author at fence for cow pasture
alongside author's boyhood home, circa 1944.

The author and his
sister, Annette.

The author as a boy
in his backyard.

Aunt Jessie Buhmann holding the author as a boy.

Baptism of Elisabeth Holt in Hazel Creek by Dennis Cole.
Photo by Don Casada.

The Angel of Brasstown and her family. Photo by Don Casada.

Four generations of the Casada family: Commodore, the author,
his daughter (Natasha), and granddaughter (Ashlyn).

Cades Cove church reunion, 1951. Openparksnetwork.org.

Downtown Bryson City in the 1930s. Openparksnetwork.org.

The Jim Shelton Family dwarfed by a giant chesnut tree in Tremont, circa 1920s. Openparksnetwork.org.

Decoration Day at Elkmont, circa 1920s. Openparksnetwork.org.

A baptism at Smokemont. Openparksnetwork.org.

Chestnuts along Heintooga Road in the Cataloochee section
of the Smokies. Photo by Don Casada.

The Chimney Tops in the morning mist.

A cold day on Nantahala.

Fall along a Smokies stream.

Fontana Lake nestled among the Smokies in summertime.

The author's garden.

Rain clouds dipping below Long Hungry Ridge, taken from Shuckstack Mountain, North Carolina. Photo by Don Casada.

Ramp patch. Photo by Don Casada.

Spring blooms.

Storm clouds laying on Twentymile Ridge. Photo by Don Casada.

The author fly fishing in Bone Valley Creek. Photo by Don Casada.

The author fishing Deep Creek. Photo by Don Casada.

Part 3

TOOLS, TOYS, AND BOYHOOD TREASURES

An amazing variety of pastimes filled my Smokies boyhood. Innocent activities such as obtaining bait for fishing—digging for red worms, catching night crawlers, chasing grasshoppers and crickets, burning out wasp or hornet nests, seining minnows, or scrambling after spring lizards—turned into great fun even before the supreme pleasure of a day's fishing got started. For me piddling became a high calling, and I pursued it with a passion worthy of a grand pilgrimage or the quest for the Holy Grail. It might be a spate of reading or working on my stamp collection if the weather was inclement, but most of my piddling took place outdoors.

Indoors or out, though, there was wholesome fun to be had, and I didn't need a vast panoply of high-tech gadgets or battery-operated gear in order to entertain myself. Relatively few material items entered into the picture, but those that did, mostly involving games, hunting, or fishing, were of surpassing importance. They were the true treasures of my youth. Some survive physically, and all endure in the savings account of my memory. Here's a look at some of the tools and toys that held places of great importance as I grew up in the Smokies.

Chapter 16

SIMPLE CHILDHOOD PLEASURES
FROM YESTERYEAR

Although I have a granddaughter of the appropriate age I have no real idea of what today's adolescents do for fun. However, I can guarantee two things. First, it costs a lot more than my youthful pursuit of pleasure: iPhones, Kindles, Wii, other electronic games, and all sorts of gadgetry that this poor Luddite, who owns a cell phone but doesn't really know how to use it, cannot even name are involved. Second, although she is an athlete of sufficient ability to garner support for her college education, I don't think her teenaged days have provided a bit more fun or as much diversity of activity than did my Smoky Mountain boyhood.

Perhaps a winsome look back at some of these youthful pastimes will demonstrate how much things have changed over two generations. It is also a quiet suggestion that today's youngsters may well be missing quite a bit of fun, not to mention a meaningful sense of connection to the good earth, because a multiplicity of joys involving an outdoor setting are vanishing like dandelion seeds caught in spring gusts of wind. All of these activities loomed large in my youth. My educated guess is that today most of them have not been enjoyed by one mountain youngster out of a hundred, although I would love to discover I am wrong.

Broom sedge sledding. From the first few hard frosts until the arrival of the greening-up days of spring, any hillside laden with broom sedge had the potential to produce a world of fun. These days there seems to be less broom sedge, a plant which thrives in highly acidic soil in places such as poorly maintained pastures or recently abandoned land, but it was as common as cornbread in my youth. Dry, slender golden stalks of broom sedge are incredibly slick, and a "ride" down a hill laden with the plant provides a thrill (and comparable speed) similar to being on a sled after a snow. In fact in some ways there's even more excitement. That's because the most commonly used device for such rides was a large piece of heavy-duty cardboard. Your "sled" contained no steering mechanism, and the ride basically involved desperately trying to hold on until you reached the bottom of the hill.

Swinging on grape vines. Wild grapes of various types—'possum grapes, fox grapes, and other varieties—can produce vines as thick as a man's wrist, and they will sometimes grow all the way to the top of tall trees as they seek life-giving light. That tendency explains why you sometimes hear squirrel hunters talk about a late-season vine-shaking expedition. Since bushytails often take advantage of a tangle of vines high up in a tree when building their nests, such hunting tactics can be quite productive.

Those stout, firmly attached vines also have offered many a mountain lad a ready-made swing. All that is required is to use a hatchet or perhaps a hand saw to cut a large vine close to the ground. Preferably the vine will be on a hillside where the swinger can take few steps uphill and launch into the air while clinging tightly to the vine. The result can be quite a ride, sometimes with the ground many feet below if the hillside is sufficiently steep. There's an element of danger should the vine break, but what red-blooded boy hasn't been tempted in that regard?

Skipping rocks. In my youth, any son of the Smokies could consistently get a minimum of ten "skips" out of a suitably sized flat river rock launched across the water so that the wide side hit the surface time and again. It was the most innocent of fun. It lent itself to strong throwing arms for softball or baseball, and the banks of the Tuckaseigee and Little Tennessee Rivers, not to mention larger creeks in the area, provided a limitless supply of ready-made throwing rocks. There's a real art to skipping rocks, with key parts of the process being the ability to select a suitable rock and also throwing it in a manner whereby it barely kisses the water on first contact before beginning a fast-paced series of skips, each one shorter than the one before.

Dam building. If I had a $100 bill for every rock I moved during my boyhood in connection with dam construction on waterways ranging from small branches to sizeable creeks, mine would be a fat bank account indeed. Most of these efforts involved three locales—Bryson Branch, Toot Hollow Branch, and lower Deep Creek. In the case of the two branches, both within easy walking distance of my home, it was actually possible for three or four boys working as a team to build a fairly impressive impoundment, one which temporarily changed the depth of the branch from a few inches to as much as three feet. Of course such engineering efforts were doomed come the first heavy rain, but in the summertime they provided hours of innocent fun.

Obviously there was nothing new in such activities, because my father loved to reminisce about the time he and his younger brother, Hall, undertook a project on this kind at their home high up on Juney Whank Branch . All went well until the water level reached a point where it flooded a yellow jacket nest. Thinking back on Daddy's description of how Uncle Hall yelled and fled when attacked by the angry yellow jackets still brings an involuntary smile to my face. "He was normally slow as cold molasses," Daddy would say, "but had he run the bases in a baseball game the way he ran from those yellow jackets, he would have been some kind of star."

As for Deep Creek, the idea was to make swimming holes a foot or so deeper or else channel the current to provide greater velocity to inner tubes as they drifted downstream. With sufficient effort from a bunch of boys, this could be accomplished. The two pools that received the most attention during my youth were the Baptizing Hole (also known as the Reeves Hole) adjacent to Deep Creek Baptist Church and the Weeks Hole a couple of hundred yards downstream. The latter was situated near the home of a good buddy, Gerald Medford, and was also a favorite fishing spot. Neither site is used for swimming today. Indeed there are signs at the former location expressly forbidding swimming, but there is another pool upstream at the rear of Camp Living Water where juvenile engineering efforts continue to this day. In readily accessible GSMNP streams on both sides of the Smokies you'll also find plenty of human construction in the form of funnels designed to make tubing a bit faster and more exciting.

Riding trees. This activity involved shinnying up slender trees until reaching a point where your weight caused them to bend and thereby allowed a "ride" back to the ground. Pine thickets, where lots of pines had sprung up after ground had been cleared and then left for nature to work her course, were most commonly used. I can remember riding poplars as well, and in each instance you had trees growing in such close proximity that when one bent over from your weight there was another one ready at hand to grab. It was great fun unless a sapling snapped. Then the trip to the ground came a lot faster than one had expected. I suspect that from time to time this pastime produced broken arms or legs, but it was sure was fun.

Making and using buzz buttons (whirligigs). These were a simple toy, easily made, that could lead to hours of pleasure. All that was required to make a buzz button was a length of string and a round button with at least two holes. The string was passed through the holes and then tied together. By flipping the button over a number of times to twist the string, then looping the string over a finger on each hand, it was possible to set the button to spinning madly by pulling the strings, releasing the pressure, and pulling again. The button hummed or buzzed when spinning. The string commonly used in my youth was black nylon fishing line, but kite string, strong sewing thread, or something similar works just as well.

Flutter mills. I never was talented enough to create a really good flutter mill on my own, but with patient help from Grandpa Joe, using nothing but wood scraps, a section or two of a small dowel, and a nail or sturdy piece of wire, a delightful toy could be created. Properly placed in a small branch, the flutter mill turned endlessly, causing constant temptation to do a bit of adjustment to make it run (flutter) faster. A really well-made one would also turn quite nicely in a stiff breeze.

Bows, arrows, and other Native American implements. I spent a great deal of time fashioning crude Indian weapons—blow guns, spears, throwing sticks (a greatly simplified version of an atlatl used to throw rocks fashioned from a dry corn stalk), and tomahawks—as well as bows and arrows when I was a youngster. The subject was of sufficient interest to me to seek "book learning" type advice for the craft, although I don't think my reading did much to improve the end products. I wasn't alone in such pursuits; most boys of my acquaintance whiled away endless hours in similar fashion.

Our bows and arrows were anything but works of superb craftsmanship, but they were sufficiently functional to provide a great deal of fun. Hickory was the wood of choice for bows, and it took considerable effort to select a young hickory sapling a couple of inches in diameter, cut it and remove the bark, allow for a bit of curing (we never let it get anywhere near dry enough), and then use a pocket knife to shape it appropriately. Arrows tended to be made of dogwood, although that was not always the case. Efforts did not extend to the addition of an arrowhead; fire-hardened tips to the arrows had to do. There were some rough efforts at fletching, but these were largely ineffective. No game animals were in danger from these creations, but they sure provided a lot of innocent fun.

Whittling. Some of the activities already mentioned, such as flutter mills and bows and arrows, made extensive use of pocket knives. The same was true of sling shots, covered below in considerable detail. But in addition to utilizing a knife for specific functions, it came into application with simple whittling for fun. Maybe it was because the old men of my acquaintance, with Grandpa Joe leading the pack, were always whittling. Perhaps it was the manner in which the importance of keeping a blade properly sharpened was a constant refrain, or possibly it was the pure pleasure of seeing a well-honed knife slice away a nice length of wood. Whatever the explanation, boys and their knives devoted countless hours to blade-on-wood activities. My educated guess is that today you'll search long and hard to find a boy who has done much whittling. Knives are forbidden on school grounds and frowned on elsewhere. Something went awry over the years, because to those of my generation and those before it, a pocket knife was a staunch companion, a wonderfully useful tool, and something you felt almost naked without.

Building forts. Thanks to the recent conclusion of World War II, the less spectacular but still impactful Korean War not too long thereafter, and in my adolescence the full-blown emergence of the Cold War, boys of my generation were preoccupied with play that had an overriding military theme. Perhaps the greatest amount of energy and effort connected with our "war games" involved the construction of forts. While a country with military matters well to the forefront of its collective imagination was no doubt a factor in fort obsession, in my case at least the primary impetus for ambitious projects came from the silver screen. Saturday matinees at the local theater always featured the exploits of one of a number of famed cowboy heroes—Johnny Mack Brown, Lash LaRue, Gene Autry, Roy Rogers, Hopalong Cassidy, Allan "Rocky" Lane, and others of their ilk—and invariably a fort or frontier stockade would be part of the movie setting.

Accordingly, boys built their own forts. Some were surprisingly complex undertakings, with pines or poplars somewhere between the sapling and log stage being the construction material of choice. Both were straight-growing trees with relatively soft wood, easily working with hatchets and available in abundance. We lacked the skill to frame a suitable door or entrance, but the finer of these edifices featured a fire ring in the center, mud caulking between the logs, and makeshift roofs formed of slender saplings covered with pine boughs. The fort might even feature an escape hole, a carefully dug tunnel of a few feet through which a youngster caught in the imaginary throes of an overwhelming siege by force could escape the enemy. Holed up in these forts with our BB guns and slingshots, with bows and arrows for backup, and provisioned with victuals such as cans of baked beans and tins of Vienna sausage, we were ready for any invading force that decided to turn its military attention to the Smokies.

Throwing sticks. Like so many other shifts and expedients of the grand trade of being a boy, I learned from Grandpa Joe about using the miracles of mechanical advantage to throw rocks for great distances. The specifics of that experience are shared below in a chapter devoted to his memory, but making a throwing stick capable of sending rocks for great distances was the essence of simplicity. The gratifying results enabled me easily to exceed, lengthwise and with a rock substituted for a baseball, any throw Mickey Mantle or Willie Mays ever made from center field.

The stick that served as the throwing implement was invariably a mature, dried corn stalk. Long, thick ones from corn described as feed, grinding, or dent grain worked best. Grandpa's favorite type of field corn, used primarily to furnish food for hogs and chickens, was Hickory King. Although for the short period of time it was in the "milk" stage suitable for roastin' ears, virtually all the annual crop was left to dry in the field before being harvested in autumn when the October beans planted with and supported by it had "made."

Fun in the snow. A decent snowfall was a glory to behold in a boy's eyes. It meant cancellation of school, and the fact that missed days would eventually have to be made up (one year after a particularly rough winter there was school every Saturday in May and classes continued well into June) mattered not one iota. You lived in the moment of beautiful white fluff hiding all winter's ugliness, a big pan of snow cream, maybe a passing nod to comments from grown folks about a slow-melting snow being good for farmers, but mostly in the myriad joys of a passing phenomenon.

There would be snowball fights, sometimes fairly serious affairs with stockpiles of ammunition and snow walls as protection from the enemy. Also, the temptation to launch icy missiles at unsuspecting adults from ambush was almost irresistible. One such escapade on my part that was hilarious at the time but now haunts me a bit involved a portly, middle-aged black lady named Elma who lived just down the street. She was the daughter of Aunt Mag Williams, a cherished friend who let me dig red worms in her chicken lot and always had something for a gluttonous youngster to eat warming on the back of her wood-burning cook stove.

A big snow had fallen overnight and I was out on my own enjoying the falling flakes and hushed world when I saw Elma on her way to town. It was surprising to see her out and about, but in all likelihood she had a spot of work to do or else she and Aunt Mag needed some food in a big way. At any rate, she was approaching slowly and with great care, taking every precaution not to slip and fall. Some boxwoods offered me a perfect hiding spot, and I was sure she hadn't seen me. Quickly fashioning half a dozen snowballs, I waited until she was well within range and cut loose. My first throw was absolute perfection—a feat I couldn't have repeated with another two hundred attempts. It caught the big hat she was wearing flush in the crown and lifted it from her head as neatly as you could have possibly asked. The resultant tirade included some verbiage I would never have associated with the deeply religious and normally mild-mannered woman, and I took the only action that seemed possible under the circumstances. I ran away like a whipped dog and hoped she hadn't recognized her assailant. Since she never mentioned the shameful assault to me, presumably she didn't.

Along with snowballing, most of it involving adversaries who gave as good as they got, there were lots of other opportunities for enjoyment. I owned a homemade sled with wooden runners Daddy had made, and the hillside pasture adjacent to the house was a perfect place to use it other than the fact your "stop" at the end of a fast ride was a dense fencerow of rambling roses. Some of my friends enjoyed the luxury of store-bought sleds, and as we reached our later teens these would often be used on the local golf course. Portions of its sloping terrain provided possibilities for long rides, although they also necessitated a lengthy walk back to the top of the hill for the next quick segment of sledding. Somehow that didn't matter to an inexhaustible youngster, and if there were girls involved, as was often the case, the uphill trudge seemed a piece of cake.

Another opportunity afforded by snow, especially if it was of the soft type unaccompanied by winds that clung to trees, was reading nature's book. When that type of snow fell overnight, I'd be afield bright and early the following morning. The white surface told its tales. Here were rabbit tracks showing cottontails going about their nocturnal business, and with care and persistence you could track them right to their daytime beds and get a shot "on the jump" as they were rousted from their hiding spots. Or the knowing eye could find the little pile of droppings where a covey of quail had roosted and store that information away for future use, determine if squirrels were sufficiently hungry to leave nests and den trees to feed, and wander along branches and the edge of old orchards seeking grouse tracks. If perchance snow revealed the passage of deer, that was a thrill beyond compare in a time when whitetails were as scarce as hen's teeth.

If the colder months brought splendor in the snow, the same held true for the recreational opportunities associated with water. Fly rodding for trout was a youthful obsession that still holds me firmly in its grasp, but that was but one of many pursuits involving nearby branches, creeks, and the Tuckaseigee and Little Tennessee Rivers. Swimming, riding inner tubes in times when the creeks got high, hunting water snakes for no reason other than to see if you were brave enough to catch one, putting catfish in boy-made pools in branches to "clean up" after they had been caught from the terribly polluted Tuckaseigee, probing tiny branches for spring lizards and seining for minnows in slightly larger ones—all of these water-based activities were part of being a boy in the Smokies. After all, it's a land with sufficient annual rainfall to qualify for the description of a temperate rain forest region, so intimacy with the water that gave such rich, varied life was only natural.

Daddy first got me a bicycle when I was nine or ten years old. It was a twenty-four-inch hand-me-down affair and a "girl's" bike as well, but to me every inch of its worn frame, including a rough weld and wire wrapping holding the front wheel to the body, was sheer loveliness. The bike featured no gear system (it was, like all bikes I was familiar with at the time, strictly a one-speed affair), peddle brakes, and a total lack of adornment until I added a basket to the handlebars. I rode it everywhere—to Deep Creek swimming holes, as far into the GSMNP as was possible before gated-off roads turned to impassable trails, to the local golf course where I worked as a caddy and then as a sort of "maintenance boy," downtown jaunts to the drugstore for a soda, or just riding around with a bunch of baseball cards clipped to the spokes making a racket.

That bike almost figured in my premature demise. We lived on a high hill and the road was long and steep enough to make for sho' 'nuff high-speed coasting. One day, as I had done untold numbers of times before, I was flying low down the hill when, maybe seventy-five yards away, a car made a left turn across my line of travel. I locked down on the brakes in a hard skid, but it was too little, too late. My bike connected with the car's right front bumper, sent me airborne, and left me unconscious on the roadside with my crumpled two-wheeler lying in separate pieces on either side of the road. I was all right, other than a slight concussion, but when I returned to consciousness the elderly driver, an outsider for whom English was a second language, lit into me about damage to his fine new automobile. That tirade ended in pretty short order when several folks gathered at the scene pointed out he was clearly at fault and muttered some thinly veiled threats to the effect that he needed to do some serious reassessment of his priorities, shut his pie hole, apologize, "and buy that boy a new bike."

The latter never happened, and when Daddy arrived on the scene, having gotten a call from some local who knew him and recognized me (the town of Bryson City was small enough that would have likely included almost everyone), his sole concern was my welfare. He did gather up the pieces of the bike and later somehow managed, with the kind of fix-it skills that served him well throughout his long life, to patch the bike back together. I continued to use it right up until heading off to college when I was eighteen.

Those innocent pursuits offer but a small sampling of the pastimes that filled my youth. All involved common features, costing nothing or next to nothing, taking place outdoors, physical exercise, and occurring without adult supervision. I garnered my fair share of knocks, cuts, and bruises, probably crossed the line between common sense and recklessness on more than one occasion, and definitely participated in a few high jinks that would have met with stern adult disapproval had I been discovered.

Set against that was the fact that I knew the meaning of freedom and self-reliance from an early age, developed solid instincts of personal responsibility thanks to wise but not overly intrusive oversight on the part of my parents, and was far too busy having fun in my spare time to come anywhere close to getting into the kind of trouble that might have been labeled juvenile delinquency. I knew the smell of campfire smoke and the heady perfume of a spring morning, the sweetness of a mountain summer and the loveliness of autumnal coloring, the soothing solitude of winter and the swish of snow in otherwise silent woods. Those were blessings provided by a love of place, the great good fortune of the time in which I came of age, and mentors who guided me seamlessly through those years of enchantment.

Many of my acquaintances would suggest that I never quite stopped being a boy, and if such is the case, that's a badge I'll wear with considerable pride. Being a boy, especially a boy growing up in the Smokies, is something I'd love to have another round at enjoying. I feel sorry for kids who have to grow up in a city. If it's not a crime against nature, it's a crime that deprives them of nature. Similarly, youngsters who are raised in households where they have anything they want and everything done for them are victims of singular disservice. Possessions and pampering don't equate to a happy, wholesome youth, and in the outdoors you don't need a great deal in the form of material goods to be perfectly happy.

Almost none of my boyhood companions owned much more than a hand-me-down shotgun or .22, an indifferent fly rod or spincasting outfit, and a bike. But we all had a limitless playground, the wilderness world of the Smokies, to call our own. That made for the kind of youth where there was minimal demand for social workers, child psychologists, and medications for attention deficit and behavioral problems, not to mention policemen, 'possum sheriffs (game wardens), and prison guards. It was a wholesome world in which to grow to adulthood.

Chapter 17

MEMORIES OF MARBLES

During my boyhood, when the gloom and doom of winter began to give way to longer days and the occasional warm, dry spell, school playground activities turned to marbles. It has been decades since I've seen youngsters playing the game, but it was an activity that enjoyed immense popularity in the high country during the 1940s and 1950s. Clearly much the same was true nationwide, because a number of terms from the simple game have entered into common usage in America. We talk about a game such as football's Super Bowl or basketball's NCAA championship being for "all the marbles," and someone who behaves in an exceptionally strange fashion is often referred to as having "lost all his marbles." We describe an individual taking a serious approach to a task as "knuckling down," and the phrase "playing for keeps" is uttered on a regular basis. All had their origin in the game of marbles.

For the uninitiated, marbles, at least in its simplest form (there are many types and variations of the basic game), involves drawing a rough circle in a smoothed patch of dirt. Each player places an equal number of marbles in the circle and tries to use his "taw," the marble that functions as a shooter, to knock other marbles out of the circle. Determining which player goes first is decided by "lagging." This involves shooting one's taw from a specified distance toward a straight line. The player's taw that stops closest to the line gets the first shot.

The taw is propelled by holding it in one's crooked index finger, placing knuckles to the ground at the edge of the circle, and flipping it with the thumb. Power is important, but accuracy even more so. If the taw remains in the circle after having knocked another marble out of it, the player gets another shot—sort of like keeping your turn in pool as long as you continue to put balls in a pocket. The game lasts until there are no marbles left within the circle.

During my boyhood there were endless variations to the game, and without exception they provided rich material for arguments. For example, an oversized taw, often known as a "dough roller," was sometimes considered to give the person who owned it an unfair advantage. The same was true of "steelies," ball bearings of comparable size to a standard marble but of appreciably greater weight. Both had the potential to chip or even break standard-sized glass marbles.

These glass marbles came in two distinct types, and each type had its adherents. For some, the only way to go was with "aggies." These were marbles, occasionally made of agate but more frequently from glass that had the appearance of agate. Regular glass marbles, especially those which were obviously of that composition, were normally called "immies" (imitations).

Beyond the basic rules mentioned above, there were a number of other things that entered into consideration. "Heisting" or lifting your knuckles off the ground was a no-no. The same was true of "fudging," which involved knuckling down within the circle rather than outside of it. The biggest bugbear of all, however, involved "keepsies" or "playing for keeps." This was an elementary form of gambling where the shooter kept the marbles he knocked out of the circle. In an uneven match played for keeps, the loser might find himself down to nothing but his taw and one or two marbles or, in a really bad situation, be left with only his taw. Teachers and parents alike frowned on keepsies in no uncertain fashion, deeming it sinful. I can still hear Daddy saying, "Don't let me hear about you playing for keeps."

Along with the standard version of marbles covered above, there were many other variations. For example, you could use "bombsies" for your first shot, which in effect meant an aerial launch into bunched marbles in the middle of the ring. Another play-for-keeps game involved dropping marbles from a waist-high level into a tin can that had a hole cut in it not much larger than the diameter of a marble. If the marble went through the hole, you kept it and received one from the can's owner; if it didn't, your marble was lost. This was a decidedly one-sided situation, with the odds weighted toward the "house" at least as much as one would expect on a slot machine in Las Vegas.

Marbles had other uses as well, with two notable ones being for games of Chinese checkers and for slingshot ammunition. In the latter capacity, thanks to their smooth and spherical shape, they were far superior to any rock and could be matched only by ball bearings.

Other than noticing vast arrays of them on display at hobby shows, I seldom see marbles in today's world. Those I have seen were mostly unearthed while tilling the soil in Daddy's garden in the years immediately prior to his death. Every time one showed its colorful face, it seemed to me a treasure, an artifact from my boyhood days and those of my brother.

Never mind the game's decline today; in days of yesteryear marbles were an important part of childhood in the Smokies. You could find bags of them in every 5- and 10-cent store as well as a tell-tale bulge in the pants' pockets of many a son of the hills. So much was this the case that I suspect anyone reading this who is over the age of fifty recalls participating in or watching games of marbles. If so, it's a simple memory, like so many others, to cherish.

Chapter 18

A PASSION FOR POCKET KNIVES

Case—Buck—Barlow—Remington—Gerber—Schrade. Once these and other brands of pocket knives were names with which to conjure. They were instantly recognizable to an appreciable percentage of the male population, at least in the Smokies. Men folks took pride in carrying, displaying, and using their knife of choice, and most males over the age of twelve felt them to be a virtual extension of their body. For that matter, it wasn't all that unusual for a tomboyish girl or a practical woman to own one.

Youngsters looked on the acquisition of their first knife as a significant rite of passage while fathers considered a two- or three-blade pocket knife as indispensable as car keys or work tools. Grizzled old codgers in country stores or beneath shade trees on small town squares swapped them or whittled with them while telling tales. It was an integral part of their daily routine during fair weather in the warmer months. Pocket knives were, in short, an important part of life.

How things have changed. A few weeks back I noticed a news piece about a boy getting in trouble for carrying a pocket knife to school. It seemed pretty innocuous, at least on the surface. A teacher apparently noticed a bulge the knife sticking out of his pocket. Nothing more. Obviously the boy broke school rules and had to face the consequences, but the hapless lad's situation speaks volumes about the world in which we live as well.

When I was a teenager in the 1950s, virtually every boy carried a pocket knife, not only when fishing or hunting but in school as well. The few who didn't wished they had one. A knife was like a billfold—something you had with you at all times. Knives, among the simplest and most useful of all tools, were highly functional and furnished entertainment. If a teacher happened to ask whether any of her students had a knife to assist her with some classroom chore, chances were excellent that almost every boy in the class would raise his hand in a fashion far more enthusiastic than their responses to academic questions.

Games of mumblety-peg were standard fare during playground breaks. Whittling contests to see who could produce items such as the best tooth-pick or finest wooden toy were commonplace. Boys used pocket knives for recreation and in all sorts of practical ways. That might involve cutting and shaping a choice fork from a dogwood or persimmon tree as the base for a slingshot. Or perhaps it meant gutting and scaling a mess of fish, cleaning squirrels or rabbits, widening the opening in a split shot so it could be easily affixed to a fishing line, making a flute or blowgun from an elderberry shoot, or performing any of dozens of chores around home. A knife blade tapering to a fine point came in mighty handy for gouging out a briar sunk beneath one's skin during an outing to pick blackberries. While it may not have followed proper medical advice, many was the time that blisters on feet beleaguered by breaking in a new pair of shoes were "popped" with a knife.

Youngsters knew practical knife safety and how to use a whet stone. They were taught those as adjuncts to the "right to carry" from the moment they first became proud possessors of a pocket knife. The standard measure of whether a knife blade was sufficiently keen involved seeing if it would easily shave the hair off one's forearm. If not, it needed additional sharpening.

While boys of my generation took pride in carrying a pocket knife, adults considered them absolutely essential. Second only to playing checkers or kibitzing while others played the board game, knives were the focal point of activity at Loafers Glory, as the town square where I grew up was known. There was constant knife swapping, with exchanges of blades vying with swapping of lies for pride of place. Genial arguments about the comparative merits of different styles such as Barlow (not only a brand-name but a two-bladed knife), Stockman (three blades), and Congress (four blades) were commonplace. The same held true when it came to allegiance to a particular manufacturer.

While such momentous discussions took place knives were in constant use whittling out whammy diddles, personalizing walking canes, or perhaps just cutting off a chew of tobacco from a section of dry twist. Those knife lovers were old men enjoying well-earned leisure after a lifetime of hard work, but the folding blades they traded and talked about were also the quintessential working man's tool.

Neither my father nor my paternal grandfather ever set foot out of the house without their trusty knife handy. That was generally true of males of their generations. Both owned a goodly selection from which to choose, and thanks to disappointment from early boyhood at not getting a knife one Christmas, Daddy saw to it that his sons and later his grandsons were always appropriately outfitted in that department. Like most males worth their salt, they simply felt naked without a pocket knife.

Even in his later years, to the age of 100 and beyond, Daddy always kept a pocket knife handy. Of course he owned several dozen of them, so access wasn't much of an issue. Still, if he misplaced the knife he fancied at a particular time (usually it slipped out of his pocket into secret hideaways of his recliner), grave concern arose. Dad kept his knives razor sharp, rightly reckoning that one which wasn't finely honed wasn't fit to carry. That was what he had known and practiced all his days, and for decades his mindset was a near-universal one.

Today I proudly carry one of Dad's pocket knives, as do my brother, all of his boys, a first cousin, and even my daughter. I can't speak for the others, but the little two-blader I favor, with its bone handles and simple design, gives me a momentary mental boost every time I take it out of my pocket. Sentimentally it's priceless, but that's only part of the overall picture.

While working on this material I paused to ponder how that knife had been used over the course of the last year or so. The varying work accomplished with it, and I know the list which follows is but a select sampling, amazed me—harvesting garden vegetables such as squash, cabbage, eggplant, okra, cucumbers, and zucchini; peeling apples and peaches; suckering tomato plants; cutting off sections of twine to tie tomatoes to stakes; gathering gladiolas, zinnias, snapdragons, and dahlias from the flower garden for household decoration; opening daily mail and shipments of books; extracting briars from my fingers; cleaning trout; removing giblets from wild turkeys; whittling a piece of wood to hold a latch in place; prying open the compartment on a balky toothbrush so the battery could be replaced; slicing an opening next to a tendon in a deer's leg to insert a game tag; and much more. Simply put, without a knife it would be difficult for me to function.

Yet today's world is one where knives seem taboo. A striking personal example makes my point. A few years back, having reached the appropriate age, I visited the local Social Security office to complete the requisite paper work associated with "retirement" (I use the quotation marks because in no sense have I retired if that means ceasing to work). A genial gentleman in uniform greeted me at the door of the facility with a cheery "good morning" and the comment: "You look like a man who might carry a pocket knife."

I thought that a somewhat strange comment yet took it as a compliment and enthusiastically replied: "Yep. As a matter of fact right now I'm carrying two." That was absolutely the last thing the guard wanted to hear. He clouded up like an approaching summer thunderstorm. With all vestiges of his smile gone, he politely but firmly informed me I couldn't enter the building carrying a pocket knife. I retreated to my truck with my figurative tail between my legs, thinking all sorts of bad thoughts about bureaucracy and muttering "what's the world coming to," to divest myself of the prized pocket knives.

Of course the same type restrictions hold true for boarding an airplane or entering many public buildings. This is a commentary on today's world as well as a pointed reminder of how dramatically society has changed since my 1950's boyhood. Mine was a rural childhood where folks lived close to the earth and a knife was considered a necessity. Today's urbanized world seems increasingly out of tune with a lifestyle where pocket knives deserved praise and held a prominent place in daily life. They are, in short, increasingly part of a world we have lost. How terribly sad.

Chapter 19

SLING SHOT MEMORIES

Recently a friend shared with me a nostalgic song from the late Randall Hylton that includes the haunting line: "Where is the boy with the sling shot who guarded the homestead back then?" It set me to thinking about sling shot days and boyhood reveries from my own youth. That in turn engendered all sorts of fond reflections of a toy that, in the right hands, became a deadly tool, for at one point the humble, homemade sling shot (or flips, as they were sometimes styled) was a staple in the back pocket of every red-blooded American boy.

A standard summertime activity for mountain kids growing up in the 1950s was spending considerable time making both toys and practical items for their own use. Obviously I have little personal insight when it comes to girls, but for them activities ranging from corn shuck dolls and hand-sewn doll clothes to items of personal attire such as dresses certainly figured in the mix. For boys, most anything that could be made with a pocket knife— flutter mills, crude spears, bows and arrows, corn stalk catapults, and wood carvings held a prominent place in leisure activities.

Certainly such was the case with me and my closest friends in those carefree years when we were old enough to run through the woods and play by ourselves yet not quite old enough to hold summer jobs, become overly preoccupied with girls, or assume the false sense of dignity that comes with being a teenager. No matter was approached with greater care and more meticulous planning than making a sling shot. In my case, at least, it was a project (or more accurately, a series of projects, since I averaged making about one sling shot per summer for several years), which involved a fair amount of adult input and supervision. Daddy offered advice and the wisdom born of having considerable experience with sling shots, while Grandpa Joe took about as much delight and was just as interested in the actual process as his adoring understudy.

The first step in making a sling shot took plenty of field research. This involved finding and cutting the fork of wood that would form the frame for the sling shot. It had to be Y shaped and of appropriate dimensions, with each fork of the limb the same size as well as the space between the forks being just right. In my excursions into armament manufacturing dogwood was always the material of choice, although other tough, tight-grained woods such as persimmon or hickory would have served quite nicely.

Primarily because Grandpa was adamant that nothing quite matched dogwood, our searches dealt with that tree exclusively. This was well before dogwood anthracnose affected area trees, so we had plenty of prospective material to examine. As we walked through the woods, checking each dogwood we spotted, Grandpa would comment: "Dogwood is about as tough and durable a wood as a man could want." Invariably he would then reminisce about a time when mountain folks used wedges made from dogwood, as opposed to metal ones, to split firewood.

Sooner or later we would locate the ideal dogwood fork, and Grandpa would saw it off with a tiny bow saw he had carried along for that purpose. "No need to destroy the whole tree," he would note, "we'll just prune out a bit for sling shot use." Often we'd select a half dozen or more forks, knowing that after they had been left to dry and cure some of them would reveal flaws unobservable at the point when they were first cut.

Once we had a suitable fork, cured and ready for completion of the process, quite a bit of close work with a sharp pocket knife was required. The "Y" of the dogwood fork had to be balanced perfectly in weight, size, and shape. Otherwise the sling shot would not function properly. We usually left the bark intact on the forks but sometimes removed it on the handle and always at the point at the upper end of each fork where the rubber from an old inner tube was to be connected.

Rubber from discarded inner tubes was readily available then, for it was long before the days of tubeless tires. You could get the necessary raw material free, or at worst for a nickel or dime, from most filling stations or tire dealerships. One inner tube, as long as it was stored properly in order to avoid dry rot, furnished the makings of dozens of sling shots.

Using the same pocket knife that had whittled the frame, two equal-sized strips of rubber about a foot long would be sliced from an inner tube. Length depended on "draw length," which meant the size and strength of the boy were key factors. The "fitting" process was just as important as one for a quality shotgun. One end of each of these strips would be secured to the dogwood frame, usually with black nylon fishing line or something similarly strong, while a leather patch with dual slits to hold the sling shot load would be affixed to the other end.

Once all of this was in place, the sling shot was ready for action. Some test shots might reveal need for minor adjustments along much the same lines involved in zeroing a rifle scope. Then came the fun and sense of self-satisfaction provided by having produced a fine tool and useful weapon.

A decided advantage to using a sling shot was that you always had an abundance of ammunition, and for the most part it was free. A pocket full of carefully selected river rocks was standard, although for pinpoint accuracy you couldn't beat marbles or ball bearings. However, the former cost fifteen cents a bag and the latter were mighty hard to come by.

Ample lack of practice notwithstanding, my personal performance as a sling shot marksman was mediocre. However, I had two older first cousins once removed who were flat-out sharpshooters. They could hit a sitting rabbit with a high level of consistency, and lest anyone doubt what a sling shot can do in the hands of a master, years ago I saw a television program where an elderly fellow used one to cut down corn stalks shot after shot.

Matters of accuracy notwithstanding, I got plenty of practice, and it was amply buttressed by boyhood flights of fancy. I warded off attacking invaders, punished transgressors, and protected hearth and home. Those were the days when a sling shot rested in the back pocket of my jeans much of the time I was out of school. I look back fondly on that lost world and realize that today's youngsters are unknowingly missing something that was once an integral part of the joy of being a Smokies boy.

Chapter 20

BOYS AND BB GUNS

Although as a boy I didn't receive dozens of Christmas gifts each year, those which did come my way from Mom and Dad were invariably practical, prized, or memorable (and in some cases, they fit all of those descriptions). Such was the case with a Daisy Red Ryder BB gun. It had some engraving identifying it with Red Ryder, the silver screen cowboy hero I had watched in action on many a Saturday afternoon at the Gem Theater, a dandy leather thong decorating the cocking lever, and the air gun came with several packets of copper pellets. The little gun, a training tool for generations of hunters and shooters in the making, immediately became a virtual extension of my body. For untold hours wandering around the yard, in fields and woods nearby, and for extended sessions of target practice, it was my constant companion. Up to a distance of twenty-five yards or so it was quite accurate, and with time and experimentation I extended that range another fifteen yards through allowing for windage and pellet drop.

No small portion of that patiently honed skill in marksmanship came at the expense of a number of silver dollars I owned. In the sometimes misguided cognition of a boy, the size of those coins pretty well matched profiles offered by the small birds which were my principal quarry. What I never stopped to think about until many years later when I added numismatics to my long-established interest in stamps, was that the first time I managed to hit one of those silver dollars it forthwith lost its value as a collectible. Today there are more than a dozen silver dollars tucked away in a drawer in my study that carry circular pockmarks all over their surface thanks to target practice long ago.

Of course, silver dollars were a far cry from my foremost interest as proud possessor of a BB gun. From the day of its acquisition forward I became an unknowing but inveterate adversary of the Audubon Society. Though there were strict parental "game laws" when it came to "game birds" (there was an open season and no bag limit on English sparrows, blue jays, and starlings—all other birds were *verboten*), but retrospective honesty, expiration of the family statute of limitations, and recognition that shameful confession can be good for the soul compels me to acknowledge I hunted songbirds with a will.

For starters, I'm now convinced that at heart most boys in their early teens who have grown up exposed to hunting, slaughter of livestock, and with the kind of closeness to the earth that life in the Smokies presented to most everyone three generations or more ago were stark realists when it came to the origins of meat. They were also about three parts poacher in early adolescence. Had I been caught in the act of hunting songbirds, I already had a detailed explanation worked out. After all, I would rationalize as I held a deceased robin, Grandpa Joe often talked of using a homemade trapping device to catch large numbers of robins and snowbirds (juncos). The trapped birds were cooked in pies or used as the base for gravy after enough cooking to make even the bones edible. Surely, I reasoned, I couldn't be admonished for doing precisely what Grandpa had once done as a part of putting meat on the table. Luckily Daddy never caught me, because I have no doubt whatsoever that the response to my explanation would have been a whopping dose of hickory tea.

Today I'm keenly and somewhat embarrassingly aware of the wayward aspects of my BB-based quests, but they did serve one highly useful purpose. As my first footsteps in the unending cultivation of a woodsman's skills, an education that never ends, those endless "sneaks" or long waits to get within range of birds provided me skill in a number of areas of considerable significance to any outdoorsman. Patience, persistence, stealth, marksmanship, understanding the habits and habitat of one's prey, and the ability to adapt to your surroundings were among those lessons. Beyond that, the incessant need for more pellets—I could go through a packet of them like a properly administered dose of salts—indirectly fostered a sound work ethic. When cash was constantly required for BBs, and later for shotgun shells and .22 cartridges, work was a ready solution and one I willingly pursued.

While I escaped unscathed from my illicit sallies after songbirds, another misstep of far greater magnitude did not go unnoticed. BB guns of the type I owned held a large number of pellets in a sort of tube that you loaded by pouring them in until it was full. To this day I have no idea of the total capacity, but it was appreciable—far too many shots for any realistic expectation of keeping count. There were two additional problems. Occasionally after a shot and recocking, a pellet would not transfer to the chamber. You could tell when you had a dry fire (the sound was slightly different) and just shaking the gun usually let you know when you had exhausted all the pellets. However, sometimes when it seemed all ammo was gone and maybe even after a number of dry fires, there would be a lodged pellet that finally found its way into the chamber.

That presented the possibility of bad things happening, or at least such was the case with a young idiot (me) who violated a whole bunch of basic rules of gun safety in a single setting. This happened while I was visiting two cousins, both a few years older and who have already been mentioned as true masters with sling shots. We had roamed the area around their farm for some time. I shot BBs with abandon while they fired at the occasional target with their sling shots.

As we headed home, my stash of BB pellets long since exhausted, I would occasionally cock the gun and take an imaginary shot at some object. Somehow the bare calf of one of my cousins attracted my attention and I "dry" fired at it from pretty well point blank range. Alas, a final pellet had somehow dislodged and found its way to the chamber. My cousin's dance of agony and screams of anguish were something to behold, but I instantly knew big trouble lurked on the near horizon. I got two solid whippings—one from their father, Uncle Walter, and a second one from Daddy when he showed up later that day to pick me up. The only positive outgrowth of this blot on my sporting escutcheon, a moment of idiocy that far transcended mere carelessness, was that it planted the message of gun safety deeply in my mind forevermore.

BB guns have well served generations of adventurous boys (and girls—my granddaughter has owned a dandy pink version since she was eight years old). They are a fine first weapon, but make no doubt about it, they are just what the word "weapon" implies—potentially dangerous. A BB gun is not a toy, and to use one in that fashion is to abuse it and the concept of gun ownership. Rather, for a kid growing up with links to the land, a love of hunting, a reverence for the backwoodsmen of pioneer times, and a fervent desire to become a sportsman, it can be a companion and an ally in an ongoing rite of passage involved in the making of a hunter.

Chapter 21

FIRST GUN

For most mountain boys of my generation, certain milestones immediately went into the treasured files of memory. They were destined to remain there permanently. "Firsts" were particularly important in this regard—first squirrel, first trout on a fly, first rabbit, first grouse, first pocket knife, first car, first job, first date, first "steady" girlfriend, first prom, and many more. I vividly recall all of these moments along with a lot of other "firsts." Even today, well over half a century after the events, I feel confident I could take you to within 100 yards of the place where I killed my first squirrel, rabbit, and grouse (all in Swain County). Similarly, I readily recall that riffle in the heart of the Park not 150 yards from Deep Creek's storied Bryson Place where I hooked and landed my first trout on a fly.

When it comes to overall impact in terms of being indelibly planted in my memory though, nothing quite matches ownership of my first gun. There had been sling shots aplenty, cap pistols, and then a treasured BB gun that saw a great deal of duty. Still, they weren't the real McCoy. I couldn't go hunting with them and expect to bring home a rabbit or squirrel, and for all that the BB played a central role in getting me ready for a gun and hunting, it didn't match up to my fervent desires.

The circumstances surrounding that joyous moment when I become the proud possessor of a real gun involved a tiny bit of trauma mixed in with a marvelous measure of pure delight. I was given the gun, a Savage Model 220A 20 gauge, for Christmas when I was ten or eleven years of age. As fate would have it, that was the only Christmas of my life, right up until I was married at the age of twenty-five, spent away from the Smokies where I was bred and born.

Mom and Dad, no doubt feeling a bit guilty as the result of one Yuletide of neglect after another, decided to travel to Winston-Salem and spend the holiday with my maternal grandparents. Wisely, the gun I was to receive was left behind in the Smokies. I was simply given a box of shells along with a card indicating what awaited me upon our return to the mountains. Never has a youngster been more anxious to return to his highland homeland, and even the throes of homesickness that seized me during the first portion of my freshman year in college paled in comparison with my desire to return to the high county that Christmas holiday. The family headed back home on December 26, but the thirty-six hours or so between when I learned I was the owner of a new shotgun and the moment I actually laid my hands on it was an extended period of marvelous misery.

By most standards of measurement, the little 20 gauge wasn't anything special. The single-barrel shotgun, choked tight as a miser's purse, retailed for under $30 in the mid-1950s. Even today with some searching you can find a perfectly functional used one in the $50 to $100 price range. Dad bought it new, possibly from the Sears & Roebuck catalog or else through Doc Woody, a sportsman/dentist who at the time owned a small local outdoor goods store. Never mind its cash cost, in my mind's eye it was and remains priceless.

I already had considerable experience hunting with a borrowed .410, and I had done some plinking with a .22 rimfire, so coming into the gun's possession, in terms of familiarity and training, wasn't exactly venturing into a brave new world. There were striking differences though, between the loaner and MY gun. The single-shot .410 had been a hammer gun, whereas the key attribute of the Savage Model 220A (which came in various gauges, barrel lengths, and ultimately, with a series of letters after the number as the basic model was upgraded and improved), at least in the eyes of the maker's advertising gurus, was that it was one of the first single-barrel hammerless shotguns to be mass produced. It had a thumb safety that was far easier to deal with than a stiff hammer that could be devilishly awkward when the matter at hand involved a fast fleeing rabbit or a covey of quail taking wing.

For years I missed far more cottontails and bobwhites than I hit with the new gun, but at least I could now get off a shot while the quarry was in range. Dealing with bushytails was another matter entirely. The super-tight choke worked wonders on a hidden squirrel high up in an oak with only a portion of its head showing. So long as I made myself wait until the animal was still before shooting, the little 20 gauge was deadly, and I became a juvenile squirrel-killing machine. Right up until graduation from high school, October twilights would find me walking through the streets of Bryson City with squirrel tails proudly sticking out of multiple pockets. That was no accident. I arranged displays of my success as carefully as a teenage girl heading out on her first date dealt with matters of makeup.

The gun also was the essence of simplicity when it came to breaking it down for cleaning, to insert a shell, or even to blow through the open barrel to call dogs. Pressing down and pulling on the fore-end readily released it, and then all that was then necessary to remove the barrel was to push the lever to the side.

Light weight in a gun can be a mixed blessing, and such was the case with my Savage 220A. Carrying it over the course of a long day afield, even for an undersized boy, presented no problems. It also had good balance and went smoothly to my shoulder. On the other hand, its thin pad did nothing to absorb recoil and even with low brass shells the gun kicked like a malcontent mule. If you mistakenly got the gun's butt on your biceps rather than snug in the armpit where it belonged, an impressive bruise was the inevitable result.

By the time I finished high school, the gun showed plenty of wear. Countless encounters with blackberry briars and floribunda roses had taken their toll on the walnut stock and fore-end, and no amount of rubbing with furniture polish or linseed oil could change that. Similarly, the bluing of the metal had long since given way to a shine closely resembling the color of a new dime or Momma's freshly polished silver all ready for her to host some special event. Some distinctly amateurish gunsmithing work on the screw holding the lever in place had further marred the scattergun by leaving tell-tale scars.

Still, fading beauty notwithstanding, the gun continued to work just fine. It saw serviceable and memorable duty not only through my youth but well beyond. One particularly cherished example came on a quail hunt, never mind how unsuitable the shotgun might have been for that sport, with a newly acquired father-in-law back when there were still wild birds. We bonded, thanks to plentiful birds, a staunch pointer, and shared passion, in a manner which up to that point had seemed impossible. He flat-out shamed me, in terms of birds in the game bag, with his semiautomatic and its improved cylinder choke. More significantly, though, at the end of the day of hunting he no longer thought of me as a hillbilly reprobate with few if any redeeming features who had taken his only child.

Then there was the matter of the shotgun and meat on the table. During four lean years of graduate school, where pizza once monthly equated to haute cuisine and when I ate enough tuna casseroles to last a score of lifetimes, that little 20 gauge gave us squirrels and rabbits with gravy, buttressed by sweet potatoes and biscuits on the side. Never have I eaten more welcome or meaningful fare. Many years later, when I owned other guns but remained firmly caught in the grip of nostalgia, I used the gun in the accomplishment of another landmark event in my sporting life—killing my first wild turkey.

Today the Savage 220A rests in honorable retirement alongside another shotgun filled with memories and meaning, the Ithaca 12 gauge double barrel Daddy used through all the years of my youth and that I inherited. I look at the two guns, now located in a gun cabinet Daddy crafted, on a regular basis. That simple act takes me back down country roads leading to old farms, abandoned fields, hardwood ridges, and rhododendron-lined spring seeps where we hunted rabbits, quail, squirrels, and grouse. The time travel is gratifying and occasionally, as a cherry atop a lifelong hunter's sundae, I take one of the guns from the case and carry it hunting.

My suspicion is that countless other sons of the mountains harbor similar memories of their first gun. If so, they are blessed, and if perchance they still own the gun they are rich with a tangible, touchable, and deeply meaningful link to their youth. Never mind what Thomas Wolfe wrote, with your first gun you can go home again.

Chapter 22

CANE POLE EXPERIENCES

The image is as enduring as it is appealing, something straight from a Norman Rockwell cover on an old *Saturday Evening Post*. A barefoot, freckle-faced country lad walks down a dusty Dixie lane with a bait bucket in his hand and a cane pole over his shoulder. Headed for a favorite fishing hole, he's as footloose and carefree as a frolicking puppy. Those fortunate enough to have enjoyed such experiences in a time of simpler days and simpler ways can look longingly back to them, while for others such images provide a bit of that comforting nostrum known as nostalgia.

Or perhaps when you think of cane poles another vision comes to mind. It is one of a battered old car or pickup truck bumping down a gravel road with a passenger-side window open. Several cane poles, all of them decorated with colorful bobbers, stick out the window. Inside the vehicle passengers, perhaps a father and his children or maybe a bunch of friends, smile as they anticipate good times to come at the old fishing hole.

Sadly, I must acknowledge it has been years since my eyes have feasted on sights of this sort. Still, this vanishing aspect of the Smokies scene is offset by glad realization that it is still possible to open a window of memory into this aspect of life in old long ago. For that matter, with a modicum of gumption and a reasonable amount of effort, you can resurrect cane pole days.

It isn't necessary to drink from the fountain of youth to do so. Cane poles remain as functional, and as much fun, as they ever were. With that squarely in mind, let's look at some of the ways in which today's fisherman can successfully ply this simple, satisfying angling tool. A logical starting point comes with the manner in which cane poles have been most frequently used over the years—for bank fishing.

A cane pole, whether used from shore or in a boat, is wielded by a simple, graceful motion in which the angler lobs the baited hook (usually, though not always, with a bobber affixed to the line above it) to a likely spot in the water. With some practice this can be accomplished with remarkable precision. The only real limitation is reach—the fisherman can get his bait in the water no farther than a distance just over twice the length of his pole. Nicely offsetting this shortcoming is the fact that a cane pole with a short length of line hanging from its end is ideal for poking into tight places such as beneath docks and piers, along shorelines with overhanging brush, or in the midst of log jams or flooded timber.

Bedding bream, for example, are notorious for spawning in places where a cast with a spincasting or fly rod faces the likelihood of getting hung up. But the length of a cane pole lets the fisherman hold it above the detritus on the surface and drop his cricket or red worm precisely where it needs to be. When there is a bite, and there is a real expectation this will happen, he hoists the fish directly into the air rather than having to worry about weaving and working it through limbs, stumps, or other impediments.

Cane poles, although more often than not used while being hand held, also lend themselves to being "set," that is to say, having the butt end jammed into the mud or sand and propped up in a forked stick cut from shoreline bushes or trees. This allows the angler to tend or watch over multiple set poles aligned conveniently along the bank. Often this will be done while the angler wields a handheld cane pole. It is a fairly simple matter, especially after one has done it a few times, to lay a pole down and rush excitedly to the set one that is getting a bite. If perchance there are simultaneous bites, and this sometimes happens with bedding bream, spawning crappie, and summertime catfish, the ensuing "Chinese fire drill" is just part of the fun. There will be time enough to deal with tangled lines and crossed poles once some fish have been landed or lost.

A variant on this multi-pole approach is crappie fishing utilizing what is often described as a spider rig. The name comes from the arrangement of poles extending from all sides of an anchored boat, giving it an appearance similar to a spider's web or the legs of a spider. The typical approach is to set the poles with the bait (almost always a minnow) for each pole at a different depth. Then, once the depth at which a school of crappie is holding has been determined, all lines can be adjusted accordingly.

Spider-rig fishing involves much the same restful, relaxing ease angling as does idling on a shady bank waiting for a bobber to bounce, but another cane pole technique involves plenty of energy expenditure. A cane pole works well for warm-weather wading in creeks or even sizeable rivers where there are shoal areas with depths of just a foot or two. The fisherman eases along, lobbing his bait or lure into likely spots, then deftly working it with the current or into inaccessible places that might be all but unreachable with a spincasting rig. This can be done with a float or through "tight lining," where the angler maintains a taut line as the sinker on his line bounces along the bottom of the stream. In slower water, a slight lift and then drop of the pole's tip suffices to change the hook's position.

This technique works for all sorts of species—trout in mountain streams, channel catfish in shoals during the heat of summer, panfish in deeper pools or slow areas of creeks, or even bass. I have fished for trout all my life and been privileged to watch dozens of skilled anglers in action. Without question, the single finest method I've ever encountered is fishing with wet flies wielded with a length of monofilament at the end of a cane pole.

Perhaps the most interesting of all cane pole techniques involves the type of fishing colloquially known as doodlesocking or jiggerpoling. It was likely pioneered by Native Americans. In this approach, a fisherman uses a cane of appreciably greater length than normal—sometimes as long as twenty feet if the individual handling the pole is strong enough. A short, strong length of monofilament is attached to the business end of the pole. To it is affixed a large surface plug, a jig-and-pig rig, plastic worm, or an actual piece of a pig in the form of pork rind.

The word "finesse" does not figure into the doodlesocker's vocabulary. This is a matter of getting a lure into or near heavy cover—along shorelines, amid flooded brush piles, adjacent to lily pads or moss beds (or small holes in this kind of cover), among log jams, alongside boat landings, or at the edge of riprap—then making a ruckus with it. One beauty of the technique is that you can keep the lure precisely where you want it, imparting back-and-forth action all the while, for an extended period of time. This is impossible with any cast-and-retrieve outfit. Strikes from bass, the target quarry with this technique, are often splashy or even of the dramatic commode-flushing variety. Expect misses, but often you can put the lure back in place and the fish will return for another go-round.

Once a fish is hooked, it is not played in the traditional sense but rather brought to the boat, hand-over-hand, by the fisherman. Indeed, a bass, once hooked by a skilled doodlesocker, may not touch the water again until it is suspended from a stringer. Doodlesocking is pretty much a two-man operation, with one individual wielding the cane pole while the other carefully and quietly poles a boat or paddles a canoe, always trying to be just the right distance from the spot being worked by the fellow doing the fishing. It can be quite effective for night fishing, especially in times near a full moon when there is enough light to allow anglers to see the spots they want to fish, and because of the necessity of getting pretty close, the technique is more effective when water is murky or has a bit of color than when it is crystal clear.

From fishing on hot, lazy "dog days" while half-dozing in the shade to holding court in the middle of a boat outfitted with a spider rig, from the excitement of jiggerpoling to the delights of wading a creek, the worthy cane pole has much to offer. With a cane pole in hand you can touch base with the past at minimal cost and while doing so have realistic expectations of angling success. As you contemplate the humble cane pole, here are some bits of trivia, along with other uses, associated with the many varieties of this wonderfully versatile plant.

The cane pole is a kissing cousin to the ultimate in craftsmanship when it comes to fishing, bamboo fly rods. The latter are made from carefully worked, tapered, fitted, and glued sections of cane, usually featuring a hexagonal shape to the rod but occasionally using the "quad rod" (four pieces) approach. The raw material is almost always an oriental species of bamboo known as Tonkin cane (from the region of its origin).

In many parts of the world cane is a favorite material in construction thanks to its strength, durability, and availability.

Cane poles, with treble hooks attached to a short length of line, can be used to snag (snare) white suckers during their spawning runs and once were commonly employed for this purpose.

A sturdy piece of cane with its light weight, predictable taper, and straightness makes a dandy handle for a frog gig.

It is also possible to "fish" for bullfrogs using a cane pole. A small piece of red cloth attached to a hook and dangled before a frog resting atop a lily pad or on a pond bank will often draw a frog "strike." Obviously a stealthy approach is essential if one expects to feast on frog legs.

Slender sections of switch canes were often used by Native Americans to fashion fish traps, and they used it in many other ways. Today river cane is much less commonthan formerly, and the Cherokees are actively involved in efforts to restore the plant and expand the acreage where it grows.

Small, tightly fitted sections of hollowed-out cane, either by themselves or in combination with a turkey wing bone, make a fine turkey call. These calls are often known as Jordan yelpers, after Charles L. Jordan, who popularized them. In truth, Indians used such devices to lure turkeys long before Jordan's heyday (circa 1900).

Should you have the misfortune to drop a cane pole out of a boat or have a fish unexpectedly drag a set pole into the water, cane has the great virtue, unlike commercial fishing rigs, of floating. It thereby gives the angler every chance of recovering his outfit. An old river rat from my boyhood named Al Dorsey would even throw the pole in intentionally on occasion when he hooked what he instantly realized was a catfish possibly big enough to break the pole's tip. He would then follow it in his flat-bottomed boat while watching for the drag of the pole to bring it back to the surface. Incidentally, he used a huge length of cane to pole that flat-bottomed boat. When he reckoned the fish was sufficiently tired, he would seize the pole and endeavor to land the whiskered behemoth.

Chapter 23

A FASCINATION WITH FLY RODDING

Daddy was a dedicated fly fisherman and one of those wise fathers who closely followed the philosophy advanced by a great outdoor writer of his era, Archibald Rutledge: "It is my fixed conviction that if a parent can give his children a passionate and wholesome devotion to the outdoors, the fact that he cannot leave each of them a fortune does not really matter so much." Daddy most definitely didn't leave me a fortune in terms of money or material possessions, but in sharing his love of fly rodding, along with a whole bunch of other outdoor pursuits, he pretty much gave me the world.

From the time I was first able to tag along without completely impeding his fly fishing, Daddy let me accompany him on short after-work outings to nearby trout streams. Within a few years that companionship expanded to all-day trips on Saturdays or during his rare days off from work, and there were even camping trips. Some indication of how seriously I took these excursions is probably given by the fact that I eagerly trained for them in advance by sleeping on the floor rather than in bed.

When I was nine or ten years of age, Daddy gave me my first fly rod. Up until that point my angling equipment had been limited to a sturdy cane pole, although that humble instrument of the fisherman's world served me quite nicely. With it I caught a bunch of bream and knottyheads, a few trout, and some catfish. Among the latter was a whiskered behemoth that almost pulled me into Fontana Lake until I got astraddle of a handy stump and used it for leverage. Once that catfish had been landed, Daddy always swore my first words were "Boy, catching a big one sure makes a fellow's legs shake." I don't know whether that was indeed the case, but if so it seems fair to conclude the episode offered an early indication of a pronounced penchant to tell sporting tales.

That first fly rod, and it was the only one I owned until I was in my late twenties or early thirties, was a simple but supremely serviceable hand-me-down. It originally came with two tips and included a primitive click drag Pflueger reel and line which had to be dried after every outing and cleaned and greased with regularity. The line wasn't silk but for all the care it required it might as well have been. Over time I broke one tip and repaired it a rough fashion, had to rewrap two or three of the snake guides in similarly inept exhibits of craftsmanship, wore the bottom of the cork handle out through foolishly embedding the point of flies in it when walking trails to and from my fishing destinations, and in many senses abused the outfit.

That neglect notwithstanding, the little seven-and-a-half foot bamboo rod made of Tonkin cane served me nicely. With it I learned to cast, being completely self-taught other than careful observation of the techniques used by Daddy and some of his buddies. It was my companion for my first trout on a fly, a keeper (barely meeting the requisite seven-inch length) caught quite close to the storied Bryson Place on Deep Creek when I was nine years old. Honesty compels me to admit I never saw the strike and hung the fish strictly by accident. It was obviously a trout deserving of removal from the gene pool, and in a fashion which would have pleased Momma, I insisted on according the little fish Mom's preferred approach to catch-and-release; namely, release to hot grease. It was part of my backcountry supper that evening, the first of countless trout I've caught and eaten over the years.

By the time I had reached the age of twelve, my skills had advanced a good bit, and my parents showed the sort of trust you would never encounter in today's world by allowing a lad to make day trips on his own. Frequently I fished with a good buddy, Bill Rolen. He was the son of a ranger and sometimes his father would drive us into gated-off areas of the GSMNP, leave us for the day, and pick us up come evening. It was a grand arrangement, but more often than not I fished by myself.

My destination of choice was Indian Creek, the biggest feeder of Deep Creek and a place which was within hard walking or easy biking distance

of home. It was the location where fabled sportsman Mark Cathey, a legendary figure constantly mentioned by locals, lived until creation of the
GSMNP. Three important moments in my later life centered on this lean,
indefatigable icon of mountain hunting and fishing.

One came when I was honored by being asked to give the acceptance
speech when he was among the inaugural inductees into the "Legends of
the Fly" Hall of Fame sponsored by "Southern Trout Magazine," a popular
on-line publication. The second came when my brother discovered, through
genealogical research, that we were distant cousins of Uncle Mark, as he
was popularly known in his later years. That in turn led to yet another in a
long series of visits to his tombstone in the Bryson City Cemetery. It bears
what has to be one of the finest epitaphs imaginable:

> Mark Cathey, beloved hunter and fisherman,
> Was himself caught by the Gospel hook.
> Just before the season closed for good.

On that particular visit to the marker I noticed something which had escaped me in all my countless previous sojourns at the site, or possibly my
brother noticed the coincidence. Uncle Mark's birthday was January 28,
the same date on which I was born. The years of our respective arrival in
the Smokies were 1871 and 1942, and that formed the third in a triumvirate
of delightful links to the man.

Cathey's Indian Creek home water, which included a nice pool bearing his name, was small and overgrown. The former characteristic made it
easy for me to wade while the latter feature guaranteed that most anglers
avoided the treacherous embrace of rhododendron and other vegetation
lining the stream's banks and forming a dense canopy over its pools. It was
there I caught my first limit of trout, learned many of the basics of how to
fish small, tight streams, and underwent most of my fly-fishing apprenticeship. Along with Deep Creek, it is and ever shall remain not only my home
water but the stream of my dreams.

My teenage years saw me progress rapidly in fly fishing ability. I became
more observant in a lot of ways, making mental notes on the kinds of cover
likely to hold trout, favored hangouts for larger fish, the fly patterns which
seemed to work best, how to avoid drag, means of producing longer casts, and
much more. As an observant angler I also was constantly vigilant not only
for any and all indications of the presence of fish but for flies (not hatching

insects but those a previous angler had left behind thanks to a wayward cast). A trout fly cost two bits at the local fly shop or $2 a dozen if bought directly from the masterful husband-and-wife pair of local tiers, Fred and Allene Hall. That was serious money when a gallon of blackberries brought a quarter, when caddying eighteen holes on the local golf course netted a $1.25, and when lawn mowing jobs averaged perhaps fifty cents an hour.

Accordingly, I became an avid "hunter" of flies which had been broken off over deep pools, left dangling out of reach in streamside trees, or otherwise lost. If necessary I would swim to examine a tell-tale piece of tippet dangling from a rhododendron bush, and should I perchance spot a fly high up in a tree I carried a thin, strong piece of cord for just such situations. With a rock tied to one end, more often than not I could throw the cord over the limb holding the fly and either pull the branch within reach or break it off. As for unwanted visits of my own flies to trees, and I was a master at what Daddy sometimes laughingly referred to as "fishing for squirrels," I would go to extraordinary lengths to retrieve them. A fly found was a quarter earned and one of my own rescued was two bits saved.

By the time I completed high school I think it fair to say I was an accomplished fly fisherman, at least by Smokies standards. Those standards, incidentally, are quite high. As I learned decades later when I made my first big-time junket to the fabled waters of Montana as a guest of that state's tourist agency, if you are proficient in the Appalachian high country you can catch fish most anywhere. I was scared to death I would prove to be a study in ineptitude in the storied setting for the Big Horn, Big Hole, Madison, Missouri, Clark's Fork, and so many other famous streams. By the end of my first half hour on the water in Montana I knew better. In that short passage of time, with a number of fine fish brought to hand, my worries were at an end.

As a teenager I caught my first true trophy trout (an eighteen-inch rainbow out of Deep Creek), increasingly enjoyed moments when the heft of my creel exceeded that of Daddy's and even, on a few occasions, those of other fly-fishing heroes of my youth. I spent hours without end in the water, sometimes leaving home before daylight and straggling back, dog-tired, at dusk. But those days astream formed a prelude to a lifetime of fly rodding which has enabled me to cast lines in Alaska, most if not all the provinces of Canada, New Zealand, South Africa, and streams without number in Montana and Wyoming. Small wonder Daddy called me "a fly fishing fool."

Part 4

PRECIOUS MEMORIES

"Precious Memories" is the title of a grand old Gospel song written by J. B. F. Wright I often heard during my childhood. It was especially popular at reunions; Decoration Day gatherings; or during church services connected with or around the time of Mother's Day, Father's Day, or Memorial Day. Portions of the lyrics have always moved me, and that is increasingly the case as my youth grows ever more distant. Certainly precious memories do linger, and there is no doubt "they ever flood my soul" even as "old home scenes of my childhood in fond memory appear."

In varying degrees all the dozen and a half selections in this section trace back to childhood scenes. In some cases they reflect specific experiences or encompass a range of particular activities; in others they treat boyhood influences which have remained strong over the decades and still stir me to the depths of my innermost being. I devote considerable space to my paternal grandfather, noting as I do so he was the most unforgettable character I've ever met. Similarly, I would be singularly remiss if I failed to acknowledge some of my most influential teachers, include a sampling of those experiences which loom especially large in memory's vaults, or ignored some of the strongest and most salient of mountain character traits. Maybe the "stock has begun to run out," as the opening chapter hints, but in some hardy folks of the region certain characteristics continue strong. If nothing more, they are well worth remembering, and to a hard-headed son of the Smokies like me they are reason for rejoicing.

Chapter 24

HAS THE STOCK RUN OUT?

A few years back a good friend who is a lifelong resident of Graham County was lamenting the fact that it seemed, in his words, "the local stock has run out." By that he meant traits that once typified mountain folks—self-sufficiency, a sound work ethic, respect for tradition, closeness to the land, willingness to perform needed tasks without looking to others, environmental concerns of a practical rather than philosophical nature, care of cemeteries, and general pride in one's forebears—appeared to be in increasingly short supply. At least from my personal perspective and through a comparison between the Smokies of my boyhood and the region as it exists today, it sadly seems that he is all too accurate.

Admittedly it's always tempting, and becomes more so with advancing age, to look back with longing to the "good old days" and compare them unfavorably with the current state of affairs. Yet it is my firmly held conviction that worship of progress can often mean adoration of a false god, and I think casting the sometimes glaring light of reality on the Smokies of today as seen through a looking glass to the past will confirm that. Ultimately judgment on whether avenues of asphalt have greater appeal than the scream of a hawk, whether an impressive bank account outweighs the simple serenity of a walk in the wilderness, whether the convenience and variety of store-bought meats and vegetables holds sway over tasty table fare you have nurtured so it can nourish, is an intensely individual matter. Yet I'd like to share some personal perspectives and in doing so hope they will, at the very least, give some pause to ponder a world and mountain ways we are rapidly losing.

Some time back a bountiful blessing came my way in the form of hundreds of slides, all of them taken by the late Bryson City resident I. K. Stearns in the period immediately prior to America's entry into World War II, being shared with me by his family. Their subject matter varied a great deal, although particular focal points included the area's largest employer at the time, Carolina Wood Turning Company; local people or perspectives that caught the photographer's eye; and scenic vistas. One readily notice-able feature in a preponderance of the slides falling into the last category was the presence of home gardens. Invariably when the setting involved distant views or an expansive background, depending on the season, there would be closely grazed pastures, flourishing gardens, or neatly plowed soil. Virtually every home shown in the images had a neat, carefully worked patch of ground adjacent to it.

Thinking along the line the slides suggested in regard to land use, I did a bit of mental time travel back to my Swain County boyhood in the 1950s. In that era it seemed almost everyone I knew, no matter whether they lived in town or out in the country, had a garden that was carefully tended—hoed, weeded, and worked with pride. Those gardens were a source of recreation, producing togetherness through combined family effort, providing peaceful relaxation and a retreat from stress, and while doing so made significant contributions in terms of putting healthy food on family tables.

In our neighborhood, every year Daddy and our next-door neighbor, local lawyer and banker Stanley W. Black, had a friendly annual competition over who could grow the finest tomatoes, potatoes, corn, and the like. Mr. Black, who also had a little orchard out in the country, took matters a step further with apples. He liked to compare the fall crop from his trees with the Golden and Red Delicious from our hillside trees as well as the har-vest from the trees of his good friend, Thurman Leatherwood, on another nearby hillside. John Price, the agriculture teacher at the local high school who lived across the road from our home, raised a big garden. So did most of the black folks living nearby. On the street below us Crawf Mahaffey grew stuff alongside Toot Hollow Branch, while Jack Lyday grew a large garden out in the country, and others had similar patches. In fact, I can only think of a handful of people living nearby who didn't have some sort of garden. This was within the town limits of Bryson City. Gardens were even more prevalent out in the country.

Take a drive around today's Swain County, or for that matter anywhere in the Smokies. You'll find that the presence of gardens is more an exception than the rule. That's telling commentary on the decline of what my grandfather would have called "plain gumption" and others sometimes styled as a "root hog, or die" attitude. Gardening can soothe the soul, represents a meaningful, maybe even matchless link with the good earth, and offers food of incomparable quality and freshness. There are few finer feelings than sitting down to a meal provided by the sweat of your brow from ground breaking and seeding, through cultivating and weeding, and finally to harvest. The exercise producing that sweat is a fringe benefit, and I'll defy you to find a headier perfume than newly plowed ground or a dusty garden when it receives the first drops from a summer shower. It's a heavenly aroma.

Indeed, you have to wonder just how those living in today's Smokies would fare if we ever face a "make do" situation resembling World War II's Victory Gardens, which required folks to raise a goodly portion of what sustained their family. Pretty poorly, I suspect, in comparison with yesteryear, although the current popularity of what is variously known as the "prepper" movement or "survivalism" is interesting.

In bygone days, raising a garden was an essential part of existence. Momma was never happy until shelves down in the basement fairly groaned with quart Ball or Mason jars holding green beans, soup mix, tomatoes, and apples. My grandparents and aunts and uncles felt precisely the same, and whenever I spent the night with a buddy, I invariably noticed a similar situation in his home.

One thing is certain. Never mind advances in technology and agricultural techniques, there's nowhere near the accumulated knowledge about gardening and farming on a small scale that existed locally two or three generations ago. Maybe that's one of the changes that defines progress, but if so, just put me down in the antiprogressive column. I genuinely believe that when we get too far removed from the chain of life, when we have minimal understanding of our connection with the earth, such circumstances are a loss to mankind.

Another changing face of the Smokies that I find troubling involves the soil lying beneath mountain feet in a strikingly different way. For reasons that I cannot fully explain, cemeteries have long fascinated me. Several factors unquestionably form part of their appeal. Cemeteries offer a tangible link to the past. They are visible reminders of life's fleeting nature as well as a silent suggestion to savor it while we can. You'll often find inscriptions, especially in older burying grounds such as those in the GSMNP, that read: "Pause, stranger, as you pass me by, As you are now so once was I." If that doesn't get your attention, then you aren't paying attention.

Other explanations of the manner in which cemeteries draw me include the peace and silence they provide, the aesthetic beauty of carefully wrought tombstones, the love that obviously went into placing even the simplest of field stones upright to mark a grave, painstakingly scratched-out epitaphs filled with love and sorrow, and the sometimes haunting nature of those epitaphs.

As much as cemeteries give me cause to pause and reverentially ponder, they can on occasion move me to abject dismay. That is especially the case when my rambles bring me to a burying ground that has been abandoned or left untended for weeds and bushes to run riot. On multiple occasions in person and in print I've roundly condemned Horace Kephart's depiction of graveyards in the Smokies, and unquestionably he resorted to rank hyperbole at the time he wrote *Our Southern Highlanders*. It pains me to write that increasingly, it seems, cemeteries marked by the shameful neglect Kephart referenced have become part of the mountain scene. Such was not always the situation.

I can't recall, during a boyhood that involved a great deal of walking and unexpectedly coming upon countless cemeteries, observing more than a handful that had been abandoned to nature. Today those rank with weeds, tumbled tombstones, and seemingly marked by general neglect have become all too commonplace. Most derelict burying places seem to be remote family plots without any connection to a church, those where few if any burials now take place, many of the scores of cemeteries located within the boundaries of the GSMNP, and small sites containing only a few graves in the Nantahala National Forest.

There are some striking and most welcome exceptions. In Graham County, where per capita income is the lowest of any mountain county in North Carolina, every cemetery is meticulously maintained. That's because Graham's political leaders have decided, in a praiseworthy manner, that honoring those gone before is a high priority.

In addition to the problem of poverty, Graham County is also arguably the most traditional of any of the mountain counties in or immediately around the Smokies whether you are speaking of North Carolina or
Tennessee. It is untouched by any interstate highway and indeed has only
a few miles of divided four-lane road. Nowhere will you find traditional
mountain talk more prevalent. So much is that the case that a few years
ago, while my brother and I were buying groceries in Robbinsville immediately prior to a camping trip on Big Snowbird Creek, the accent of
the young woman who checked us out, redolent of the accent and speech
mannerisms we heard so often as youngsters, struck us immediately. My
brother was so impressed that he said: "I think I'm in love with you. You
are the first young person I've heard speak the old-time mountain way in
a long time." That old-time mountain way to which he referred was one
where cemetery maintenance was pretty much a given.

Thanks in part to ready research tools, genealogy currently enjoys considerable popularity. Yet even as that aspect of interest in our ancestors
thrives, it seems that in some cases traditional family devotion to cemetery
care barely survives. That is sometimes explained in part by a family line
running out or all family members having moved from the mountains to
distant locations, and it must be emphasized that there are plenty of splen-
didly maintained burial grounds that are in some cases almost showplaces.
Those connected with and in close proximity to churches are usually neat
and well groomed, and the same holds true for those looked after by local
authorities (such as the countywide situation in Graham) or by some type
of perpetual care arrangement connected with a funeral home. Yet small
mountain churches have historically had pronounced tendencies to come
and go, and many older cemeteries in the mountains were family plots or
perhaps associated with a small local community as opposed to a formal
town with an established political structure.

Sometimes the size of the cemetery and level of neglect can be of appreciable magnitude. Until fairly recently, even the final resting place of
many of Swain County's most famous and important citizens, variously
known as Bryson City Cemetery or School House Hill Cemetery, had no
formal arrangement for maintenance, and efforts by town officials to keep
it mowed and in good order had become increasingly sporadic. Now a
formally organized nonprofit group, Friends of Bryson City Cemetery has
made it something of a showplace of respect for our past and those who
peopled it. It is a laudable model that merits widespread emulation, as does

a group that cares for the Lauada Cemetery where many originally buried in what became the Park were reinterred. One wide-ranging problem with these and similar organizations is that many of those most active in them are senior citizens. The key question is whether coming generations will carry the torch.

Admirable standards of care definitely are not the norm for cemeteries throughout the Smokies, however, and that's something which should be a source of considerable embarrassment to all of us with deep ties to the region. I have two aunts and an uncle buried in a private cemetery that merits more frequent attention than it receives, and similar situations are widespread. The cemeteries located in the GSMNP receive what could charitably be deemed a marginally acceptable level of care. If you visit them just before the annual Decoration Day, things will appear just fine. On the other hand, many receive only that single cleaning over the course of an entire year, and it doesn't take much imagination to realize what can happen when a given cemetery has Decoration Day in May and then gets no further attention for the rest of the growing season. Just take a short hike to any of the Park cemeteries located along U. S. Highway 441 as you leave Cherokee headed to Gatlinburg and chances are fair, if it is late summer or early fall, that you will encounter somewhat overgrown plots.

Some of the blame rests squarely on the shoulders of GSMNP officials, but they are by no means solely responsible. While access to the cemeteries along the drainages emptying in Fontana Lake's north shore is difficult and presents a situation where Park assistance is essential (it is provided once a year for each cemetery), others can be reached with minimal effort. Admittedly there are barriers, some of them understandable, others onerous, to individual maintenance efforts. But if I understand the terms of the documents connected with creation of the GSMNP correctly, there's ample latitude for descendants to care for graves of their loved ones. That isn't being done with any appreciable degree of consistency, and the ultimate responsibility for this rests not with bureaucracy but with family and locals with a love of the past.

There are cemeteries on private land in my native Swain County where the standard of care can only be described as somewhere between deplorable and nonexistent. Failure on this front is definitely an example of "the stock running out." It pains me, but such is reality.

Another troubling development in what seems a gradual erosion of traditional mountain outlooks comes on what might be loosely characterized as the economic front. Although written with eloquent persuasiveness, for me J. D. Vance's *Hillbilly Elegy* misses the mark in many ways. The same is equally true for a rejoinder to Vance, Elizabeth Catte's *What You Are Getting Wrong about Appalachia*. Admittedly their Appalachia is far wider than the scope of this volume. They focus more on coal country and lifestyles far removed from the hills and hollers of the Smokies. Historically folks in the region in which I grew up worked at the local mill or scratched out a piecemeal living with a mixture of hardscrabble farming and sporadic paid employment.

Still, some of the matters they address, such as drug addiction, disappearance of a traditional work ethic among younger people, and a dwindling sense of community are common to the Smokies. To me, the key element of this disturbing trend focuses squarely on economic issues. Mountain people have always been poor in material wealth, but offsetting that was a glorious sense of fierce independence, pride, the blessings of living in a place of breathtaking beauty, and a subliminal sense that everyone in the community had your back in times of real trouble. As surely as he would never ask for help, a man instinctively knew that when he was down on his luck help was there in the form of a type of togetherness that translated to reaching out to those who were sailing seas of misfortune.

Even in the darkest times of the Great Depression "mountain proud" held strong. Hardy Smokies folks weathered the takings connected with the original creation of the GSMNP, decidedly shoddytreatment by the Tennessee Valley Authority when the flooding of Fontana added to the Park, failure of some local banks where monies from the takings had been deposited, and the toll of chestnut blight. A lesser breed would have been destroyed by those cataclysmic and near simultaneous developments. But with the coming of Lyndon Johnson's Great Society, welfare checks, food stamps, government handouts, and increasing bureaucratic intrusion into daily life, the Appalachian way of life changed irrevocably. Pride in self declined while crime multiplied exponentially. The myriad societal woes associated with single-parent homes enveloped the area like the mists of an August morning, but there was no bright sunlight to break through the gloom. The stock ran out a bit more.

The temptation to pontificate on this general theme presses hard on me, and the sociological observations above come from nothing more than the mind-set of a mountain boy grown old, personal perspectives dating back to the middle of the last century, and deep concern about the future of some of the brightest and most beguiling of Smokies traditions. So, with a few closing observations, I'll abandon my pulpit, mindful as I do so that Daddy was often fond of suggesting I "could talk the ears off a Georgia mule."

For those who do care about the direction of today's society in the Smokies, here are a few more conundrums to consider.

> What's the role of the church in daily life compared with the situation three generations ago?
>
> What has been the impact of a vast, ongoing influx of retirees and part-time residents, many of whom harbor strikingly different perspectives on life and even strong desires to "change" or "improve" mountain people?
>
> Is mountain culture losing its distinctiveness and becoming ever more polyglot thanks to supposed progress?
>
> Are educators in Smokies schools of today so enamored of technology and all things new that they fail to pay due obeisance to the past?
>
> Are we watching the means of communication that Joe Hall studied and Michael Montgomery has chronicled in their splendid *Dictionary of Smoky Mountain English* become as strange and distant as Chaucerian English?

For me, as someone who is helplessly, hopelessly caught in a lifelong love affair with the mountains, these are deeply troubling questions. I don't want the stock to run out, and I rage against the mere thought of that happening. That leads to a final question, one for which I have no ready answer. What can each of us do, and what minor miracles can be individually wrought, to guarantee that our precious, priceless heritage survives? This book is one man's tiny tilt against the whirling windmill of passing time.

Chapter 25

OLD-TIME SURVIVAL TECHNIQUES

In today's world phrases such as "back to the earth," "grow your own," "sustainable gardening," "cultivating heirloom varieties," and the like are bandied about with increasing regularity. Indeed, as an indication of just how prevalent survivalist thinking has become, a few years ago a lady connected with National Geographic television programming contacted me seeking advice on "a new television series on eating wild and living off the land." I'm not sure exactly why she thought I would be qualified to provide insight, other than the fact that the subject is of considerable interest to me and I've written on it in magazines from time to time. I must admit though that I chuckled a bit given the fact that what National Geographic had in mind is, in essence, what mountain folks have done for generations.

Most of today's popular heirloom varieties of tomatoes survive thanks to the fact that generations of frugal folks saved seeds. They did so because the cost was right (nothing) and they knew through dint of experience which varieties grew well, produced abundantly, had solid disease resistance, and were tasty. A case in point would be Cherokee Purple tomatoes. The variety is in my studied opinion about as fine a tomato as you'll ever slice and lay atop a piece of bread en route to one of the finest culinary treats imaginable, a tomato sandwich. While I don't know the details of its origin, the name strongly suggests the Cherokee Purple might well have historic links to the Smokies.

When it comes to meritorious qualities in apples, once again oldies are truly goodies. Both Grandpa Joe and Daddy often talked of vanishing varieties they had once known as commonplace dwellers in mountain orchards—Sheepnose, June apples, Limbertwig, Pippins, Russets, and the like—and today there is renewed and fairly widespread interest in apples of this sort. In season you can even buy them, usually at exorbitant prices, in upscale city food markets. They are normally touted as being "organically grown," but what always intrigued me was Grandpa and Daddy mentioning that old-timey apples had little if any need for spraying and were resistant to blight, insect damage, and the like. Often they were also highly productive. They were organic long before the term was "cool."

One specific link to apples dating from boyhood still opens the floodgates on my salivary glands every time I think about it. An elderly lady named Lillie Quiett who lived catty-corner across the street from Grandma Minnie and Grandpa Joe had a massive June apple tree at the edge of her place. Every year, without fail, it produced an abundant crop, never mind that it was never pruned, sprayed, or fertilized. I was always permitted to pick up as many windfalls as I wished. Some were eaten on the spot, but most went into apple sauce or, better still, the filling placed between layers of Grandma's delectable stack cakes. Those stack cakes have to rank as my all-time favorite in the dessert sweepstakes.

Although they didn't graft apples, at least in my lifetime, both Daddy and Grandpa saved a number of types of seeds from annual vegetables and melons they grew, knew how to root various plants, and in general practiced both frugality and a common man's equivalent of selective breeding. When it came to saving seeds, a standard aspect of raising crops, they worked wonders. Getting special attention were productive beans or peas, tomato plants that outdid themselves when it came to size and quality, watermelons and cantaloupes that were exceptionally large and sweeter than the average run of melons, along with numerous other fruits and vegetables.

The favorite storage medium to protect seeds from insect damage was snuff. Both beans and field peas would be allowed to dry on the vines. They would then be dried in the late summer sun, shelled out, put in a recycled mayonnaise or peanut butter jar, covered with a dusting of snuff, and sealed with a screw-on lid. Grandpa also saved a bunch of other types of seed—pumpkins, kushaws, both red and yellow pear tommytoes, hot peppers, candy roasters, and for a number of years field corn. Uncle Hall Casada stumbled on a type of okra that did exceptionally well, and it immediately went on the "save the seed" list as well.

They supplemented saved seeds with store-bought ones, but that was an exception rather than standard practice. In at least one instance Daddy came to regret relying on the convenience of store-bought seed. For years he regularly bought and planted a variety of nonclimbing green bean that sort of fell between bunch beans and half runners. The variety was known as White Princess. Then one year, inexplicably, seeds were no longer available. For the remainder of his life he groused about his shortsightedness in that regard.

On the flip side of the bean-saving equation, some years ago a good friend from over Topton, North Carolina, way, Ken Roper, first introduced me to a climbing green bean that, in my view at least, tops both White Princess and a longtime local favorite, Mountain Half Runners, in terms of taste and productivity. It is a vigorous pole bean he originally obtained from an old-timer who said it originated in the Nantahala community and had been around for more than a century. All I know is that they are incredibly productive, mighty tasty, and something I've saved annually from when I first obtained the seed. I've decided to call them Nantahala Runner Beans, and believe me, they know how to climb. My brother went to considerable pains one summer to provide a climbing apparatus for them made of lengthy canes. I've got a picture of him perched precariously on the penultimate step of a king-size step ladder reaching high above his head to pluck beans from the vines. They had to be 12 or 14 feet off the ground and above him vines are still reaching heavenward in real-life "Jack and the Beanstalk" fashion.

Similarly, I have a variety of clay peas (also known outside the Smokies as field peas, crowder peas, zip peas, hulling peas, and by other names) which have been a mainstay in my garden for at least forty years. They originally came from a woman who was in a crafts group with my wife. She didn't have a name for them, but they grow like nobody's business, are exceptionally easy to shell and freeze, and are delicious.

In today's world it is relatively simple to obtain heirloom seeds and plants, although they do tend to be on the pricey side. But the true mountain approach to such matters has always been one of save and share. You save anything that has proven to be a winner for you, share with friends and family, and make do with what you have even as friendships bring you new varieties. The approach reminds me of something I once heard Grandpa say about expressing gratitude: "Thank you's cost nothing, but they go a long way." Saving seeds is likewise free, and the ramifications in terms of shared goodwill, learning of new varieties, and exposure to previously unknown foodstuffs is virtually limitless. Saved vegetable seeds, in short, bring pleasure, cultivate friendships, and belong in the catechism of every gardener. The same holds true for cuttings, root stocks, or other means of propagation for flowers, fruits, or indeed anything that grows.

Taking the self-sufficient approach is easier today than ever before, because placing dried and cleaned seeds in a Zip-loc bag and then freezing them is an ideal storage medium. This concept of heirlooms that has become all the "new" rage is in truth as old as the hills. It reminds us in a most gratifying fashion of how our hardy, self-sufficient forebears knew the ways of living close to the good earth and practiced them. These ways, with seed saving being a grand example, were integral and vital parts of Smokies life. It's heartening to see ways of old enjoying a revival.

Chapter 26

A GARDENER LOOKS BACK

"Why he ain't no professor; he's just an old dirt dauber." Several decades ago that's how a plainspoken woman simply known to locals as the "plant lady" described me to another customer when that individual happened to mention I taught at the local university. Seldom if ever in my life have I been paid a finer compliment than being styled "an old dirt dauber." It's a badge of honor, one I'll wear with great pride.

Living close to the land runs as a bright, meaningful thread through the fabric of my life. Some of my fondest memories of a Smokies childhood revolve around helping Daddy and Grandpa Joe plan and plant crops in the spring. In my teenage years, this metamorphosed to tending a small garden plot of my own. Well before adulthood I had become part of the timeless, rewarding cycle of plant, nurture, and harvest that traces back to the point when mankind first made the transition from hunter-gatherer to an agricultural existence. To this day recollection of the first time Grandpa let me cut up seed potatoes alongside him, using my first pocket knife (a Christmas present a few months earlier), warms the cockles of my heart. I still adhere to his simple advice: "Cut a good chunk of tater, son, and always make sure it has at least two eyes."

Each of the four seasons in the Smokies has its distinctive and appealing characteristics when it comes to working the land, but most gardeners, including this one, would likely pick spring as their favorite. Earth's reawakening brings bountiful blessings in myriad forms—a profusion of wildflowers, fresh wild and garden greens in the diet, fried mountain trout fresh from the stream, a bait of ramps or poke salad doing double duty as a spring tonic, and increasingly balmy weather that makes being out and about while communing with nature an exercise in pure pleasure.

Even administration of traditional spring tonics such as sulfur and molasses or sassafras tea sweetened with sourwood honey has a certain appeal. In tandem with wild vegetables of early spring they seem to cleanse the system or, as old-timers often put it, "cure what ails you." Most of all, though, the beginning of another cycle in earth's eternal rebirth means soaring spirits connected with planting time and promise of bountiful crops in coming months. Such links to the land and mountain folkways, often subconscious but nonetheless emotionally powerful, have succored and sustained me all my years.

The aroma of freshly plowed ground is finer than the costliest perfumes, and feeling humus-rich soil in your hands soothes the soul like a blessed balm. A garden not only provides wholesome meals and the time-honored satisfaction of "putting food on the table." For me it has always offered a place of quiet refuge to escape daily stresses while reestablishing loving links with the past. Although gardening's myriad pleasures are better experienced in person than explained in print, all these blessings provided by getting hands in the dirt and seeds in the soil have figured prominently in my having raised some type of garden almost every year since I was eleven or twelve. The only exceptions were years devoted to undergraduate and graduate studies. So strong is my love affair with the land that when my wife and I were finally able to afford a modest home, the key consideration for me was not design, interior amenities, or square footage. Instead, my one nonnegotiable "must have" was the availability of sufficient land for a large garden, fruit trees, and berry bushes.

Certain gardening principles have always guided me. My gardening mentors never specifically mentioned "three sisters" cultivation, but they practiced variations of it by planting corn, climbing beans or field peas, and pumpkins or winter squash in a harmonious relationship. For those unfamiliar with the concept, it emphasizes a symbiotic relationship between plants adapted from Native American approaches to agriculture. Corn provides a means for beans to climb; those members of the legume family in turn fix nitrogen from the air and are beneficial to the soil; large leaves of pumpkins keep weeds at bay.

While carefully adhering to the three sisters gardening method, my overall approach has followed a different triumvirate—the three "Cs" of continuity, change, and cultural tradition. The continuity involves adhering faithfully to things taught to me well over half a century ago and doubtless passed down for many generations before that: slicing seed potatoes for planting, removing all suckers on tomatoes except the first one, saving proven seed from year to year, regularly rotating crops, frequent additions of leaf mulch, infusions of wood ashes, shaking tomato vines to assist pollination, "collaring" vulnerable seedlings to frustrate cutworms, and dozens of other tricks of the gardening trade.

Yet it's wise not to get too "sot in your ways." Accordingly, there's change in the form of trying a few new plants each year. In that regard a renaissance of heirloom varieties and increasing availability of long-forgotten seeds has been a boon. There are new "old" varieties of tomatoes to try every year, different creasy or cutshort beans to test, and occasional major blessings such as introduction to Cherokee Purple tomatoes and Oriental persimmons. This spring will see candy roaster seeds go in the ground, evoking warm memories of pies and preserves from boyhood There will be some ground cherries, a reminder of those days when I walked through sere September corn fields with Grandpa Joe with those tasty treats always at my feet. Old favorites like climbing crowder peas will be sown, as will perhaps a total of forty varieties of fruits and vegetables. I'll watch blueberry plants now approaching fifty years of age and up to ten feet in height bloom once more and in due course bring their predictable bounty. Fig bushes continue to flourish in carefully chosen, protected places. Flowers, some of them perennials and others annuals for which seeds are saved and sown each year, will bring their visual flavor to the gardener's feast.

Most of all, though, my gardens (one for food, one for flowers) are places to pause and ponder, to observe in unhurried wonder, as I ceaselessly derive an ample measure of pleasure from miracles wrought by soil and sun, water and wind, and my helping hands. There's no finer treat for the troubled soul, and the sense of satisfaction to be derived from putting some fine victuals on the table or sharing garden truck with friends and neighbors adds meaning to life. An integral part of mountain culture, it's one of the greatest of many gifts given to me by the Smokies.

Chapter 27

PICKIN' NATURE'S BOUNTY

Some of my fondest childhood memories center on countless spring, summer, and early fall days spent plucking the fruits of nature's labor. Berrying picking gave me precious pocket money and fun days involving environs such as briar patches, elderberry-laden branch banks, old fields and field edges, high elevation balds, and more. My labors in these locales provided the basic essentials for all sorts of tasty treats that emerged from the kitchens of Momma and Grandma Minnie.

Of all these wild wonders, my personal favorite has to be the strawberry. It grows in areas that are easily accessible (although keeping a watchful eye out for old Mr. No Shoulders is advisable), carries no protective armament in the form of briars or thorns, is easily picked as long as your stooping mechanism is in good functioning order, and has a heavenly taste. Izaak Walton, quoting a friend named Dr. Boteler, summed up its virtues quite nicely well over three centuries ago: "Doubtless God could have made a better berry, but doubtless God never did." Humankind has succeeded in producing a bigger berry, but when it comes to taste and texture, the wild strawberry has it all over its domesticated cousin. Adorning late-spring meadows and abandoned fields, these delectable scarlet jewels could convince even the most xenophobic of Texans that bigger is not necessarily better.

Wild strawberries belong to May, and one of the next berries to ripen is a child of June sometimes known as June berries. This is the serviceberry, so named because of a link with circuit-riding preachers. The first services by these men on horseback, conducted after cold weather and impassable winter trails had kept them away for several months, closely coincided with the distinctive white flowers of the tree bring a welcome splash of color to gray, dull woodlands. I've never eaten any type of dish prepared with serviceberries, but finding a streamside tree laden with ripe berries provides a welcome snack during a break in a day of trout fishing. They offer a mild, ever so slightly tart taste, and if you chew them thoroughly, the rather large seeds carry a hint of almond flavor.

Another berry to make its annual ripening appearance about the same time is one of distinctly humble origins. The child of farmed-out land and barren patches of red clay, this black beauty is often overlooked. Yet connoisseurs who welcome the dewberry's seasonal return with a joy born of past experience recognize and welcome the its estimable merits. Few if any poets have sung the dewberry's praise, but virtues it has and in abundance. The glories of a dewberry cobbler are such that it may be just as well relatively few have experienced them. Better appreciated in the taste than in the telling, such a cobbler will, as I've heard some old-timers describe it, bring tears of pure joy to a glass eye.

The glorious ecstasy of a dewberry cobbler, or maybe a handful of fresh ones topping a bowl of home-churned vanilla ice cream, more than offsets certain disadvantages the plant has. Once established, dewberries are devilishly difficult to grub out of fields. Their small but super-abundant briars can wreak havoc on even the toughest pair of brush britches or Duxbak pants. The vines, which grow horizontally just a few inches above the earth's surface, are Mother Nature's ultimate trap or tripping device. Make a misstep or get in a hurry while wending your way through a patch of dewberries and you are begging to take a tumble.

More than once I've made an almost instantaneous transition from walking or running to using my nose as a plow point while amid dewberries, but the finest example I've ever witnessed of just how tough and unyielding the runners can be involved a boyhood friend, later one of the key researchers on the team that developed Viagra, by the name of Jackie Corbin. Known during his youth as "Grubby," thanks to his penchant for grubbing out an extra yard on the football field or going through briar patches or other vegetative impediments as if they didn't exist, he was a regular on rabbit hunts organized by Daddy.

On this particular occasion a shot he took had crippled but failed to kill a cottontail. Since his gun was a single-shot one, Jackie took out after that fleeing rabbit with precisely the same sort of quickness and determination that earned him a football scholarship to fund his undergraduate studies. Unfortunately for him, the rabbit ran through a big dewberry patch, and that was Jackie's undoing. He tripped, turned a complete flip in the air, and somehow managed, using his gun to help with leverage, to land on his feet. It was a sight to behold, and it took Daddy a full fifteen minutes of diligent attention to clear Grubby's gun barrel of the mud jammed in it.

Dewberries are closely related to what is far and away the best-known of the wild brambles, the luscious, omnipresent blackberry. Old Will Shakespeare, who seemed to know something about everything, once wished that "reasons were as plentiful as blackberries." He was right on the mark. Botanists indicate that there are literally hundreds of subspecies of blackberries, and anyone who has done much picking of them likely has noticed subtle variations in their appearance and nature. In fact, genetic engineering has even produced a thornless blackberry, but like seedless watermelons these are also-rans in the taste sweepstakes. Moreover, no self-respecting berry picker feels that he has fulfilled all the requirements of his job until his hands are well-scratched, briar-riddled, and stained a lovely purple-black hue.

When it comes to blackberries, "no pain, no gain" is certainly the operative truism. But even if picking them results in occasional occupational hazards such as a bunch of chigger bites or getting into a wasp nest, they are well worth the effort. Realization of that fact comes the moment you take the first bite from a piping hot bowl of blackberry cobbler swimming in cream, slather an ample amount of jam or jelly on a buttered biscuit, or yield to the tremendous temptation to eat a luscious handful during the pickin' process.

The next berry to ripen is the wild raspberry. They come in two distinct types in the Smokies, red and black. These vary markedly in their growth habits and favored habitat, and while both are delicious, they differ appreciably in taste. Black raspberry canes are slender and grow quite tall. In the winter they are readily noticeable because their stems have a purplish tint. Their favored habitat seems to be field edges and roadsides at lower elevations.

Red raspberries, on the other hand, grow on shorter, sturdier canes and seem to prefer higher elevations. They are commonplace along maintained trails that offer openings to the sun. For example, they grow all along the path that winds up to the observation tower crowning Clingmans Dome, and at ripening time in late summer there's a treat ready at hand for those who know their berry lore.

Another berry found in great plentitude in the Smokies and indeed over much of the country is the elderberry. Even though it lacks the thorny protection of some of its brethren berries, it is sadly neglected today. Yet gathering the big clusters of berries requires nothing more than a sharp pocket knife, and washing and removing them from the collection of stems forming the cluster is an easy task. Once these things are accomplished, elderberries lend themselves to a variety of uses. They make a quite passable pie, toothsome jelly, and a wine cordial that is sheer nectar. As a bonus, if patience isn't your strong suit, the distinctive white bloom clusters, generally known as elderflower, can be used for fritters, wine, and numerous nostrums to treat allergies, colds, and other ailments. Elderberry juice or concentrate is also a widely recommended folk medicine.

Once elderberries have come and gone, the best of the summer's berrying is past. Gooseberries remain, however, as do blueberries and their cousins, huckleberries. The latter two berries grow primarily at high elevations and are prominent in the areas known as balds scattered throughout the Smokies. For sake of completeness, I probably should mention deer berries and mulberries. I love the latter, which ripen fairly early, although you've got to be on the ball if you plan to beat the birds to them. Daddy would never touch a mulberry, declaring, "You could cut a hundred of them open and find a worm in every single one." That was quite possibly the case, but as a youngster getting a bit of protein with my berry seemed just fine. I'd stuff myself with mulberries from a fine tree on our property to the point where my lips betrayed me every time.

Each year the arrival of winter's cold posts a seasonal "no picking" sign, but sons and daughters of the Smokies in yesteryear knew that with spring came renewed pleasure and mouthwatering delicacies from pickin'. Meanwhile, they had canned berries for pies and cobblers, jellies and jams to decorate biscuits with distinction, and maybe even some berry leather for snacks or use in making berry dumplings. Berries were a dependable, welcome, and important part of the mountain diet in most high country homes. For me, they were profitable as well, and even now, all these decades later, I derive a great deal of quiet satisfaction from a few hours spent in a berry patch.

Chapter 28

SUMMER DAYS AND
WATERMELON WAYS

As should be clear by this juncture, two elderly individuals who figured quite prominently in my boyhood were my paternal grandfather, Joe Casada, and a wonderful colored lady who lived just down the road from us, Maggie "Aunt Mag" Williams. In addition to being of quite advanced age as I entered my teen years (Grandpa was born in 1878 while Aunt Mag was born in 1863), they shared several things in common. Both loved to eat fish. Both had lived hard lives in which poverty played a prominent role and in which hard work was taken for granted as a part of their existence. Aunt Mag had been born when slavery was still legal, and Grandpa had married a woman who was bound (an indentured servant). Both lacked much in the way of formal education (Aunt Mag was illiterate), but they were incredibly rich in folk wisdom, practical aspects of eking out a hardscrabble, root-hog-or-die existence, and a deep understanding of things closely connected to the good earth. One other commonality was a shared appetite for watermelon, which was obviously a lifelong culinary love affair.

Their enthusiasm for watermelon was one I shared, and some of my warmest memories of high summer revolve around feasts of ice-cold watermelon. Although it is possible, in today's world, to buy watermelons most any time of the year, in the 1950s they didn't show up in local grocery stores or roadside stands until late June. Homegrown melons wouldn't ripen until the latter part of August. For roughly three months, though, feasts of the luscious red flesh were in the offing, and it didn't take much of an excuse for either Grandpa Joe or Aunt Mag to enjoy this wonderfully tasty example of earth's bounty. Every aspect of the experience comes back to me in vivid fashion.

In my mind's eye I see Grandpa toting a watermelon home from town in a tow sack, straining with the weight of forty pounds or more across his stooped shoulder. Or there's Aunt Mag quietly mentioning that her daughter, Elma, had bought a watermelon the day before and I might want to stop by after a day of fishing to "holp me eat it." Of course, it went without saying that a mess of fish was the price of admission.

In each case they chilled the watermelon to perfection by placing it in a wash tub surrounded by water in which big chunks of ice floated. I'm not sure how Aunt Mag procured ice, but Grandpa got it from the ice plant located right alongside old U.S. Highway 19 at the point where Kirklands Creek empties into the Tuckaseigee (I prefer the traditional spelling) River a short way above Bryson City. Ice boxes, both in homes and at places where soft drinks were sold, were still in the process of giving way to electricity, and there was a solid local market for twenty-five and fifty-pound blocks of ice. With a few licks with an ice pick Grandpa would reduce one of those big blocks into chunks ideally suited for chilling a melon to perfection.

Mind you, these were real watermelons, giants of their kind with appealing names such as Georgia Rattlesnake, Charleston Gray, and Green Cannonball. You didn't see any of today's popular individual or "baby" melons. These were behemoths of the watermelon tribe, and Grandpa was a master when it came to looking at the bottom of one, studying its stem, and thumping it a few times to determine ripeness. Along with a sweeter, more fulfilling taste, those melons had another distinctive feature often missing in today's "dumbed down," less tasty descendants—they came with a full complement of seeds, not in sissified seedless form.

Once a melon had been properly chilled and was ready to cut—usually in the afternoon of a sweltering day—there was almost a ritualistic formula to the process. A long, keenly sharpened butcher knife was the instrument of choice for the operation. Even the knives were works of mountain craftsmanship. Grandpa Joe used one he had made from a saw blade. It featured wooden handle held together by brass rivets, and the knife had been used so long and sharpened so much it had begun to resemble the profile of the ice pick he had used a few hours earlier.

The moment the knife pierced the thick rind, you knew whether the chosen melon had reached ruby red perfection in terms of ripeness. A fully ripe melon would split asunder with a most satisfying sound, and before you lay two pieces of dewy, scarlet perfection—almost round in the case of Cannonballs and oblong ovals if it was a Charleston Gray or Georgia Rattlesnake.

Each half would then be carefully cut into slices, salted if you were so inclined, and messy, juice-dripping, stomach-filling magic ensued. I was always good for two slices and sometimes three and had sticky juice running from ear to ear, along with plenty dripping down my bare belly. Grandpa happily anointed his work overalls while Aunt Mag took the precaution of donning an apron before eating. Even when one was full to repletion, there remained the considerable joy of watermelon seed spitting contests.

Aunt Mag considered such antics beneath her dignity, possibly because her rather sparse equipage of teeth mitigated against any long-distance seed expectoration. But Grandpa Joe competed, with contests involving both accuracy and distance, just like he was still a boy. Come to think of it, in many ways he was a boy at heart, and whenever possible he ignored the limitations posed by an old man's body. On top of that, thanks to his pro-nounced predilection for "chaws" of dry twist tobacco, he had a great deal of experience and expertise in forcible ejection of spittle (or seeds) from his mouth.

Watermelon feasts and the ensuing seed-spitting contests had useful side-lights inasmuch as the free-ranging chickens both Grandpa and Aunt Mag owned delighted in dining on the seeds. They also welcomed rinds on the menu, although often there was human competition for them. Both Aunt Mag and Grandma Minnie made a point of putting up runs of watermelon rind pickles every summer. Then too, yet another option at Grandpa's was to feed rinds to the hogs. In other words, every part of the watermelon was put to good use.

Those were wondrous days, and simple anticipation of a watermelon feast was enough to carry me through row after row of hoeing corn. Similarly, I remain convinced now, as I was then, that no monarch on his throne, no high society folks dining in high-dollar restaurants, ever found a greater measure of culinary pleasure than a mountain lad digging into a watermelon in a stage of dead-ripe perfection. Or, as the inimitable Mark Twain put it through the words of Pudd'nhead Wilson, watermelon "is chief of this world's luxuries, king by the grace of God over all the fruits of the earth. When one has tasted it, he knows what the angels eat. It was not a Southern watermelon that Eve took; we know it because she repented." Indeed. Watermelon is heavenly bliss.

Chapter 29

THE AMERICAN CHESTNUT—VANISHED

For all of us who cherish the good earth and care deeply about the future of the natural world, the American chestnut offers a singularly sad tale from the past as well as a glimmer of hope for the future. Fortunately today's youngsters have a realistic opportunity of being an integral part of a grand conservation success story—the return of the majestic tree that once graced forests up and down the Appalachians and far beyond.

A century ago the beautiful, versatile chestnut adorned vast areas of forest in the eastern United States. From Mississippi and Alabama north all the way to Maine, spreading outward from the mountainous spinal column we know as the Appalachians, it was *the* dominant tree in vast tracts of hardwood forest. From pioneer days onward, and for that matter long before Europeans put down roots in the New World, the chestnut held a special place in American life. Among the most predictable of all the nut-bearing trees when it came to consistent crops year after year, chestnut mast provided food for man as well as for many of the animals, wild and domesticated, upon which he relied for meat.

Homesteads in the Smokies routinely nestled close to groves of chestnuts, and giants of the species were common boundary markers. These landmark trees with saw-toothed, spearhead-shaped leaves afforded welcome shade from the summer heat and a gathering spot for friendly barter, banter, or gossip. Among the best-known lines in all of our country's poetry are those from Henry Wadsworth Longfellow's "The Village Blacksmith":

Under the spreading chestnut tree,
The village smithy stands . . .

The verbal scene drawn by this titan of American letters was one intimately familiar to our forebears. Quite simply, in days gone by, the chestnut was a vital part of life for millions of rural dwellers, and almost everyone who resided in the Smokies had considerable dependence on this mighty monarch of the forest.

With that thought in mind, perhaps interjection of a personal anecdote is appropriate at this point, because my own boyhood was filled with tales revolving around the sad saga of the American chestnut. Grandpa Joe was a hickory-tough old man hardened by a lifetime of arduous work eking out a living in the rugged hills and hollows of North Carolina's Great Smokies. He wasn't a fellow much given to demonstration of emotion, but whenever the vanished giant of the forests he had known as a boy and man was mentioned, there would be a catch in his voice and a tear in his eyes. "Son," he said to me countless times in rocking chair sessions on his front porch looking out at the mountains, "the chestnut was life's blood to mountain folks during my youth and the prime of my years. It gave us sustenance in more ways than you can imagine, and when that awful blight struck it was like the biblical plague had come to the high country."

He would reminisce about the way the chestnut was an integral part of life for him, his family, and countless others living in similar circumstances in the Appalachians. He ruminated on fattening hogs on chestnut mast; gathering the nuts by the bushel to get cash money (those nuts, sold to local brokers, went by rail to cities where vendors sold roasted nuts on street corners); eating them raw, roasted, in soup, in bread, and in dressing; cutting trees for acid wood (they were a favored source of tannic acid at leather works); making split rail fences and roofing shingles out of them; building barns and sheds from rough lumber; and hunting squirrels, deer, and turkeys which fed on them. In short, the tree, as a foodstuff, income producer, and lumber source was central to Grandpa's existence.

Most authorities estimate that the species composed at least twenty-five percent of all the eastern hardwood forest, and over extensive areas, including the Smokies, it was even more prevalent. There it grew in virgin splendor and even when lesser ones were cut as acid wood the largest trees were carefully nurtured and protected. Marching in verdant ranks up sloping hillsides and steep ridges, ever soaring majestically skyward, chestnuts were the crowning glory of the Great Smokies and the Blue Ridge, Plott Balsam, Black, Nantahala, and Unaka mountains.

Beloved for their staunch serenity, ability to attain incredible size, and standing as a seeming constant in a world where the wolf of poverty was never far enough from the door, they were inextricably intertwined in the existence of those living close to the good earth. Grandpa Joe was in his early fifties when the virulent fungus widely known as "chestnut blight" first reached the Smokies. Accidentally introduced in seedlings from the Orient that arrived in New York City in the first decade of the twentieth century, its spread had been rapid. As the blight reached deadly tentacles southward down the Appalachian chain, it became an all-too-realistic version of the "yellow peril" that preoccupied many political thinkers during the interwar years. In the mid-1920s one major national magazine described the fungus in just such a fashion: "Americans routed all along the line! Orientals advancing irresistibly! Devastated area steadily widens as triumph of invaders is complete!"

It was an apt description of the course the fungus took. It resisted all efforts (and to a certain degree continues to do so) aimed at curing it or curbing its advance. Grandpa knew little of this; all he experienced was an incalculable loss and dramatic disruption to his way of life. The same was true for everyone he knew. Quite often Grandpa would bemoan the demise of the chestnut and comment with great sadness: "You'll never know the wonder of chestnut woodlands."

Nonetheless, Grandpa and Daddy gave me many vicarious encounters with chestnuts. One of my favorites among Grandpa's vast store of stories, and it never became an "old chestnut" no matter how many times he retold it, involved his squirrel hunting experiences in stands of chestnuts. According to his lively accounts, never quite the same in the retelling but always carrying the ring of authenticity, killing a dozen bushytails from a large chestnut tree when the nuts began falling was commonplace. "All you had to do was pick a good spot, keep alert, and pick your shots with care." He noted that during the glory days before the blight's arrival squirrels were incredibly abundant, thanks in no small measure to having a predictable and abundant source of food.

Another cherished story connected with chestnuts came from my father. He and his brother made a studied practice, during the peak of nutting season in autumn, of observing ground squirrels closely. They didn't hunt the ubiquitous rodents but rather carefully watched them as they stored chestnuts against the coming hard times of winter. Mentally marking holes and storage burrows where chipmunks harbored nuts, they knew they could return later and find anywhere from a quart to a half gallon of chestnuts. "One good thing about those nuts," Daddy remarked, "was that they were always sound. Somehow both gray squirrels and ground squirrels recognized rotten or wormy nuts when they first picked them up, and those would never form part of their store."

Even in its death throes, for Daddy, untold numbers of handymen, and the furniture industry in general, the worthy chestnut offered one farewell benefit. As the trees died and eventually fell to the forest floor, tiny worms ate their way through the logs. Still, the dead chestnuts, thanks to the high tannin content that had made them so valuable to the leather-working industry, resisted rot. It wasn't long before foresters and woodworkers recognized that "wormy chestnut" was a wood of surpassing beauty. The worm holes gave the lumber an eye-catching pattern of infinite variety, and the lovely patina with which it glowed once planed, sanded, and finished gave wormy chestnut a softness and warmth matched by few woods. Moreover, furniture or paneling from wormy chestnut had an aura about it, a mystique if you will, as if it lived on after death.

The mountain home in which I grew up featured a mantel and desk, both made by my Dad, lovingly crafted from wormy chestnut. Similarly, in his final years he presented his great-granddaughter, the only one of that generation born before his death, a magazine rack he had made from the wood. For a number of years it was on display in a local museum that highlighted mountain crafts, but now that she is old enough to appreciate this part of a Smokies heritage, it rests in her bedroom.

Throughout my boyhood the mentors who first introduced me to hunting, fishing, and the delectation of being in the outdoors always took pains to point out chestnut sprouts, along with those of its kissing cousin, the chinquapin (both are of the genus *Castanea*), whenever we encountered them. Looking back, I realize this was their way of mourning the passing of a treasured friend, of paying richly deserved tribute to a stalwart companion that had been a constant ally in the struggle for survival.

Small wonder then that those familiar with the lost legacy of this vanished giant hope that the miracles of science, through crossbreeding of isolated blight-resistant survivors with other members of the same family, will eventually bring about its resurrection. We are getting closer each year, and already organizations devoted to the American chestnut's return are producing seedlings for replanting.

Maybe, just maybe, for all Grandpa Joe's acumen, his gloomy prophesy in regard to the American chestnut being "gone forever" will prove to be wrong as the tree continues traveling the comeback trail. Such thinking is soul-satisfying and sustaining, and meanwhile, each Thanksgiving I pay my own special tribute to the one-time leafy lord of the Smokies land. Using the nearest thing available to the "real McCoy," I prepare cornbread dressing liberally laced with Chinese chestnuts. The recipe comes from Grandma Minnie, and with each scrumptious bite the past beckons and memory marches triumphant.

Chapter 30

THE JOYS OF NUTTING

When pioneers first settled North Carolina, initially in the coastal plain and eventually expanding across the piedmont and then into the deep hollows and remote coves of the high country (much of the migration into the upper piedmont and mountains followed the spine of the Appalachians southwestward, as opposed to being a strictly westward expansion), they relied almost exclusively on their own gumption to survive. Living *off* the land, as Native Americans had done for untold generations before them, these hardy individuals became closely attuned *to* the land. Their linkage with the earth involved subsistence crop farming along with keeping some chickens, hogs, and cows for eggs, meat, and milk. Also, these folks for whom self-sustenance was a way of life relied heavily on nature's bounty. They hunted, fished, and trapped. Along with utilizing the valuable food provided by game and fish from field and stream, they relied on wild vegetables, berries, fruits, and nuts.

The latter food from nature figured prominently in life during autumn, and fall's gradually shortening days were particularly busy. It was harvest time, with corn to be put in the crib and fodder in shocks, pumpkins to be gathered, apples and pears to be picked and prepared, molasses to be made, hogs to be butchered, vegetables to put in root cellars, the last green beans to be dried for "leather britches," grains such as buckwheat and rye to be cut and winnowed, and field legumes such as October beans to be stored. On top of all this crammed rush of getting in crops, the hunter's moon of October beckoned with almost irresistible allure. As it crested the eastern horizon at nightfall, burnished bright as a huge golden coin, no mountain man worth his sporting salt could avoid thoughts of putting some extra food on the table in forms such as squirrel and gravy, a bear roast dripping with fat from the old bruin's feasting on summer's berries, or maybe a succulent haunch of venison.

It was a time for both preparation and celebration as another cycle of the earth's bounty came to an end and before the lean, mean times of winter began. All too soon bluebird skies and pleasant temperatures of Indian Summer would give way to biting winds and bitter frosts. One of the hallmarks of relatively brief but bright and beautiful autumns in the Smokies, an exercise that combined genuine pleasure while taking full advantage of bountiful nature, was what most simply knew as "nutting." It formed a splendid example of the important art of "making do," and while the necessity that once underlay expeditions to gather nuts belonged to a world long since vanished, the practice loomed large in my boyhood and, for that matter, can still do so today. The gratifying end results embrace simple fun, opportunities for togetherness among family or friends united in common cause, and some wonderful eating.

Nutting, especially as a family outing or social event, likely had its beginnings when the American chestnut was plentiful. Whole families, particularly in the high country along the ancient spine of the Appalachians, gathered bushels of the predictable, prolific mast. They used the nuts to fatten hogs, earn a bit of welcome cash through sales (vendors of roasted chestnuts were once common on city street corners in the winter), and of course for their own consumption. All the males in my father's family loved to talk about the time when chestnut was king, but as eminently practical individuals they acknowledged the loss and turned their attention to substitutes.

The American chestnut may now have been gone from the Smokies for a full three generations, but fortunately such is not the case with other nuts. Many of them are both delicious and readily available. Perhaps the best example is the black walnut. Early in the squirrel season Daddy and I would look for trees or for stained white belly fur on bushytails we killed indicating that they were feeding on walnuts. That information was duly filed away with plans for a family outing in the not too distant offing. It was something Mom and Dad continued to enjoy long after their willing helpers were grown and gone.

Readily identifiable (it is one of the first trees to shed its leaves, sometimes before the nuts fall), the black walnut is common along fence rows and the edges of fields in river bottoms. The task of gathering walnuts and then preparing them for cracking, while not physically demanding, consumes considerable time. Hulls need to be removed, and this is best done several weeks after the nuts are gathered. Otherwise, with hulls still green and holding moisture, they will leave your hands stained. If you have any doubts, give it a try and deal with the "Mission Impossible" involved in trying to return your hands to their normal color. After all, dyes from walnut hulls and those of the butternut were once favored for coloring homespun clothing.

Drying hulls for easy removal involves patience more than anything else, and most veteran "nutters" have a favorite method to accomplish this. They can spread nuts out atop a tarpaulin or on the ground to allow them to dry in the warm sun of an Indian Summer, and then mash the hulls off by foot one nut at a time Or, once cured and with the hulls dry and crunchy, they can be placed in a tow sack, hung from a handy tree limb, and whacked repeatedly with a section of two-by-four. As a boy I enjoyed this approach, although a 34-inch Louisville Slugger baseball bat was substituted for the piece of sawed lumber. Perhaps the simplest approach, and it works surprisingly well, is to spread nuts atop gravel or hard ground and run a vehicle over them repeatedly.

Once the hulls have been removed, it is time to crack the walnuts and pick out the meats. My grandfather used to muse: "The man who figures out a device to crack black walnuts cleanly, leaving big pieces of nut meats, should make a fortune." We still await such an invention, although a good friend up in the mountains who is a machinist with an inventive knack, Ken Roper, made a quantum leap in the right direction that used a flywheel off a car and an attached handle to apply leverage, with the device fixed to a wooden base for stability. It's ingenious, but he only made a few of them, saying he was having to machine almost all the parts and that few folks wanted to pay the price he had to ask. It doesn't produce perfect halves, but it sure beats the dickens out of smashing them to smithereens with a hammer or compressing them to the breaking point in a vise. I'm just happy I got one while he was making them, and as Ken later joked, "Maybe you've got you a collectible."

The method Daddy employed for cracking involved a vise and a hatchet. He placed nuts atop his shop vise, always being sure to turn them at a certain angle, and then cracked them with the back of a hatchet I had been given one Christmas. As I grew up some of that chore became my responsibility, but Daddy was so much surer, faster, and less inclined to hit the nuts too hard that he still handled the bulk of nut-cracking duties. We would crack a peck or maybe even a half bushel of them. Then came the slow, tedious work of getting the meats out. This effort, known as "nut pickin'," was almost always a group one. Sometimes it involved relatives, but the mainstays were Mom and Dad, my sister, Annette, and me. When it was just immediate family we often listened to the radio. If relatives were present, laughter, telling of tales, and remembrances of nutting in their childhood punctuated the congenial process.

The considerable effort involved in getting a few pints of walnut meats was well worth it. Merely thinking about it conjures up visions of a batch of Momma's oatmeal cookies, still warm from the oven and studded with walnuts and raisins. Similarly, a properly made walnut cake with walnut icing is a delicacy sure to bring tears of pure joy to a country boy's eyes, while on a hot summer's day home-churned walnut ice cream is near-frozen nectar from the gods.

Grandpa Joe loved everything connected to walnuts, as was, come to think of it, pretty much the case with anything edible that grew, swam, ran, or in any way existed in the limited geographical world with which he was intimately familiar. Had he been taken out of the Smokies he likely would have been a lost and lonesome soul, but on his home heath it was a markedly different story. He seemingly had some kind of thoughts, folk wisdom, or insight to share with me no matter what the plant or animal.

I loved his description of walnuts. A number of young trees lined the pathway leading from his house to the chicken pen and then on to the hog lot. We walked that path times without number, but seldom did we make the familiar trek without him pausing alongside one of the walnut saplings for a bit of a nature lesson. "Son," he would say, "look at those trees. I'll be gone about the time they start bearing lots of nuts, and it will be at least sixty years before they've grown enough to be cut for timber. This here's (that is the way he said it) fine river bottom land, real rich soil, and it will grow stuff about as good as anywhere in these old mountains." Based on the quality and quantity of the produce his garden produced, that was accurate information. "But walnuts demand patience. They ain't going to be rushed and they ain't going to grow fast. I reckon you could call them a three-generation tree." By that he meant that it took slow-growing black walnuts a full three generations to reach a size where they provided one or possibly two fine saw logs.

He would then woolgather for a moment on the importance of forbearance. I always sensed that underlying the lesson on walnuts was a subliminal message directed at an often impatient and always boisterous boy. "If you wait," Grandpa noted, "walnuts will eventually reward you. They make beautiful wood for furniture, and you know those two guns I've stored away up at the house? Well, their stocks and fore-ends are made of fine-grained walnut."

Grandpa knew woods and their uses. If today he could somehow walk that garden path from long ago, he'd light up with that soft grin that was about as close as he ever came to a real smile. The old house has gone through multiple owners, but some of the black walnuts Grandpa admired (and likely planted, although I don't know that to be a fact), have now reached the three-generation status he so often mentioned. They are tall, straight, and handsome trees, precisely the kind that bring significant sums of money from folks anxious to have select wood from mature black walnuts.

As a family we dabbled with other types of nuts as well, and our yard sported a Chinese chestnut tree that grew so rapidly it progressed, in the course of only a couple of decades, from a nut-bearing source of considerable pride to a nuisance that eventually had to be cut down. Kudzu-like, it was threatening to engulf both the driveway and street serving our house.

Hickory nuts, which come in a number of varieties, some just about as tasty as walnuts, were incredibly abundant. It's no wonder Native Americans relied heavily on them, and stands of hickories along with nutting stones are frequently found near Indian mounds. Numerous types of hickory are plentiful in the Smokies, and come autumn you can't miss the vivid golden leaves of these sentinels of fall. If anything, however, they are more difficult to crack and pick meats from than black walnuts, and the amount of food you get for your labor will soon have you concluding they are the nutting world's equivalent of truffles.

Hazelnuts, a hillbilly cousin of the filbert, grew widely along creeks, rivers, and branches during my boyhood, and they were among the most predictable of the nut crops in terms of bearing a solid harvest year after year. They were bushes—ranging up to fifteen feet or so in height—rather than trees and were simple enough to harvest. The only problem, and it was significant, involved squirrels. Once bushytails started cutting on them, they would work nonstop until the entire crop was gone. Our way of besting the treetop tricksters, which normally began cutting on hazelnuts in mid-September, well before the nuts dropped from their husks, was to gather them in the husks and let them dry for a couple of weeks. At that juncture nuts fell out easily and were ready to crack. One of the advantages of the hazelnut was that its meat came out whole in a single piece.

Three other mountain nuts deserve at least passing mention. Two of them, chinquapins and butternuts, have become increasingly difficult to locate, while a third, beechnuts, can be quite unpredictable when it comes to production. Chinquapins, which were fairly common during my youth, are seldom encountered today. A bush-like relative of the chestnut, they were to some degree affected by the blight that destroyed the American chestnut, but they were frequently found on open, south-facing hillsides and particularly in what mountain folks called "fire scalds" (places where a wildfire, sometimes set by arsonists and frequently found in portions of the GSMNP, had burned hot enough to kill everything). For some reason chinquapins were a prominent succession plant in such areas, and they were quite plentiful thanks to a few local n'er-do-wells setting fires out of pure meanness or in hope of being hired by the GSMNP or U. S. Forest Service to help fight the fires.

Those fires occur with less frequency today, but anyone who covers much off-trail ground in the Smokies will still find bushes bearing the round, deep brown nuts that look like a miniature chestnut and are enclosed by the same type of protective burr. Growing up I often heard someone say, "She's got chinquapin eyes," and by that they meant luminous, shiny eyes resembling pools of molten dark chocolate. For some reason I've never heard the term applied to the eyes of a boy or man.

Butternuts have a mild taste slightly reminiscent of home-churned butter, and perhaps that is where they got their name. The nut hulls were once used to dye cloth, with the finished product having a buttery hue. The butternut attire associated with soldiers in the Confederate Army gives an indication of how widespread its use for dying purposes was a century and a half ago. Another name, one I heard frequently years ago but which seems to have passed out of favor in modern parlance, was white walnuts.

Butternut trees and their foliage indeed look somewhat like a walnut, although the nuts are elongated rather than oval in shape. The wood of the tree was so prized, and such remains the case, that it was unusual to find a grown, heavily bearing specimen. Today the tree is in trouble after a fashion somewhat reminiscent of the chestnut's plight. A disease known as butternut canker showed up half a century or so ago, and by the arrival of the twenty-first century biologists estimated that it affected as many as three-quarters of all butternut trees. Even those that were not dead were, in most cases, so afflicted they had stopped producing mast.

Then there's the lordly beechnut with its slick, silvery bark so admired by lovelorn males anxious to carve their name, along with that of their sweetheart, into the parchment-like outer layer. Perhaps the best indication of the appeal of beechnuts from the standpoint of edibility comes from the way they attract wildlife. Squirrels, chipmunks, deer, bears, grouse, wild hogs, and turkeys all will flock to them, ignoring any and all other types of food whenever they are available.

The little three-sided nuts develop inside burrs, but for some reason roughly three seasons out of every four the nut hulls are either hollow or the mast fails entirely. When they do "make," though, and you can readily tell by checking a nut or two in late summer, beechnuts are well worthy of human attention. For my part, I always check a few giants of the species growing along a little branch that wends its way through some property I own, and on the relatively rare occasions when they carry a fine nut crop I know two things—I'm going to enjoy some tasty treats and I'll see plenty of deer from a stand strategically placed nearby.

While they can be used in various types of dishes, beechnuts are probably best when eaten on the spot. Just do it in moderation because the fact that they are arguably the sweetest of all nuts notwithstanding, ingestion of too many raw ones can create gastric distress. Grandpa Joe somehow knew this, and he'd warn me whenever I seemed hell-bound to overindulge on mast from the massive beeches that lined the river bank near his home. "Son," he would say, "if you keep eating raw nuts you're about to have another episode like that one with the green apples a few months back." A couple of those green apple bellyaches were of sufficient severity for painful memories to linger, or maybe it was just Grandma's castor oil remedy that stuck in my memory. Anyway, I'd follow his advice. We'd gather a bunch of nuts, parch them atop the stove, and then enjoy a real treat.

Heat destroyed the toxic saponin glycoside in the nuts, and once we had a bunch of them roasted, Grandpa and I would get down to serious gustatory business. Beechnut hulls are tender enough to be removed with one's teeth, and while it takes considerable effort to get at the little tidbits, the work was well worth it.

I now realize that memories of nuts and nutting took Grandpa back to a time he held dear. That explains, at least in part, why he spent so much time talking with me about nuts and gathered them at every opportunity. More often than not when we went squirrel hunting at day's end there was little if any heft in the game bags of our coats, but the side pockets of our jackets and front pockets of our pants were dramatically different. We almost always stuffed them with whatever mast we came across. When Grandpa said, "There ain't no need to be peckish in the fall woods," he was acknowledging the ready availability and importance of nuts in his mountain world.

Today we can still sample and savor such times and the delicious treats they produced. To me, venturing afield for a few pleasant, productive hours of nutting is a fine approach to perpetuating a worthy example of old-time mountain ways.

Chapter 31

SCHOOL DAYS

In my case the tired old chestnut about walking a mile uphill to school both ways held an appreciable element of truth. The walk to school was indeed a mile, and it involved a hill in each direction, so going meant finishing my journey by climbing up School House Hill while the afternoon return home necessitated getting to the top of Black Hill. Bus rides were out of the question for such insignificant distances, although today the idea of a first grader trudging a mile to school and crossing multiple streets without the aid of either a red light or guard would occasion cries of parental outrage, have the public incensed about dereliction of duty on the part of the school board, and generally create turmoil. In the Smokies of the 1950s, the situation was simply an accepted part of life. No one, whether they lived in town or the country, gave so much as a passing thought to mile-long walks for school kids. Indeed, in some of the more remote rural areas, students would take shank's mare appreciably further in order to reach their bus stop.

Looking back on those years initially at Swain Elementary and later Swain County High School from the perspective of many decades summons thoughts of teachers and how they shaped me as a person and a writer. They are comforting ruminations and remind me of the ample blessings that caring, competent, and committed teachers bestowed. As someone who spent some three decades in the classroom, I know that my shortcomings as a teacher were legion. Yet it is my fervent hope that periodically along the way my presence and tutelage touched the occasional student after the fashion in which a number of teachers touched me. Others must judge my competence as a professor, but whatever virtues I brought to the classroom, any life I breathed into subject matter was a direct product of the guidance and instruction provided me on all levels in my own days as a student.

Recognition of some of those who had a particularly marked impact follows. Their names will mean nothing to most readers, although maybe it isn't too much to hope that the occasional individual will have been blessed by their diverse strokes of pedagogical genius. In a broader sense their collective excellence and the roles they filled, along with the era in which they taught and the place education held in remote regions of Appalachia during the middle decades of the twentieth century, reflects a period of time that seems almost as distant as the dawn of the Industrial Revolution.

These teachers, and thousands of kindred spirits up and down the spine of the Appalachians, sent untold numbers of bright-eyed boys and girls off to ivy-clad walls and ivory towers as first-generation college students. Similarly, the professors who walked hallowed halls of learning in higher education did their part in shaping and molding me and so many others. They took eager young minds on the cusp of adulthood, both burdened and blessed by backwardness and naiveté, and exposed them to theorems and equations, laboratory experiments and world literature, which the parents and certainly the grandparents of the majority of those students would have thought as remote and alien as the dark side of the moon.

My teachers were worthy educational soldiers marching in ranks led by the likes of Jesse Stuart and Cratis Williams. Today, as individuals, they are pretty much forgotten to all but family memory and recollections of former students like me whom they influenced with a touch of magic, a hint of mystery, and the immense gift of a love of sharing knowledge. Once lords of the lectern and belles of the blackboard, they are now but names on old report cards stored in dust-laden boxes or in many cases engraved on a tombstone atop a Smokies hill. That they are largely forgotten is a shame.

That is the justification underlying remembrances of mentors, long gone or else in the Decembers of their days. It is an attempt by a son of the Smokies to capture the surpassing importance of mentors. Almost without exception my elementary and high school teachers were caring, most were competent, many were devoted to their craft, and a select few were flat-out paragons of excellence. Although I would love to be wrong, I suspect similar comments are far less widely applicable for those teaching in today's public schools.

It should also be noted, and this relates not only to those mentioned here but to the entire cadre of teachers who nurtured me through twelve years of classes in Swain County, that I was surprisingly well prepared when I went off to college. No doubt a great deal of independent reading helped, but I had been endowed with the basics in all disciplines. For example, my high school French teacher's pronunciation may have been execrable, but I didn't know that until college when I had a professor who spoke the language with complete fluency and had used it as her *lingua franca* during many years in the missionary field. Yet my high school teacher, Lillian Thomasson, knew the basics, even if her verbal offerings of French involved an accent that did not quite hide her mountain roots. Her pronunciation would have raised eyebrows in Paris or Quebec along with a hushed, heartfelt *mon dieu* or two, but she laid the groundwork well enough for me to breeze through two years of college French with A marks.

I'm too far removed from modern education to venture expert explanations as to why current public education seems to be such a mess, although I do feel low pay, serious restrictions on disciplinary measures, too much emphasis on standardized tests, major sociological problems associated with students from one-parent families, and socioeconomic issues tracing back to the so-called Great Society of Lyndon Johnson lie at the heart of the matter. I can't solve anything in today's education, but perhaps looking at a number of teachers who made the classroom come alive and who guided and educated me in multiple ways will offer some food for thought. They are primarily covered chronologically in the order in which I appeared in their classrooms, and they are identified by name because they deserve to be. I have every confidence that these individuals had a deeply meaningful impact on far more students than this writer. They merit remembrance for that lasting service and as stellar representatives of a noble profession.

Before getting to the specifics of their impact, however, it is probably appropriate to perform a bit of what is styled, in the legal world, "qualifying the witness." I was never a pupil who made a teacher's job easy. A few months back, while rummaging through some long-forgotten mementoes, I came across report cards for all twelve of my years in public school. Like she did with so many things associated with her children (though alas not my brother's baseball card collection), Momma had saved every one of them.

They told a tale, in the deportment or citizenship category, which must have caused her and Daddy considerable angst. One grading period after another, over the years, there would be a listing of grades in subject areas, mostly A marks along with the occasional B or B+. Behavioral grades were another matter entirely. Too often in the early years citizenship merited an indifferent S (satisfactory) mark rather than the preferred E (excellent), and on a few occasions there was the dreaded U (unsatisfactory). Comments suggested I had problems with "listening without interrupting" and lacked willingness to "share rather than force ideas." In my final year of high school the first of three reporting periods had the cryptic remark from my homeroom teacher: "Conduct grade lowered by five teachers and Mr. Rice (the school principal)." In other words, I was a disciplinary pain in the posterior.

While I lack sufficient introspection to understand my wayward behavior, and it was inexcusable any way you look at the issue, I've got some pretty sound ideas by way of partial explanation. Boredom was definitely a factor, and it's probably no accident that some of the teachers I recall with the greatest degree of fondness realized as much. More to the point, they figured out ways to counter that indifference. Another factor was a degree of insecurity rooted in small stature (I did not get my major growth spurt until my senior year in high school and freshman year in college) and a compulsion to want to be recognized and at the center of things. On top of that I was a bit impish by nature, and even now I derive considerable pleasure out of simple pranks or joking.

Periodically my waywardness resulted in a spot of trouble transcending negative notes on report cards. The most memorable occasion came in my ninth grade English class. The teacher, Thad DeHart, was mild-mannered enough, but he tolerated neither fools nor foolishness gladly. His teaching equipment, in addition to chalk, erasers, note pads, and the like, included a leather razor strap kept in a cloakroom at the back of the classroom. Periodically when someone got out of line he would threaten them with "six of my best" using that instrument of corporal punishment. Today such threats, much less the actual action, would be an instant career ender. That was not the case in the late 1950s, and occasionally he actually applied the strap to the south end of wayward students facing north.

Such was my fate only once, although other boys got multiple six-lick doses (he never had to whip a girl and almost certainly wouldn't have done so no matter how badly one behaved). I have no recollection whatsoever of the nature of my transgression, although I have every confidence that the administering of six of Mr. DeHart's best was richly deserved.

When he made the decision to give me the punishment, and whippings were always administered in full view of the class *pour encourager les autres*, he had to go to the cloakroom to retrieve his razor strap. That was when a moment of singularly misguided inspiration seized me. I always wore a Duxbak cap to school (but never inside—that was taboo) and it was stowed beneath my desk. I hurriedly grabbed it and stuffed the thick cap in the seat of my pants to ease the coming pain.

Apparently my padding effort was readily visible, because Mr. DeHart whaled the daylights out of me. It was bad enough to cause bruises, but rest assured there was no sniveling, snarky teenager who couldn't wait to get home and report how he had been manhandled. That might be an almost predictable reaction in today's world of sheltered snowflakes, but I knew beyond a scintilla of doubt that letting Momma and Daddy learn of my punishment would result in a repeat performance. I took it in precisely the way it was intended—as an action to deter further misconduct. Far from alienating me, Thad DeHart became one of my all-time favorite a teachers.

For reasons which partially elude me to this day, some teachers and professors who were hardest on me in both a disciplinary sense and academic demands were among those who made the greatest impact educationally. Thad DeHart, who administered six of his best to my nether parts, was a prime example. He was one of a number of pedagogical geniuses who had influence in molding and motivating a boy who stumbled, at times myopically, towards an adulthood where reading, writing, and teaching would be his world.

A key component of DeHart's English classes found students being handed, the first day of classes in their brave new world of high school, a lengthy list of words. These weren't just run-of-the-mill parts of the English language already forming part of his students' reading or even speaking vocabularies. Instead, they were what he labeled "ten-dollar words," hundreds of them. Most were as unknown to children of the Smokies as the streets of San Francisco. The majority contained several syllables, and personally I doubt if I knew the meaning of one in twenty of them.

There were multiple requirements associated with the words on that handout. Students had to learn their pronunciation, meaning, and spelling as well as be able to use them in cogent fashion (cogent was one of the words). Ample extra credit was available through finding the words printed in a book, magazine, or newspaper. This yearlong excursion into the wonders of the English language served multiple purposes. It enhanced the vocabulary of every student and for me marked the onset of a lifelong veneration of words. It expanded our horizons through reading and modes of expression, and some indication of the lasting impact of this teaching technique comes from the fact that seemingly every student who ever took this class remembers the word list, most with fondness.

Thad DeHart influenced me in another fashion that might have been described as extracurricular even though it directly related to the teaching of English. From an early age, never mind temporarily forgetting how to read during the summer between first and second grade, I devoured books with an appetite as insatiable as it was eclectic. So voracious and wide-ranging was my craving for books that by the time I reached high school I had exhausted everything the local public library had to offer in multiple subject areas. (Incidentally, the library was founded and bears the name to this day of my childhood next-door neighbor, Marianna F. Black.) Those included hunting, fishing, all types of outdoor adventure, travel, and geography. I had read everything available by Zane Grey, devoured other Westerns, exhausted books for juveniles such as the Walton Boys series, and knew Arthur Conan Doyle's tales of Sherlock Holmes's sleuthing almost by heart. Writers such as Rudyard Kipling, Robert Louis Stevenson, Richard Henry Dana, and Edgar Rice Burroughs were old friends, as were poets including Robert Service, Robert Burns, and Sidney Lanier. Venturing into new territory, I had just begun to make the acquaintance of some of the era's great mystery writers when I chanced to mention my interest in exploring new literary domains to Mr. Dehart.

Recognizing a likely (and somewhat rare) prospect when he saw one, he poured out names of "possibles" on a frequent basis. More than that, he regularly inquired about what I'd recently read and showed genuine interest in a student who read for the sheer fun of it. Through his guidance I first made the acquaintance of Erle Stanley Gardner, Agatha Christie, S. S. Van Dine, Sax Rohmer, Raymond Chandler, Ross Macdonald, Dorothy Sayers, and a host of others. He always had new suggestions, and not just in the arena of mysteries. I was encouraged to branch out into regional literature including Olive Tilford Dargan (*From My Highest Hill* is set in the Smokies), Wilma Dykeman's *The French Broad,* and the novels of John Fox Jr. and Charles Egbert Craddock (the pseudonym of Mary Noailles Murfree—I was also taught the meaning of the word "pseudonym" and given an explanation of why Ms. Murfree likely used one). He tried to turn me on to Thomas Wolfe, but in that one instance Thad DeHart failed. Wolfe's writing still leaves me cold, although authors whom I admire, such as Pat Conroy, sing his praises to the angels.

For all his considerable and lasting influence though, he was not the first teacher to reach that hidden part of me that craved vicarious adventure through literature. Pride of place in that regard belongs to my seventh grade teacher (in those days one teacher covered all subjects during the first eight years of school), Mildred Wood. A local by birth, she regularly reminded her students of how difficult college had been for her and how important it was for us to prepare in the best way possible during our upcoming high school years. Implicit in what she said was an assumption many of us would go to college. That was something of a leap of faith, and I have no doubt whatsoever that she knew it. Still, it represented her fond hope that many of us from the hills and hollows of the Smokies would wend our way to institutions of higher learning. It indicated her conviction that living back of beyond in no way equated to possessing a backward or inferior mind.

The implications of her gently prodding students toward a bright future did not dawn on me until much later, but she had an immediate impact in another fashion. Although through Grandpa Joe and Daddy I had already been exposed to what was in some ways an advanced exercise in the art of storytelling, it was Mildred Wood who brought home to me the magic that literature could convey when offered in oral form.

She seemingly knew all of Edgar Allen Poe's terror-filled short stories by heart, and she could tell them in an edge-of-the-seat, heart-pounding fashion. Occasionally as a special reward or perhaps just for a break in classroom routine, she would set aside a period of time for a "visit with Mr. Poe." Invariably she seemed to choose a day when dark clouds scudded across the Smokies skies, and on at least one particularly memorable occasion thunder and lightning provided sound effects for her story. Over the course of a year she shared "Murders in the Rue Morgue," "The Black Cat," "The Tell-Tale Heart," "The Pit and the Pendulum," "Some Words with a Mummy," "The Gold Bug," and more. By doing so she left a deep mark on the mind of an impressionable young boy—tales well told carried an aura of magic.

Although he didn't influence my eventual emergence as a writer, tenth grade biology teacher Clifford Frizzell sure knew the way to attract and hold an outdoors-loving lad's attention. Each semester, in addition to regular classroom and textbook material, he assigned students a major project. In the fall that was dissection of a frog and all the learning of parts attendant to scalpel work amid the stench of formaldehyde, but it was the spring project I embraced with fervor.

That endeavor involved flora of the Smokies. In concert with greening-up time in the mountains each student was to locate as many plants as possible, remove a leaf or perhaps a flower to be pressed into a scrapbook, and provide both common and scientific names for each plant. Extra credit could be obtained by provision of information such as whether the plant was edible (lots of spring greens were), produced edible fruit or berries, had medicinal uses, could be toxic, or enjoyed special links with some species of fauna (pawpaws, for example, are the host plant for caterpillars of the zebra swallowtail butterfly).

Today much of that project, other than actually gathering leaves, would involve little more than Internet research. In the 1950s, however, it not only got students out of doors but required them to trundle down informational corridors where they likely had never ventured. Grandmothers who had grown up close to the land and handled daily family diet and "doctoring" were a rich potential source of information on medicinal plants, edible herbs, what caused disease like milk sickness in cows, spring tonics, and much more. Grandfathers could provide details on which woods split and burned best, which trees produced lumber well suited for anything from carving to construction, which bore edible nuts and which nuts were best, differentiate between the many types of pines and oaks, and even get into minutiae such as what type of wood was especially hard (dense ones such as dogwood or persimmon) or soft enough to lend itself to whittling (basswood, butternut, or maple). Parents knew much of the same lore.

On top of everything else, it forced students to get out in the wonderment of nature which was the Great Smokies. That meant first-hand exposure to a land of temperate rain forest with unrivaled variety in its plant life, healthy exercise, and at least for me, a type of learning so enjoyable as to be pure pleasure. The entire project captured me and brought realization of just how wonderful the learning process could be when properly presented and pursued.

One of my high school teachers was a man who, in the opinion of many peers including my siblings, did not possess a scintillating presence in the classroom. Yet for me John Wikle was memorable and impactful for two reasons. First, in addition to being a teacher by profession, he wrote regularly as a stringer for the *Asheville Citizen-Times*. He may not have been anything approaching "big time" when it came to freelance writing, but for me seeing the byline of someone I not only knew but had daily exposure to in the classroom was impressive.

Even more impactful were words he wrote in red atop an essay. In this particular instance students could write on a topic of our choosing. Predictably, I selected a subject of great interest to me—squirrel hunting. I don't recall the grade awarded the finished product, but Wikle's comment was indelibly imprinted in my mind: "This is the kind of material, in much more sophisticated form, which the outdoor magazines buy." A seed had been planted. It took two decades to sprout and begin to flourish, but from that momentous day in my senior year I dreamed of writing on subjects related to the outdoors.

The final high school teacher who must be praised, Lillian Thomasson, was a tried-and-true veteran of the classroom. She was consistently clever in luring unsuspecting students into her clutches of wisdom. A few years ago at a high school class reunion some classmates remarked on what they considered my uncanny ability to draw her off subject. Thinking about their comments later, it dawned on me that my supposed ability to distract her was a straw man. She just gave the appearance of being led away from the subject matter while playing me like a well-hooked trout as she provided insight that was far more enduring than sterile textual information.

A prime example came in a class of hers in either civics or American history. A teacher in the local school system for upwards of four decades, Thomasson often taught two generations of the same family, and quite possibly there were instances of her having three generations in her classroom. The only breaks in her lifelong dedication to classroom teaching came when she pursued graduate studies and a short-term federal job helping out poverty-stricken locals during the worst times of the Great Depression. In the latter instance, she remained involved in education by doing double duty as a government worker while serving as principal of a county elementary school.

One day, I somehow managed to work mention of the previous weekend's rabbit hunt into class discussion. At the time I thought I had played her like a puppeteer; I now realize it gave her a grand opportunity for a special teaching moment. She seized it immediately.

Smiling in her characteristic fashion, Mrs. Thomasson said: "Let me tell you a rabbit hunting story." Her account went back to a point in the early 1930s when she regularly drove around the county checking on the impoverished, perhaps providing carefully couched advice about how they might improve their lot, and sometimes offering surplus foodstuffs which the government shipped in by rail. Usually these comestibles involved items such as cheese or flour, but on this occasion a load of grapefruit had arrived.

In the course of an early morning drive to distribute grapefruit to destitute area residents, she hit a rabbit with her vehicle. Her husband was out rabbit hunting that day and she had a sudden inspiration. Stopping her car, she checked on the dead cottontail and found the meat apparently undamaged. Mrs. Thomasson promptly field dressed it, stowed it in one of the bags which had held grapefruit, and placed the animal in her car's trunk. It was a chilly winter day and she knew the carcass would keep just fine. That evening, when her husband arrived at home after a fruitless day afield, she had fried rabbit and all the fixin's on the supper table. "It was welcome," she said, "because we enjoyed tasty meat we didn't have to buy, and I could tease my husband about who was the family's real hunter."

That was only part of the story though. Mrs. Thomasson then seamlessly transitioned into what happened as she made her rounds the following week. She asked one of the recipients of grapefruit how the family had liked them. The remarks of that voluble housewife pretty well summarized the general reaction to grapefruit: "They's right purty to look at," the woman commented, "but I biled 'em and I biled 'em. They never did get fit to eat."

Many years later realization would dawn on me that Mrs. Thomasson had, with the tale of the rabbit and the grapefruit, given a striking example of Smokies life during hard times. She brought to the classroom a glimpse of how little local residents knew about the wider world through providing an example of culinary ignorance along with a reminder that even in her family, which was better off than most, frugality and practicality were important. Of course, that tale drew a laugh from students, and she laughed with us before adding a cautionary note: "The way I handled distribution of grapefruit was a mistake on my part. I should have known those needy folks would be unfamiliar with grapefruit, and by failing to tell them how they should be eaten I did them a disservice, caused some embarrassment, and, worst of all, wasted perfectly good food in a time of need. It taught me a lesson I've never forgotten about respecting others and giving thought to their knowledge and condition."

She pulled such stunts of teaching legerdemain on a regular basis, and beyond that Mrs. Thomasson's contributions to students and community were exemplary. Over the years many friends, mostly female, have told me how she introduced them to music, art, and other aspects of culture through tea parties, arranging trips to performances in Asheville, or encouraging them to draw (she was a skilled and trained artist). As she neared retirement, Thomasson assumed a sort of unofficial mantle as the local historian. Her book, *Swain County: Early History and Educational Development,* while having scattered factual flaws, was diligently researched and remains the standard source on the subject. She figured prominently in the celebrations connected with Swain County's centennial, wrote plays, designed brochures for local government officials seeking outside investment, ran a motor court, and was a leading figure in the Smoky Mountain Bible Conference.

Intensely proud of her milieu, late in life she wrote: "Swain County has been an obsession with me for the greater part of a lifetime; this must be due, to some degree, to an ancestral background of rugged pioneers with economic, religious and educational interests and a desire for adventure. Education, teaching experience, hobbies, and historical events have played an important role in directing my activities." Much of what Thomasson wrote was applicable to every one of the teachers who exerted early influence on me. All of them had long-standing family ties to and had grown up in the region. They could have pursued careers elsewhere, but the bosom of the mountains held them in comforting closeness. There can be few places where the word "home" looms larger in the consciousness than in the Smokies, and these teachers implanted that concept in me in blessed fashion.

Transition from high school to college brought many differences, but one common factor was exposure to superb teachers. My undergraduate education took place at King College (now King University) in Bristol, Tennessee. Then and now it was a Presbyterian-affiliated institution, and Presbyterians enjoy a richly deserved reputation as fine educators. In my case some wonderful professors did their best to mold the poor piece of clay they had been given, and today I look back on those days with great fondness. In the early 1960s King was small, and as Dr. R. T. L. Liston, the president at the time, repeatedly stated, "a place of the mind." Rules were strict, chapel attendance mandatory (and the roll was sometimes checked), and any hint of wayward behavior was strongly discouraged. Merely holding hands with a coed would bring frowns and maybe stronger disapproval.

For my first three semesters in college I was, to put the best possible face on matters, an indifferent scholar. Two developments led to a dramatic change. One was a heart-to-heart conversation (if a conversation can be held with only one of the two individuals involved having anything to say) with Daddy at the onset of the second semester of my sophomore year. He let me know in no uncertain terms that my performance was unacceptable, that he had no intention of providing further support in the form of tuition or anything else if my efforts didn't show marked improvement, and he reminded me that there was a war going on in Vietnam. I got the message, and for my final four semesters at King College I made the dean's list.

An appreciable portion of the credit for this turnaround goes to Daddy and a bit of much-needed maturation. I also figured out, at least partly, how to balance studies with the social "education" I was receiving thanks to the presence of two women's colleges in Bristol, a college-owned golf course within walking distance, and the sport of soccer. But another significant factor was King College's Dean of Women, Inez Morton. She did double duty by teaching in the English Department, and the second semester of my sophomore year I had her for a course in American literature.

A native of the area who had grown up on a farm alongside the nearby Holston River, she was, to put it in the mountain vernacular, "big on manners." Yet beneath a sophisticated exterior that knew precisely how to hold a teacup, what was and was not appropriate behavior for the sometimes boisterous young women who were her charges, and an imposing presence who almost invited a rapscallion like me to try some kind of juvenile prank to test her acuity, there beat the heart of an incurable romantic. Miss Morton had a deeply rooted passion for nature, and she knew how to convey it in the classroom.

Among her favorite poets was Emily Dickinson, and one day in class we were discussing some of that strange but talented woman's verses. The poem in question included some type of allusion to an unidentified songbird. I instantly recognized the bird as a wood thrush and understood the metaphor that was either of complete disinterest or else totally unknown to my classmates. I ventured some thoughts on spring, songbirds in general and wood thrushes in particular and then alluded to how earth's reawakening witnessed dramatic changes in the behavior of many birds and animals. Enthralled, Miss Morton immediately revised her opinion of me. I underwent a transition from a rather boring, burdensome undergraduate to someone in whom she took a real interest.

She encouraged some of my early ventures in writing through comments on papers done for classes she taught, and more significantly, she said to me on more than one occasion: "Jim, you could be a writer some day." I have no doubt she proffered similar encouragement to a great many students, but for this one those words "took holt" like a cocklebur on a flannel shirt.

Another way in which she influenced me would likely have seemed mind-boggling to anyone who knew me at the time, but she gave me a love of theater and the spoken word. I've never done any acting, but class trips to the nearby Barter Theater in Abingdon, Virginia, were immensely enjoyable. Although I dreaded the moments at the time, her requirements for "speechifying" in one of her classes had real meaning. I was petrified then, but today I'm completely comfortable speaking before crowds and don't need any technological assistance of the type you too often see with major political figures. I can speak without a prompter, usually without notes, and always without some device in front of me showing me the proper words.

My other major influence during those halcyon undergraduate years between 1960 and 1964 was Dr. William J. Wade. He was my advisor, mentor, and teacher in a number of classes in my major, history. We've stayed in touch over the ensuing years and not long ago I was overjoyed to take a trip to Bristol to participate in a series of events connected with his ninetieth birthday. He's still active, sharp as a properly whetted Barlow knife, and keenly interested in the "doings" of all his former students. In the aftermath of his birthday celebration he sent me a letter that was as gracious and meaningful as about anything I've ever received.

The ways in which he affected me aren't in some senses as readily definable as was the case with teachers back home in Swain County or with Inez Morton, but they are pervasive. He encouraged me in connection with a term paper somewhere along the line where I addressed Horace Kephart's misrepresentation of much about daily life in the Smokies, gave me real appreciation of the give-and-take of a seminar setting, but most of all was and has remained a calm, steady, and genteel voice devoted to scholarship.

Although I'm sure it meant almost nothing to him, a memorable moment in our connection came when, some years back, he purchased a copy of one of my books to donate to the King College Library, saying, "They need to have this." Then there was the occasion, fifty years after my graduation, when I finally got up the nerve to call him Bill instead of the Dr. Wade I'd always used. I told him that henceforth I was going to call him Bill, saying that while I might be taking liberties and probably hadn't completely earned the right to that degree of familiarity, I was still going to do it. I noted I had earned a Ph. D. so was on equal footing educationally and then added that having reached my seventies maybe I could get by with it. He just chuckled in his gentle, winning way and said: "Oh, the need for that title went away once you were no longer a student of mine."

I've already alluded to some youthful larks that got me into trouble, but before leaving the subject of misbehavior, I should note that while I was sometimes a wayward lad, in no way did I have a monopoly on mischief in my high school or college days. During my undergraduate years, she-nanigans of all sorts were commonplace, and likely the nature of students at my alma mater in the early 1960s was a contributing factor. Most of us were from the poorer parts of Appalachia; a fair portion belonged to a group who perversely somehow seemed particularly inclined to devilry, namely PKs or MKs (preachers' kids or missionaries' kids); and of course there was the eternal problem of transitioning into the world of adulthood. It's little short of amazing what a collection of bright and in a fair number of cases flat-out brilliant minds, all hovering between adolescence and maturity while struggling to get their sense of judgment in balance, could produce in the way of pranks. Had comparable energy, enthusiasm, and intellectual effort involved in capers associated with my college years been directed toward academic achievements, unquestionably some of my buddies and yours truly would have graduated with highest honors.

King College was a highly moral, intensely conservative, and rigidly strict institution of higher education. Almost no students owned automo-biles, freshmen were not allowed to go home until Thanksgiving, most of us were first-generation college students, and the vast majority of students lived on campus. Through size and circumstance we became a close, tight-knit community. There was none of today's situation of mass exodus every weekend creating a "suitcase campus." We stayed on campus, participating in about every cultural event available, and since no one had much spend-ing money, our pleasures were simple ones.

There was one television set on the entire campus (it received three channels), dormitories had a single pay phone each along with one local phone per floor, showers and bathroom facilities were communal (at each end of the hall), and almost everyone had some kind of job (they were called workships) requiring a minimum of ten hours labor per week. Over my four years I washed dishes, worked on the ground crew, locked up academic buildings, and stoked coal-fired furnaces in a job that nightly left me coated head-to-toe with coal dust.

Still, there was time aplenty for capers, and what follows is a sampling of some of the things that transpired during my four years at King. Since over half a century has passed, I'm pretty sure that the statute of limitations has run its course in connection with these events. Besides, I'm not saying I was (or wasn't) involved in any of these episodes. Obviously, though, in every instance I had "inside" knowledge.

Volkswagen beetles were the car of choice for many faculty members, and a young math professor had one of which he was inordinately proud. One night a sizeable group of male students carried his vehicle a hundred yards or more and, with considerable maneuvering and no small measure of engineering ingenuity, deposited it on the floor of the only gym on campus. Since the gym floor was at the foot of several steps, getting the vehicle out was no simple task. As was often said of Queen Victoria, the owner was not amused.

King had a small dairy farm on land the college owned adjacent to campus, and at one time the herd had supplied milk for the students. That was no longer the case, but some of the maintenance staff kept milk cows there. One Saturday night when most of the student body had gone to a basketball game, several n'er-do-wells who remained behind cornered a cow in the pasture, got a rope around her, and dragged the poor bovine back to campus. "Daisy" was fairly compliant until the apprehending party reached one of the two men's dorms and decided to lead her up three stories to its top floor.

Things changed then. There was no elevator, but it's amazing what enough manpower, with plenty of pushing and tugging, can accomplish. No calf with a chronic case of scours ever left more calling cards than that beleaguered milk cow, and she protested by bellowing every inch of the way. Somehow though, the work party got her to the top floor, tied her off to a railing, and then vanished like milkweed spores in a dust devil.

It was just as well. Some sanctimonious, self-important snitch had alerted the dean, and he soon showed up with the bursar in tow. Once they got over their collective shock, with the dean repeatedly muttering, "This is too much, this is just too much!" maintenance workers were summoned to maneuver the cow back down the stairs. This proved an even more arduous task than the cow's earlier ascension, and gawking, gesticulating students didn't help matters.

Another memorable event took place on an unusually balmy March day during my sophomore year. The warm weather was particularly welcome,

since there had been a big snowstorm just a few days earlier. Air temperatures were sufficiently pleasant for the windows of the college chapel to be
open, and since chapel was mandatory, most students were in attendance.
However, the open window and a student who had decided to "skip" the
service combined to create irresistible opportunity. While chapel was in
progress, the miscreant student fashioned a fine, icy missile from vestiges
of snow still lingering on the building's north side. Then, with uncanny
aim, he lobbed it through the open, beckoning window.

On this particular morning some members of the college's board of
trustees were in attendance at chapel. Their presence was probably in connection with one of the board's periodic meetings. By sheer chance the
snowball caught a particularly officious trustee, one who considered himself the epitome of decorum and was generally deemed to be a bit uppity,
squarely in the back of his bald head. For anyone who has ever enjoyed the
pleasure of reading the diary of Samuel Pepys, it records an episode where
the end result was similar.

Under the cover of prayer Pepys made unwanted advances on a young
maiden seated next to him in a church pew, and she retaliated by giving
him a solid jab in the posterior with a hat pin. Pepys reacted with an oath
and virtually leapt into the pew in front of him shouting "My God, my
arse." The trustee did much the same, shouting out what, given the setting,
was a singularly inappropriate oath. That particular chapel session ended
in disarray, and the next one brought a stern lecture from Dr. Liston.

Another chapel-related incident came in early May of my junior year
when, once again, windows were open. One of the two men's dorms sat
catty-corner to the chapel and not more than thirty or forty yards away at
the nearest point. It so happened that one of the residents of a room in that
closest corner owned a stereo equipped with two massive speakers. While
chapel was in progress, someone jimmied open the door to the room, placed
Jerry Lee Lewis's "Great Balls of Fire" on the turntable, turned the volume
to maximum level, dropped the needle, and hastily exited the room while
locking the door behind him.

The auditory effects, as far as decibel level was concerned, were worthy
of the Mormon Tabernacle Choir in full voice. The dean arrived on the
scene with a degree of alacrity no one who knew this plodding individual
would have thought possible. He knocked loudly on the door, shouting,
"Open up! Open up!" Of course there was no one to open the door. He
kicked it down and disengaged the needle on the record player. Once again

there were stern words in the next chapel service, but the culprit remains unidentified to this day.

Another memorable episode occurred in the lone women's dorm. One coed always waited until the absolute last possible moment before rushing to the toilet to do her business. This habit and her haste on such occasions were sufficiently obvious for others to observe. Then there came the fateful day when she scurried down the hall only to find every stall but one locked. Of course she entered, it but when taking the throne, she discovered the seat had been coated with Vaseline. According to those within earshot, her utterances were a joy to hear. "Whoops! Whoops!" was followed by a loud crash as she slid from the seat.

In the autumn of my senior year, a student who lived within thirty or forty miles of King had his parents come to pick him up and take him home for the weekend on a regular basis. He managed to raise the ire of a whole bunch of guys living in his dorm by returning late on Sundays with a bushel of fine apples (the family apparently owned an orchard) and showing them off without offering to share. Eventually several of us had enough of his variation on the Garden of Eden's temptation. One Saturday while he was away several of us managed to open the locked door to his dorm room and, with a great deal of community effort requiring several hours of coordinated labor, hauled load after load of leaves up flights of steps to his third floor room. With the room almost packed with leaves from floor to ceiling, we closed the door but left a transom over the door open. Through it we dumped a final few loads of leaves, carefully swept up every vestige of evidence that might have suggested anything was amiss, and waited for the apple king's return. His reaction when he opened the door, only to be swamped by an outflow of leaves, was priceless. There was a second round of widespread joy at his dismay when he eventually dug his way in far enough to discover a sign on his bed which read: "It doesn't pay to be stingy with your apples."

There was more fun, most of it relatively innocent, although anyone who got caught would have been in serious trouble with a no-nonsense administration. There were a couple of abortive panty raids that produced nothing more than a worn-out bra or two and some panties that had seen better days. Although Ray Stevens's hilarious song "The Streak" would not be released for another decade, there were two or three nighttime male races across the campus oval with the participants as bare, except for covered heads, as Lady Godiva.

One morning campus awoke to find that the air had been let out of all four tires on every car on campus. I think the powers in charge hired someone with a compressor to come out and take care of matters. Then there were midnight excursions into the dining hall through a window conveniently left unlocked after supper. The target of those raids was a special cache of food kept in a refrigerator and used to feed the ground crew (they ate better than the students). Such were those days of youthful fun.

Although the subject is one I admittedly approach with trepidation, for every youngster growing up, no matter what the geographical setting, youthful ventures into romance form a part of school days. Accordingly, I'll conclude this lengthy chapter with a few thoughts on courting rituals, adolescent romance, and the whole matter of boy-and-girl as they existed in the 1950s, noting at the outset that I was a study in hopelessness when it came to honeyfuggling.

Most social interaction outside of school settings took place at birthday parties, school-sponsored dances, church youth groups, or informal gatherings at local hangouts (in Bryson City these were Bennett's Drug Store and Na-Ber's Drive-In restaurant). At parties there were kissing games such as spin the bottle or post office, with the accompaniment of considerable giggling and general foolishness of the sort that seems to be the exclusive domain of teenagers.

The first "girlfriend" of whom I have any real memories was Sue Hyde. There was an earlier crush on a comely colleen by the name of Paula Jo O'Brien and interest in a red-headed lass whose name eludes me, although I do remember her mother taught school. They don't really count, however, because I was so shy Paula Jo didn't know I existed, and obviously my failure to recall the redhead's name suggests her allure involved transitional fixation at best.

On the other hand, thanks in part to her being a good friend of my sister and also as a result of her subsequently having demonstrated her love for family and her home by writing and publishing a quartet of books (in order of publication they are *Blue Willow Dishes: Recipes and Remembrances; Gone Full Circle: More Recipes and Remembrances; From the Kitchen, From the Heart;* and *Where Cedars Sing*) that blend personal memoir, mountain culinary ways, and a tribute to her Smokies roots in alluring fashion, I've maintained contact with Sue over all these years.

In my parents' later years she catered multiple birthday parties or special events for them at the Calhoun Country Inn, owned by her family and which she operated for a time. When I was reading a number of fine books written by her older brother, Herbert "Hub" Hyde, and eventually writing a profile of him, she was helpful with family reminiscences and photos connected with a man who gained appreciable political stature on the state-wide level in North Carolina and was often described as "the last of the great orators." In her first book Sue wrote a story about my sister entitled "Annette's Aria," and in the course of telling that tale she states: "Incidentally, her big brother was probably my first real boyfriend! I think he was the first boy to ever break my heart. Even now I remember him ever so fondly!" I don't recall the exerciseas heartbreaking although such tiny tragedies are recurrent themes in childhood romances.

Later girlfriends from high school days varied quite a bit. There was a lovely girl named Joyce Dugan who was part Cherokee. She involved my first encounter with the concept of "going steady." I recently mentioned the term to my granddaughter, who is now of the age I was when dating Joyce, and she clearly had no idea what I was talking about. In this case I do remember shamefully two-timing her and getting caught. She returned a medallion I had received as a bench-warming member of a high school basketball team that was good enough to reach the final round of competition in the North Carolina state playoffs. It was the symbol of our "going steady" courtship, and she put it back in my hands, rightly letting me know that I had broken the faith of steadiness. Other than one final night when Joyce was my date for the junior-senior prom, that sweetness of high school wooing had come to an abrupt end.

Then there were other girlfriends—Wanda Walsh and for the briefest of times on the senior class trip to Washington, Maxine Freeman; Judy Vance, Sally Van Sweden, and Marty Moore during college years; and more. Oddly enough, and I have no idea whether this is a commentary on personal peculiarities or a testament to some threads from youth staying strong throughout one's life, but over the years I've maintained some type of contact, either directly or through mutual friends, with almost all of the girls mentioned above.

Whenever I look back to those days of innocence, my thoughts always trend toward comparative thinking. I know Daddy, right to the end of his 101 years, could recall names of girls he dated, and in his memorabilia were photos aplenty not just of him and Momma in their courting days but of earlier romances. They were a part of coming of age in the Smokies, an ongoing education in the school of life.

Chapter 32

THE LORDS OF LOAFERS GLORY

During the late 1940s, throughout the 1950s, and on into the 1960s, the shaded area of the Bryson City town square across from the old courthouse and adjacent to a five-and-ten-cent store was locally known, at least in politer circles, as Loafers Glory. The name was an apt one, although the location had another, equally applicable but less genteel name—Dead Pecker Corner. In the days before widespread availability of television, much less the Internet and today's communications technology, such gathering places were common throughout the Smokies. Sometimes it was town squares, with country stores, gas stations, and community buildings being other favored locations. The names for these areas where old-timers gathered (males only—they were strictly a male preserve) varied from place to place, with the word "liar" often figuring in the equation, but they were popular and well populated. Indeed, they formed a fundamental, almost indispensable part of the mountain social scene.

Loafers Glory was well populated with local characters throughout my boyhood and beyond. From the time when spring afternoons became warm enough for it to be comfortable outdoors, on through summer and continuing to the end of the glorious October days of Indian Summer, it was a favorite gathering place for old men. Some were regulars; others, with

Grandpa Joe being among their ranks, appeared periodically whenever they traveled to town.

On Saturdays, boys who lived in or near town often joined the group. I spent many an idle hour there, and I remember a number of friends and classmates who enjoyed the company of the oldsters as well. Sometimes we would even have a chance to participate in a keenly competed game of checkers, one of several activities enjoyed by the fellows I like to think of as the Lords of Loafers Glory. Personally my skills at checkers were so inferior as to present little challenge, but there were a few teenagers who could more than hold their own.

Any competitive checkers game would likely draw half a dozen kibitzers. On Saturdays when there might be two dozen or more folks present, there would be several games going on.

Along with checkers, another favorite pastime was knife trading. Every self-respecting male, man or boy, carried a pocket knife, and two or three of the regulars were always bargaining with one another or any casual passer-by curious enough to get involved in the trading. Knives were also used for whittling, a perfect activity to accompany the arguments, philosophizing, and political opining that went on nonstop. Some of the whittling was just idle rendering of sizeable sticks into toothpicks, but other wizards with a knife crafted small animals, sling shots, whammy-diddles, and more.

I always enjoyed stopping by Loafers Glory, whether in company with Grandpa Joe or by myself. It was most decidedly a place where youngsters were to be seen, not heard, and any time one of the regulars saw fit to recognize your presence or mention you in the course of conversation was a moment for quiet pride.

The topics of conversation varied greatly at Loafers Glory, but local and national politics, any scandal involving someone personally known by the regulars, upcoming elections, religion, and trials at the nearby courthouse all received full and often brutally frank airing. Nothing, even the moral fiber of area ministers, was sacrosanct. Along with what amounted to local gossip, although anyone describing Loafers Glory conversation with that word would have immediately become persona non grata (gossip was something womenfolks did), there was also plenty of telling of tall tales. Much of the storytelling fell into the outdoor genre, with recollection of grand hunting and fishing feats. When a venerable Nimrod like Granville Calhoun or Bear Hunter Watkins stopped by, they were especially welcome as were their stories.

Whenever district or federal court was in session at the courthouse across the street, benches at Loafers Glory would be full to overflowing, because trials brought extra folks to town as well as providing plenty of fodder for conversation. One court-related occasion I recall with a mixture of irritation and embarrassment, never mind that the better part of six decades has come and gone, gave the regulars an opportunity to enjoy some innocent fun at my expense.

In company with several other boys, I made the mistake of easing into court as a spectator. After all, a veteran mountain lawyer of the ilk of Felix Alley or Herbert Hyde could provide first-rate entertainment with spellbinding defenses and sparkling moments of oratory. A few hours in court, with the right kind of case and a good stem-winder lawyer in action, could be pure joy.

However, the entertainment on this occasion focused not on lawyers but on a gaggle of youngsters who had dared enter court attired in what were then known as Bermuda shorts. It didn't matter that we were reasonably clean and far neater than some of the audience clad in brogans, overalls, and shirts that hadn't seen the business end of laundry work for some time. That was the type of workday clothing worn by Loafers Glory regulars and much of the general male population. Shorts, on the other hand, were strictly taboo. When the presiding judge noticed us, he ordered the bailiff to usher us out of his presence immediately. News of this action got across the street to Loafers Glory almost instantaneously. I can still hear Al Dorsey, who wasn't exactly a paragon of sartorial splendor or cleanliness, chuckling as he commented: "I guess the judge showed you boys who was boss!"

Old Al was one of the regulars, as were a couple of fellows who had some problems with addiction to painkillers. In fact, they were notorious in trying to convince boys to go to the drugstore and get patent medicines such as Hadacol or Yellow Jacket Pain Pills for them. For his part, Al Dorsey had a decidedly checkered history, having spent time in the state penitentiary for murder, but I never heard his time in prison discussed at Loafers Glory. On the other hand, his catfishing exploits were a regular topic of conversation. For their part, the addicts were tolerated, but whenever one of them started pestering a youngster, some of the more stable regulars would soon set them straight in no uncertain fashion.

While gatherings of coffee drinkers, whittlers, and storytellers around wood-burning stoves at crossroads stores are often mentioned as being part of the tapestry of American history, I suspect that outdoor gatherings similar to Loafers Glory were likewise once commonplace in small communities across the nation. Certainly the men who gathered at the square in Bryson City were a colorful lot, and I now realize that I was privileged to have been a fairly regular bystander at their daily gatherings. It was a marvelous microcosm of mountain ways, a front row seat at lengthy sessions of fine storytelling, and part of a delightful world of yesteryear.

So much was that the case that one of many regrets focusing on my youth is that I didn't pay more attention to the men and the milieu. Now that I have attained the years of the fellows who were the Lords of Loafers Glory, I know that those were shining days in the mountain sun.

Chapter 33

TOWN SQUARE BIBLE THUMPERS

During warm weather months in the Smokies of my youth, itinerant preachers were fixtures on town squares. Virtually all their preaching was done on Saturdays. On that day their potential audience grew considerably. It was "come to town day" when rural folks did their shopping, bought their groceries, got garden plants and animal feed at the local Farmers' Federation or whatever cooperative served their region, and simply enjoyed the opportunity to be out and about. During the summer there would likely be a goodly sprinkling of goggle-eyed tourists, awestruck by this local eccentricity of religious celebration, as well.

These wandering purveyors of the Gospel were universally known as "Bible thumpers," thanks to one of a number of tactics they employed to gather an audience and then keep its attention. They carried a massive Bible and would, with some regularity, raise it aloft with one hand then give it a resounding thump with the other. The best of them could deliver a whack that made a Bible pop like an exploding firecracker.

In my personal experience wandering preachers seldom if ever mentioned a particular denomination and probably did not belong to one. Few if any were ordained other than that they had decided, on their own, to answer a calling. They were strangers to formal theological training, had likely never darkened the doors of a seminary or Bible college, and were in many ways men of mystery. No one seemed to know their origins (I never knew a Bible thumper who lived locally) and seemed, at least in my youthful eyes, men of great strangeness.

Their uncertain backgrounds and lack of formal credentials notwithstanding, all possessed salient characteristics, and the best of them were amazingly persuasive. To a man, although they would likely have given anyone mentioning the phrase "stage presence" a blank stare, they instinctively understood the concept. Let one of the more passionate among their ranks really get down to business and he was something to behold. Along with periodic thumping of his primary prop, an oversized Bible, there would be mesmerizing gesticulation to punctuate or emphasize particular points, spittle would fly as verses were spouted, and wayward human behavior invariably formed a critical part of the subject matter.

The finest of the street preachers had a certain rhythm to their delivery, with the phrase "Let me tell you, brother" being repeated countless times. It would almost always be followed by a mighty smack of the Bible and an utterance (I'm not sure it was a word) that sounded to me like "Huh!" or "Ha!" There were periodic pauses to wipe the sweat from their brow with large handkerchiefs, and the overall level of showmanship rivaled that of a carnival barker or purveyor of patent medicine. There was never any question of a speaking permit, impeding traffic, or anything like that. The verbal offerings were variously viewed as serious religion, welcome entertainment, and sometimes an opportunity to debate religious issues.

I must confess that I don't recall a great deal about doctrinal discussion or the text of sermons these preachers offered, and even if I could, it's likely thematic coherence wouldn't have been a strong point. But those from the Bible thumper ranks who garnered large crowds and keen listeners had a definite proclivity for the "hellfire-and-brimstone" school of delivery. A skilled thumper could paint verbal visions of Hades and word portraits of Satan sufficient to scare the bejeebers out of a small boy. You could almost smell sulfur and feel heat as they ran through a litany of sins serving as a guaranteed passport to the portals of the underworld. I recall almost no references to good works and ways to enter paradise. Devilish deeds and damnation, along with myriad examples of sinful shenanigans, were standard fare on the square.

Never mind that Swain was a dry county at the time, as were most others in the Smokies on both the North Carolina and Tennessee sides, alcohol topped the lengthy list of sins the thumpers would enumerate. Many of these itinerant peddlers of the Gospel had a colorful array of descriptions for intoxicants—John Barleycorn, tanglefoot, golden moonbeam, demon rum, stump water, squeezin's, and devil's brew were among them. They would rail about ruined homes, abused wives, ill-fed and poorly clothed children, general slovenliness, and more in association with vile drink.

Some weighed in heavily on the evils of tobacco as well, but that didn't go over particularly well with the benchwarmers of Loafers Glory, for almost to a man they either smoked or chewed tobacco. When the subject matter turned to that "vile, stinking weed," there would be audible grumbling and rolling of eyes in the audience. Many years later I would learn that during the early seventeenth century, especially in the reign of King James I, similar fulminations regarding tobacco were standard fare. Had the Bible thumpers known of Robert Burton's characterization of the plant in *The Anatomy of Melancholy*—"'Tis a plague, a mischief, a violent purger of goods, lands, health: hellish, devilish, and damned tobacco, the ruin and overthrow of body and soul!"—they would surely have quoted him. As it was, this particular lamentation was pretty much a nonstarter, for not only was the primary audience addicted; many of them or their kinfolk grew burley tobacco as a cash crop.

On the other hand, titillating tales of lust, chastising of chasers of women, and condemnations of adultery played exceptionally well with audiences. Dancing was another frequent target. It was a social activity inviting all sorts of lurid descriptions, although the best I ever heard was in a class by itself. One particularly articulate preacher excoriated any and all dancing at considerable length, concluding with a thunderous statement that it was nothing more or less than "a vertical position for horizontal desires."

Flashy or revealing attire—anything from Bermuda shorts to ladies wearing fashionable slacks, from penny loafers to pegged pants—provided fine verbal fodder. But my favorite moments came when some particularly daring or devoted thumper, lacking any verbal filter or acquaintance with diplomacy, took it on himself to start pointing fingers. He would single out some hapless passerby as a specific example of a soul whose evil ways were made manifest by their manner of dress and hector that individual in merciless fashion.

The Loafers Glory crowd, ever alert to an opportunity for comic relief or perhaps conversational meat for the coming week, often played bit roles on such occasions. It was interactive theater, so popular in England during the Elizabethan era, brought to the mid-twentieth century. No sooner would a preacher direct his attention to someone who seconds before had been sauntering innocently down the sidewalk than he would get support known as "aggin' and hissin'." Cries of "You tell 'em, brother," "Preach on, preacher," "Tell it all, brother, tell it all,"or just heartfelt "Amens" would ring out from the audience.

More often than not, those individuals who drew such unwelcome attention slunk along the sidewalk in shame, but on one memorable occasion a local woman noted for her outspokenness and eccentric behavior turned the tables in dramatic fashion. She always carried an umbrella, and when the thumper directed shaming comments at her, that parasol instantly turned into a weapon. Carrying it before her like a soldier charging with a bayonet-equipped rifle, she marched up to the offending preacher and accosted him. Emphasizing every word with threatening pokes of her weapon, she unleashed some decidedly unladylike language, called the itinerant a "sanctimonious son of a bitch," and threatened to beat him to the ground. The hapless fellow, used to having the upper hand, was caught on the horns of a dilemma. He could hardly take physical measures with a woman, and it was abundantly clear she had no intention of leaving or ceasing her frontal assault. After perhaps thirty seconds of being the target of withering abuse, he ignominiously fled the scene to the accompaniment of laughter and applause from the Loafers Glory contingent.

Other than this single instance, I don't ever recall any verbal counterattacks aimed at the street preachers. However, old men in the audience felt perfectly comfortable in shaking their heads in disagreement or in suggesting to someone sitting next to them that the Bible thumper was venturing into questionable religious territory. Similarly, a real stem-winder of a preacher expected and received plenty of positive responses with knowing nods or along the lines of "I hear you, brother."

Confrontational tactics were standard among the thumpers, and this method of conveying the Gospel message found widespread usage throughout Smokies churches as well as on the streets. A cherished, oft-told tale from my family's own store of lore involves a great-grandfather who was a fire-and-brimstone Baptist. A relatively young man in his community notorious for his carousing lifestyle died unexpectedly, and his family asked my ancestor to handle the memorial service. He tried to beg off, frankly mentioning the well-known sinfulness of the deceased, but the family was insistent that he was the man to handle the funeral.

He eventually relented, agreed to preach, and the first portion of the service went smoothly enough. The congregation sang a hymn or two, there were readings from Scripture, and then Reverend Casada got down to serious business. Looking down from the pulpit to the open casket situated just a few feet away, he pointed at the deceased and pronounced: "There lies one who has gone to Hell!" That shocking statement was immediately followed by him turning to the family seated in the front rows of the little country church and shaking a finger at them with the admonition: "And there sits a bunch more traveling down the same road unless they change their ways." Oral tradition does not provide details of what happened next. But since other members of the family from that general period appear in court records for affray, and given the clan's notoriety for tempestuousness, it probably wasn't a placid scene.

Curiously, with the notable exception of the umbrella-toting lady, I don't recall women ever paying much attention to the thumpers. They would walk past a street preacher while going about their business without much more than casting a glimpse in his direction, if that. On the other hand, old men with nothing better to do, and young boys en route to the Saturday matinee at the nearby Gem Theatre, were prime candidates for a captive audience. More than one of the Bible thumpers railed against the evils of movies, although I don't think it had any impact whatsoever. I know that personally my dime (later twelve cents when the price for enjoyment of a cartoon, a serial, and a fine Western went up) always got spent, and there was never a street preacher of sufficient quality to make me miss a movie. Still, these wandering purveyors of the Word were an integral and interesting, though not necessarily important, part of the Saturday scene in Bryson City as it was in the years between the end of World War II and sometime in the 1960s. Friends from that era who grew up elsewhere tell me they were a common local feature throughout the Smokies. As the Age of Aquarius arrived, Bible thumpers disappeared from the mountain scene. Their days in the sun had come and gone, but for at least two generations they brought color, entertainment, and a particular brand of fervid religious outlook to the high country scene.

Chapter 34

VANISHING ASPECTS
OF THE MOUNTAIN SCENE

Increasingly with the passage of time I find myself reflecting on things I did as a youngster. In one sense at least the bulk of this book's contents involve ruminations on those glorious days in the Smokies sun. Most recreational activities were simple, inexpensive, and relied more on youthful ingenuity, along with a good dose of suggestions from Grandpa Joe and others, than any of the store-bought junk—video games, all sorts of technological gadgets, and electronic gizmos—that pass for entertainment with today's kids. My looks backward, and I'll happily acknowledge they are longing ones, almost always bring to the mind thoughts as to how many other folks have been privileged to know the joys of these Smoky Mountain pastimes.

Accordingly, as a supplement to activities that have already been covered, here's a sort of addendum in the form of a list asking whether you ever participated in a given game, enjoyed a particular experience, consumed some type of food, or have this particular recollection stored on the shelves of your memory's storehouse. For each reflection, I'm simply asking of the reader: "Did you ever?" A few such activities loom so large in my personal memories that separate chapters have been devoted to them, but I hope this further listing will leave no doubt that my Smokies boyhood offered richness and variety.

Did You Ever?

Boil eggs at Easter and "fight" them for keeps—the egg that broke went to the proud holder of the one that remained intact after the small ends had been knocked together. Of course there was always some wiseacre who managed to slip in a guinea egg—about the only way they would lose would involve being matched against a rock. The shells of guinea eggs are that hard. A good "knocker" egg could produce the makings of a big bowl of egg salad or a batch of deviled eggs in short order.

Play rolly-bat with either a real baseball or a suitably sized rock wrapped with old socks and tape. In order to be the batter, you had to field the ball and then throw or roll it toward the bat. The bat had been laid out on the ground sideways facing the field. If your roll hit the bat, or if you caught a fly ball or line drive hit by the batter before it hit the ground, you took his place at bat.

Play war—with imaginary armaments such as grenades that were may pops (passion flower fruit), white pine cones, or magnolia seed pods; home-made bows and arrows; forts built from pines or other trees you had cut; and sling shots.

Trap cottontails with box traps known as rabbit gums.

Convince a visiting cousin or some poor city slicker soul to take a bite of a persimmon that had turned orange but was still a long way from being ripe.

Enjoy the indescribable delight of a properly made persimmon pudding, something as delicious as a green persimmon is disgusting.

Ride a bike back and forth across traffic count strips countless times with the idea of misleading the state department of transportation in a big way.

Buy fish hooks, shotgun shells, or .22 cartridges individually—all could be purchased that way in the 1950s.

Come across an old still (or maybe an active one) while wandering through the woods. On a personal note, I once got too close to one that was clearly in operation. A couple of rifle shots through the trees overhead, along with a distant shout, "You boys don't need to be here," conveyed an all-too-clear message.

Get a good dose of hickory tea. Or maybe two doses—one at school and a second one when your parents learned of your transgressions. I must admit, back in the days when corporal punishment as part of the educational process was not only accepted but actually appreciated by most parents, that happened to yours truly on more than one occasion.

Walk carefully on sidewalks in order to avoid cracks, guided by the adage "Don't step on a crack or you will break your Momma's back."

Hear grown folks talk about an elderly family member who was a bit "quare," "not quite right," a bit "addled," or "poorly." This was a standard way of describing dementia.

Listen to any of the grand old radio programs such as "Gunsmoke," "The Lone Ranger," or "Amos and Andy."

Make a particular point of listening to programming associated with the Grand Old Opry or Louisiana Hayride.

Go to a drive-in theater (and sometimes try to sneak two or three "extras" in by hiding them in the trunk).

Go to Belk's (or a similar local clothing store) for a year's worth of school clothing.

Browse dreamily through the major mail-order catalogs from Sears & Roebuck and Montgomery Ward.

Live in or visit a house that did not have electricity.

Make the cold trek to an outhouse on a winter night.

Participate in May Day or Sadie Hawkins Day festivities when they were a standard part of spring at many schools.

Visit someone's home, usually on a Friday night, to participate in making music or maybe just taking care of the grinnin' while others did the pickin'.

Participate in square dances with a local band, maybe just a pianist, or even a record player providing the music while a caller hollered out the next movement in what could sometimes be an intricate undertaking.

Listen to traditional square dance songs such as "Under the Double Eagle," "Down Yonder," "Soldier's Joy," or "Buffalo Gals" at those gatherings.

Watch or participate in a turkey shoot.

Grow your own popcorn and enjoy the special treat of shelling and popping it.

Go on a 'coon hunt and enjoy the hallelujah chorus of a pack of dogs on a hot trail or the tales of old men harkening back with longing to their respective "dogs of a lifetime."

Participate in drawing names" for Christmas in your class in school (this was standard practice when I was in elementary school).

Go "sanging" (gather ginseng for sale).

Go "gallacking" (gather galax leaves to use in wreathes or as table decoration, especially at Christmas.

Find a case holding praying mantis eggs while out hunting in the winter and bring it home.

Skate on leather-bottomed shoes across frozen ponds or places where water had frozen on a sidewalk or driveway.

Make your own fishing outfit from river cane you had cut, with the lead covering of roofing nails used for sinkers and a bottle cork for a float.

Find yourself on one of the two business ends of a cross-cut saw.

Use a go-devil to split wood, or, if you really want to reach back in time, split wood using wedges made not of metal but of dense woods such as dogwood.

Split kindling from rich pine (lighter wood) to use as a fire starter.

Lay the kindling each night in a wood-burning stove for cooking breakfast the next morning.

Get involved in hog killing and butchering.

Gather eggs from the family chicken house.

Put a glass egg in a nest to encourage a laying hen to set.

"Blow" an egg and refill it with hot sauce to deal with an egg-suckin' dog or an egg-eatin' snake.

Take part in a rat killin' at the family corn crib.

Pull weeds to feed hogs.

Sucker tomatoes.

Sucker tobacco or mash tobacco worms.

Get stung by a packsaddle.

Knock down a hornet or wasp nest after smoking it or dig up a yellow jacket nest after pouring gasoline down the entrance hole—all to obtain some prime fish bait.

Trap 'coons, muskrats, mink, possums, and fox for their fur.

Go skinny-dipping in your favorite swimming hole.

Burn your belly with a "belly flop" or your bottom with a "cannon ball" jumping into a swimming hole.

Use a rope tied to a convenient tree limb to launch out into a swimming hole.

Get a bad case of chiggers or poison ivy.

Find an abandoned old home place in early fall where there was fruit on apple or pear trees and enjoy a field snack.

Eat a hunter's lunch of tinned sardines or Vienna sausage with saltine crackers.

Drink the finest spring water imaginable from some remote seep high up in the Smokies.

Listen to someone recite wonderfully lyrical poems from the likes of Rudyard Kipling or Robert Service around a backwoods campfire.

Hear a recitation of Stephen Vincent Benet's "The Mountain Whip-poorwill" and identify with half the lines in the poem.

Mow grass with a reel-type push mower.

Have a secret crush on some curly-haired little girl but be far too timid to look her in the eye, much less speak to her.

Play spin the bottle or similar boy-girl games at parties.

Run a trot line, throw line, limb line, or jug fish for catfish.

Attempt to smoke rabbit tobacco.

Enjoy a crackling fire in the family room or food cooked on a wood-burning stove.

Eat a supper consisting of nothing but cornbread and milk (either sweet or buttermilk). Those who haven't enjoyed this culinary pleasure might think it constitutes mighty slim pickin's. In truth, a big chunk of cornbread made from slow-ground, stone-ground meal and crumbled in a glass of cold milk is a taste treat of great delight.

Enjoy home-churned butter, nicely salted and pressed in an old-time wooden mold.

Milk a cow.

Churn butter.

Eat fried pies with filling made from dried apples or peaches folded into a round piece of dough folded like a half moon to hold the fruit. Slathered with butter, such fare is fit for a king or any son or daughter of the Smokies.

Pour molasses over soft butter and mash it all up before applying the resultant mix to a cathead biscuit. The trick is to get just the right amount of molasses and butter for the biscuit, although missing your measurement isn't a tragedy. It's just an excuse to eat another biscuit.

Eat fresh pork sausage for breakfast.

Enjoy the genuine privilege of eating tenderloin from a recently butchered hog.

Have hamburger and milk gravy, with cornbread, as a main dish. That was one of Mom's favorite ways of making a relatively small amount of meat go a long way.

Eat old-fashioned stick candy in flavors such as horehound.

Buy loose candy by the piece.

Take a hefty dose of sulfur and molasses or maybe a cup of sassafras tea as a "spring tonic."

Drink syllabub at Christmas time.

Slop hogs.

Toss scratch feed to chickens.

Shell corn you have grown to fatten hogs.

"Plug" a watermelon to check its ripeness. I never really understood this process; once the melon was plugged it had to be used.

Eat sauce or pies made from some of the winter squash and pumpkins that grow wild in the mountains. Among them are candy roasters and cushaws.

Feast on country ham your family has cured, with the obligatory side dishes of red eye gravy and biscuits.

Eat sawmill gravy (a milk gravy, usually made with drippings from sausage and plenty of sausage bits left in for good measure).

Savor a properly made stack cake, with at least seven thin layers of cake, each one separated by spiced sauce made from dried apples or maybe black-berry jam.

Participate in a cake walk.

Attend an all-day singing with dinner on the grounds.

Go to a brush arbor revival.

Prepare homemade pickled peaches.

Pick up ripe honey locust pods from the ground and eat the meat that surrounds the seeds.

Find a prime patch of hazelnut bushes and gather the delicious nuts.

Gather fox grapes to make jelly.

Find a patch of ripe pawpaws and enjoy a woodland feast.

Eat the sweet-sour flesh surrounding the seeds of maypop fruit.

Sample liver mush, scrapple, head cheese, or other foods made from the parts of animals that frugal "waste not, want not" mountain folks put to good and tasty use.

Go to school where someone who has eaten a bait of ramps was in attendance. Suffice it to say you'd find your sense of smell works all too well on such occasions.

These are but a sampling of the experiences that come to my admittedly disordered mind as I look back, with longing, to a world I can only hope we have not completely lost. If these are pleasures you enjoyed as a youngster, you were truly blessed.

Chapter 35

TALE OF AN OLD COFFEE CUP

For hunters, fishermen, and outdoor enthusiasts of all stripes there comes a stage in life where they either own pretty much all the gear they need or else cannot afford it. I've long since reached that stage, although honesty compels me to acknowledge that a fly fisherman really never has too many rods and the hunter always welcomes just one more gun. Of course spouses often have markedly different outlooks, and based on personal experience I can tell you it's mighty difficult to justify another fly rod when you own a dozen or an additional shotgun when you already have at least two of every gauge from 10 to .410. Those who are outside the ranks of the sporting cognoscenti simply cannot understand that there are differences, far transcending the cosmetic or appearance, in a double barrel and semiautomatic of the same gauge.

Such particulars and peculiarities of paraphernalia being duly recognized, once in a while an item comes along that is truly special thanks to being handcrafted, having unique attributes, or possibly just being something that evokes warm memories. That happened to me a few years back when, the week before Thanksgiving, a package arrived in the mail bearing the return address of my lifelong friend and boyhood fishing partner, Bill Rolen.

We had stayed in touch by e-mail, phone, and occasionally in person

263

over the years, and Bill helped me appreciably with photographic support and informational details when I was writing what I consider one of my most important books, *Fly Fishing in the Great Smoky Mountains National Park: An Insider's Guide to a Pursuit of Passion*. A substantial portion of my early "pursuit of passion" was in his company—just two boys living a dream on Deep Creek, Indian Creek, Luftee, Bradley Fork, and other Park streams. During those carefree teenage years both of us added treasure beyond measure to the vaults of our respective memories.

Yet in my wildest dreams I could never have imagined a tangible link to those days in the 1950s that would be so meaningful, much less one that would resurrect happy days in my own life as well a whole world of sport in the Smokies of yesteryear. The contents of the box Bill mailed me were simple—twenty or so trout flies in old-fashioned patterns such as Yellarhammers tied on long-shanked hooks and legendary mountain angler Mark Cathey's favorite instrument of feathered deceit, Grey Hackle Yellows, along with an old coffee cup.

The flies, tied by Bill, a master of the vise since boyhood, meant a great deal, but in terms of significance they paled in comparison with the coffee cup. At first glance it seemed just another rather nondescript example of once popular backcountry cookware featuring dark blue enamel with white specks. The enamel was worn away in a spot or two, with rust showing through, although the cup is still perfectly serviceable when it comes to holding a steaming cup of coffee or hot chocolate beside a backcountry campfire during evening tale-telling time.

What set this cup apart, to use one of those ten-dollar words high school English teacher Thad DeHart drummed into my thick skull so many years ago, was its provenance. The cup came from a set of utensils that stocked the cabin the Civilian Conservation Corps (CCC) built in the 1930s at the Bryson Place on Deep Creek. That structure replaced an earlier building first a farm family then hunters and fishermen utilized for decades—certainly from early in the twentieth century and possibly earlier.

The cabin constructed by the CCC was still standing in my youth, and some of the most memorable of my many camping trips with Dad were spent there. To me, even as a boy, it was hallowed ground. After all, the spot was one where icons of sport in the Smokies—men like Mark Cathey, Sam and Waitsel Hunnicutt, O. P. Williams, and Granville Calhoun—had camped in pre-Park days while on bear hunts or fishing trips.

Sometime around 1960 the Park, in one of many examples of misguided madness involving destruction of historical artifacts (old homesteads, out buildings, and indeed any and all evidence of the human presence had been leveled and burned in the 1930s), ordered the ranger at the time to burn down this legendary gathering spot for sportsmen. That Deep Creek ranger just happened to be Bill Rolen, the father of my pal, and I have no doubt whatsoever that this was one of the toughest duties he undertook over the entire course of his career. After all, he was a man with deep roots in and an abiding love for Swain County and the Smokies.

Rolen carried out his orders to burn the Bryson Place but also decided to save a bit of history. In an act that, had it been known at the time, doubtless would have brought the wrath of his superiors over at Sugarlands down on his head (fortunately today's Park leadership has a decidedly different approach to historical preservation), Bill removed a few items before setting that historic structure ablaze. In due time those artifacts were passed on to his son and namesake, and young Bill's letter accompanying the cup resurrected memories so meaningful to me that they shine as brightly as if they occurred this past summer. "We certainly had our times," Bill reminisced, "rattlesnakes, soaking rains, long backpacking trips." He recalled the anglers we idolized—Claude Gossett, Hop Wiggins, Levi Haynes, Alvin Miller, Ernest Smiley, and my father—and some of their favorite pools on Deep Creek. He relived our good times together on Indian Creek, Deep Creek's Left Fork, and elsewhere. Then he wrote, in simple yet for me deeply moving words: "I've only had two fishing partners; you, during my younger years, and Levi Haynes after I passed my half-century mark. I was privileged to have both of you as fishing/camping partners."

Then Bill added, "Along with the flies I've included a cup from the old Bryson Place. I can think of no one else who would appreciate this more than you. Don't think of these things as gifts. They are just a way of recognizing and remembering our past."

I'll honor Bill's wishes and just call the cup and flies mementoes, but they are more meaningful than the most precious of gifts. After all, it's possible, even likely, that those fly fishing heroes of my youth drank from the coffee cup. Indeed, it's not much of a stretch to reckon that Mark Cathey, after a long day astream performing his mesmerizing "dance of the dry fly," may have mixed a goodly dollop of snakebite medicine with his post-supper coffee in this very cup.

I'd like to think so. Certainly every time I look at that old cup, every time I gaze on those enduring mountain fly patterns, they will take me magically back to endearing angling days and enduring angling ways.

Chapter 36

THE ANGEL OF BRASSTOWN

Most chapters in this collection of memories focus on a boyhood of surpassing bliss and beauty spent in the Smokies. However, I have felt an exception is merited for coverage of arguably the finest representation of adherence to the old ways in the high country to be found in today's world.

Roughly a decade ago I was first introduced to a daily blog produced by a woman named Tipper Pressley, a resident of Brasstown, North Carolina. It was like finding a pot of mental gold, and early each morning a visit to her blog lifts my spirits and provides me with as fine a start to the day as Grandpa Joe's scalding hot cup of chicory coffee ever gave him. I'm carried swiftly and surely back to the place that shaped me and that remains the source of my soul.

Folks commenting on Tipper Pressley's daily blog, "Blind Pig & the Acorn," often refer to her as the "angel of Brasstown," a description coined by my brother, Don. The geographical part of the description is easily explained. Brasstown is a crossroads community in Clay County, which lies in far southwestern North Carolina. It's not exactly a hotspot of tourism or a destination featured regularly in travel magazines. In fact, Brasstown is a location probably best known as the site, for many years, of an annual

New Year's 'possum drop and especially for that bastion of preserving and perpetuating Appalachian folkways, the John C. Campbell Folk School.

The angel part of Tipper's moniker is a bit more demanding and open to multiple interpretations. Among them are an angelic face seemingly graced by a permanent smile; a character and approach to life that conjures up recollections of the old quote from Loweezy in the Snuffy Smith comic strip, "gooder'n airy angel"; and her keen interest in crafts depicting angels, such as corn husk angels and highly decorative paintings of them for use in Christmas decoration. But where Pressley really shines in earning earthly angel wings is her passionate devotion to celebrating and preserving all things connected with our rich and varied Appalachian heritage. As she puts it in describing her blog, which has appeared daily since 2008, "All you really need to know is I'm crazy in love with my home in Appalachia—the people, the food, the music, the colorful language, the sustainable lifestyle, the soaring mountains, and the deep dark hollers." She claims to hear "voices—young, old, male, and female, all with the same urgency encouraging me to continue my endeavor (her daily sampling of mountain lore) so that their memories might live on at least in the language of Appalachia."

In truth there's a great deal more to know than the barebones of a passionate love affair with a region and its way of life. Tipper is a marvelous cook specializing in traditional high country foodstuffs who occasionally teaches culinary classes at the John C. Campbell Folk School and in other settings; a talented musician who hides her light as a bass player while showcasing the songwriting, singing, and instrumental talents of her twin daughters, Corie and Katie, brother Paul, and the grand legacy of her late musician-father, Jerry; skilled photographer with an exceptional eye who often renders the ordinary or overlooked extraordinary; serious student of mountain history; writer; storyteller; and seminar speaker. It should also be noted, almost as an afterthought, that she has a full-time job with a foot solidly planted in today's world of technology.

Tipper's interests, although invariably attuned to her passion for place, range even more widely than her abilities, and day after delightful day they are on display in Blind Pig & the Acorn. The blog's title, aptly taken from a common Appalachian adage suggesting that even a blind hog will occasionally have the good fortune to root up a tasty morsel of oak mast, enjoys considerable popularity, and the coterie of folks who get their morning fix of all things Appalachian is an ever growing one. Performing a delicate balancing act that includes almost magical monitoring of comments to avoid the venom and vituperation so common in many blogs, Pressley manages to educate and entertain on a daily basis even as she celebrates southern Appalachia's myriad attractive attributes. In that context, one reader spoke for many in a recent heartfelt comment: "You have done so very much to make me proud of my heritage."

Fostering that pride involves a wide range of topics, and one of Tipper's strongest attributes is her ability to take some seemingly inconsequential topic and infuse it with interest. Another is her insatiable curiosity. When a perceptive reader mentions some rapidly vanishing mountain custom, alludes to an old-time fruit or vegetable, or inquires about some obscure subject once commonplace to the steep ridges and deep valleys of the Smokies and neighboring Appalachia, you can pretty well count on the topic being covered somewhere down the road.

Although Pressley's interests are encyclopedic in scope, a number of threads run as consistently bright strands through the entire fabric of Blind Pig & the Acorn. A personal favorite is the monthly "Appalachian Vocabulary Test" where five words or phrases are offered to see if readers use them in their own daily speech or at least are familiar with their meaning. She also has someone use the word in a sentence while speaking it out loud.

Another recurring theme is music. Her twenty-something twins ("Chitter" and "Chatter" in the blog) possess ample quantities of the family's deeply entrenched musical talent, and they now perform regularly at regional church gatherings, fairs, folk festivals, and other venues. They play traditional string instruments of the region—guitar, fiddle, and mandolin—while offering exquisite harmony reminiscent of the likes of the Louvin Brothers, Don Reno and Red Smiley, or their grandfather and Uncle Paul. Tipper's father, the late Jerry Wilson ("Pap" on the blog) and his brother, Ray, were an acclaimed regional singing duo and recipients of a North Carolina Heritage Award in 1988, while Paul is an accomplished guitarist, singer, and songwriter. Readers of Blind Pig & the Acorn can savor scores of selections from the family musical archives while reading the latest blog post.

Given her love of the land, gardening is another prominent theme. Her husband Matt (the blog's "Deer Hunter"), a skilled jack-of-all trades, enters the scene doing everything from simple tilling to greenhouse construction.

From winter's seed-starting time right through to fall harvest, there are regular updates on everything from herbs to "tommytoes," cabbage to corn. Use of crops on the family table and for canning, drying, preserves, and pickles also looms large. Although it hasn't yet happened, given the wealth of cooking lore Tipper shares, a cookbook with a title along the lines of "In the Kitchen with the Blind Pig Gang" seems likely to appear at some point in the future.

Traditional mountain crafts form another area of prominence on the blog. Periodically some craft project is covered, and over the years during the Christmas season Tipper has offered family creations for sale. Among them have been knitted and crocheted items made by her mother ("Granny"), CDs from various members of this musical clan, and jewelry, handmade soaps, oils, and balms from the twins.

Unassumingly selfless in person but tirelessly strident in promoting mountain heritage, Tipper generously shares links to other Appalachia-related blogs in her "Sit a Spell" section. There are frequent historical posts with coverage ranging from Civil War letters back home to stories underlying popular ballads, from forgotten customs such as dumb suppers to Decoration Day or all-day singings. Yet the Blind Pig involves more than "pause and ponder" reading material leavened by ear-soothing music.

The blog's visual impact sometimes stirs the viewer's soul. Pressley's keen photographer's knack for capturing commonplace scenes from strikingly different perspectives often draws immediate attention. Daily comments from readers provide insight and information. Where responses on many blogs deteriorate into sniping, here there's a sense of shared love and something of an aura of oneness. Readers feel they are part of an extended family. As a personal example of this togetherness, I've obtained heirloom candy roaster seeds from fellow Blind Pig fans, received helpful suggestions on troublesome gardening problems, and been reminded of how tasty springtime pigweed (purslane) can be.

Adding a bit of spice to Tipper's heady literary brew are occasional guest posts. The quality of these varies, but unfailingly they come from the heart and evoke a deep, abiding love for Appalachia. That affinity for Appalachia, masterfully molded and melded by a true Appalachian angel, forms the essence of Blind Pig & the Acorn.

To date well over three thousand blogs devoted exclusively to heralding all that is good and gracious, enchanting and exciting, about the mountain way of life have appeared. Quantitatively only John Parris's storied "Roaming the Mountains" newspaper column from the *Asheville Citizen-Times* in yesteryear surpasses that figure in terms of extensive, ongoing coverage of mountain ways. Now in her mid-forties, Tipper Pressley likely will give us stories on the glories of Appalachia for many a year and yarn to come.

Chapter 37

A DAY AT DEVILS DIP

In many ways Grandpa Joe was a boy trapped in an old man's body. Full of tricks as a pet 'coon, tough as a seasoned hickory sapling, and imbued with seventy-plus years of wisdom accumulated by living close to the good earth of the Smokies, he possessed an unflagging sense of adventurous spirit when it came to outdoor pursuits such as hunting or fishing. On many of these sporting outings I enjoyed the great good fortune of being his sidekick.

Somehow Grandpa had a knack for turning something such as an afternoon's fishing in the Tuckaseigee River, which flowed by his home, or a day spent in pursuit of squirrels, into grand enterprises involving the two of us as a dauntless duo. For all our boisterousness and bravado, those escapades didn't always work out as planned. Often as not we came home from a day in the autumn woods without a bushytail between us. Our fishing outings were somewhat more predictable in terms of fish on the stringer, but the day which brought one of our finest catches ever turned into something of a disaster. It involved an early spring afternoon trip to a big pool, locally known as Devils Dip, in the nearby river.

Deriving its name from powerful hydraulics and a strong backwater that gave it the appearance of a whirlpool, Devils Dip lay just a short walk downstream from Grandpa's house. We had fished it many times before, and almost without exception the south side of the pool, on the same bank as Grandpa's house, was good for a few knottyheads. On this particular day, however, yielding to the Sirene-like appeal of a growing stringer of fish, the two of us ventured into uncharted territory. Hopping from one rock to another, we went farther out on the shoals adjacent to the turbulent water of the whirlpool than ever before. At one point, scared a bit by the nearby torrent, I commented to Grandpa: "If we aren't careful we'll fall in."

He nodded in agreement before settling matters as far as both of us were concerned. "You might be right, but every time we move we catch more knottyheads." It was difficult for a small boy to argue with that logic, especially given the fact that Grandpa was completely accurate. It seemed that every time we hopped from one rock to the next, two or three more knottyheads graced what had become an impressive catch.

Alas, my prophecy came true. I'm not sure whether I slipped and grabbed Grandpa or if he fell and reached out to me. Whatever the case, both of us were fully immersed in the frigid waters of Devils Dip. We scrambled out immediately, shaken and chilled but no worse for wear other than the fact that Grandpa had lost his straw hat. Purchased just the day before with hard-earned cash money, the hat made four complete circles in the circling current of the whirlpool with my erstwhile mentor trying to snag it with his long cane pole at each passage. The fifth time around the hat caught the current and headed downriver to Fontana Lake, never to be seen again.

By that time both of us were shivering and dreading the coming confrontation with Grandma Minnie. My paternal grandmother was a tiny woman, weighing 100 pounds at most, but she had a 300-pound temper and when riled up a tongue that could flay the hide off a razorback hog. The family in general, and Grandpa Joe in particular, stood in a constant awe of her wrath. Everyone did their level best to avoid being the focus of one of her periodic eruptions, and for the most part all were successful except Grandpa and me. We had a seeming knack for evoking her ire. Muddy shoes, being underfoot at the wrong time during cold weather, and a spouse who seemed to delight in acting like he was still a boy were unquestionably part of the explanation.

As we walked to the house, still dripping water and chattering from the cold, we passed the hog pen and chicken lot and then made our final approach along the path intersecting the garden. We both knew that each step brought us closer to impending doom. Showing up on the doorstep looking like a pair of half-drowned muskrats was going to earn us a tongue lashing of the first order. Grandpa acknowledged the inevitable by muttering, "They ain't going to like this one bit." The "they" to whom Grandpa referred was Grandma Minnie. Somehow in situations such as this he found it comforting to use an impersonal pronoun rather than her name.

I nodded in silent agreement with his foreboding and followed close on his heels. Sure enough, Grandma met us at the door and what I now realize was a millisecond of relief immediately gave way to rage. For some reason she directed her initial verbal sally towards me. Punctuating every word by poking me squarely in the solar plexus with her gnarled, arthritic index finger, she said, "The only thing worse than a young fool is an old fool." Then, having switched suddenly to prodding her spouse with the same finger but with added emphasis and impetus, she quickly added, "Here stands a matched pair."

At that moment I dared chance a glance sideways to see how Grandpa was reacting, only to discover he was slowly retreating while never breaking eye contact with Grandma. I wasn't about to be left alone to face her fury and forthwith moved to join him in what threatened to turn into full flight. As we backed through the doorway and out of sight, Grandpa grinned, winked at me, and whispered quite softly: "I reckon they won't be cooking any fish tonight."

We had cold cornbread and milk for supper.

Chapter 38

HOG FEEDING AND
LESSONS LEARNED

Grandpa Joe offered a study in character contrasts. Though easygoing and soft-spoken, he was mule stubborn. Similarly, while tough as leather and seldom given to shows of emotion, he could be wonderfully patient and tenderhearted with his adoring grandson. Fiercely independent, Grandpa wouldn't labor under the supervision of another man. Yet he possessed an admirable work ethic comprised of pure grit, keen understanding the wisdom inherent in "making do with what you've got," and sharply honed survival skills developed during a lifetime of living in close harmony with the land.

He epitomized the mountain description of "quare," but in my eyes he possessed an abundance of admirable traits. Those included being full of tricks as a pet coon; willingness to give endless quantities of that most precious of assets, time; and in some senses, just being a boy trapped in an old man's body. One sunny September afternoon all these qualities coalesced in unforgettable fashion.

We were in the cornfield of his tiny farm along the banks of the Tuckaseigee River near Bryson City, amid rows of towering Hickory King corn, pulling red-rooted pigweed and gathering inferior pumpkins for his hogs. The corn had already "made" and awaited storage of cobs in cribs and fodder in shocks. Our labor was hard, dirty work, made even tougher by the possibility of stings from packsaddles and certainty of encounters with razor-sharp edges of dry corn leaves. To me, none of that mattered.

There were ripe ground cherries for a snack, samples of Grandpa's rich store of tales to nurture the mind, and treasure from his memory to stir the soul. The pigweed and pumpkins for the hogs were, along with a steadily increasing ration of corn, part of a fattening-up process that would conclude with killing day come the first strong cold snap in November. Then the whole extended family—my grandparents, mother and father, aunts and uncles, along with any cousins old enough to help who lived in the area—would put in an extended day of labor processing from six to eight hogs, utilizing, as Grandpa put it, "everything but the squeal."

As was often the case in such settings, Grandpa used the setting to indulge in some reminiscing. In this case he drew from his rich memory bank to discuss days when hogs roamed free and fattened to prime bacon perfection on chestnut mast. Anything touching on the subject of chestnuts was a deeply moving one for him. As he became a bit misty-eyed and developed a catch in his voice, I became increasingly troubled. Having faced such scenarios before, I knew that the best approach was an abrupt change of subject. On this occasion what proved to be misguided inspiration led me to mention of one of my fondest ambitions. "Grandpa," I said, "I sure do wish I could throw a rock all the way across the river."

Shedding his mantle of painful nostalgia, he chuckled and responded: "Why that's easy. I can throw one all the way over to the mouth of Deep Creek" (which entered the river directly across from his home). With youth's endless enthusiasm and sometimes woeful innocence, I immediately seized on that seemingly ludicrous statement.

After all, Grandpa was bent with age, had never completely recovered from a hip shattered while out hunting in the snow, and to my knowledge possessed no throwing ability whatsoever. Impulsively I stated, without even thinking about a quid pro quo should he fail: "Grandpa, I'll pull pigweed, shell corn, and slop the hogs by myself for a week if you throw a rock across the river."

Having duly offered the bait and suckered his grandson into taking it, the family's grand sire muttered a favorite phrase. "You'll learn," he said, as he opened his Barlow knife to cut down a particularly long cornstalk. After stripping the fodder he trimmed the stalk down to a length of about eight feet and carefully carved a notch near its small end.

We then walked to river's edge and, after considerable scrutiny, Grandpa selected a stone. Fitting it into the notch, he drew back the cornstalk and launched his donnick. The rock was still rising when it reached the opposite side of the river at its confluence with Deep Creek. Turning to me with that sly grin I had seen so many times before, Grandpa said: "Son, things ain't always what they seem. I reckon you best get to pulling pigweed." He left me in my crestfallen misery for what seemed an eternity, then softly chuckled: "Go ahead and get busy now, but I'll help you. Next time you get a case of the big britches, though, you might want to remember to think a little bit before you open your pie hole."

Chapter 39

IN PRAISE OF PORCHES

One of many blessings folks living in the Smokies tend to take for granted is that they can enjoy their porches on balmy spring days, throughout the summer in early morning and from late afternoon until bedtime, and well into autumn when Indian Summer holds sway. With a fan or shade trees, even midday in the summer can be tolerable. Similarly, a flannel shirt or lightweight sweater makes fall evenings perfectly comfortable. Such is not the case everywhere, and the lengthy annual run of what might be styled the "porch season" in the high hills of the southern Appalachians is a real blessing.

In today's world of air conditioning, near addiction to television or computer screens, and a seeming compulsion to be indoors, porches don't loom nearly as large in everyday life as was once the case. Yet I'd like to sing the praises of porches, and much of my tribute comes directly from countless wondrous hours spent on them, mostly on the ones at my boyhood home or that of my paternal grandparents. Of course there were porches aplenty elsewhere—summertime courtships where I had neither the money nor the transportation to do anything but visit (they provided a welcome bit of privacy), pickin' and grinnin' sessions on summer evenings, visits with friends or relatives, and much more.

When visitors came a-calling, weather permitting we adjourned to the porch overlooking the town and offering vistas of Frye Mountain, the head of Kirklands Creek, and the beginning of the Alarka range on the opposite side of the Tuckaseigee River valley. The porch was a grand place to be when thunderstorms threatened. On countless occasions when a good shower would have been most welcome, we watched rains falling on the opposite ridgeline, sometimes so heavy they hid Frye Mountain, with flashes of lightning momentarily brightening the sky. We seldom enjoyed the benefit of those evening showers, because typical summer rain patterns brought rain from the southwest, moving up the river.

That porch was almost a second home to my sister. She would sing and rock for hours on end, and on one occasion when Daddy accidentally ran over a cat in the driveway, she purt nigh drove the rest of the household crazy with mournful tunes that in essence amounted to unending dirges. It was also a place to watch lightning bugs as light gave way to night, to observe "goings on" in downtown Bryson City, or during the day to watch birds go about their business. A pair of screech owls that raised several generations of young in a huge white oak located nearby added to the overall appeal and ambiance, and during the summer there was always a chorus of grasshoppers, katydids, and jar flies as background music.

Porches were a place for relaxation at day's end, but they also witnessed plenty of work. Indeed, quite often labor and rest went hand in hand. Sometimes a number of family members would gather to talk, but when they did so, more often than not their hands were busy. The job might involve stringing and breaking beans for a run of canning the next morning; shelling crowder peas or lima beans with the same end result in mind; peeling and quartering apples, either for drying or canning; working up a bushel or two of corn (shucking, scrubbing away silks, then cutting from the cob) for soup mix; cutting up okra; going through peaches beginning to go bad that Mom had bought for a song to make preserves; and the like. More often than not a prelude of porch work was part of the overall process of canning.

Occasionally, usually on a Sunday afternoon, there would be a run of hand-churned ice cream. I don't ever recall doing this at home, but it happened periodically at the residence of Grandpa Joe and Grandma Minnie, usually when a bunch of cousins from out of town visited or maybe when a lot of us got together for a family meal.

Most memorable of all for me were porch sitting sessions with no one involved except Grandpa Joe and me. Sometimes this came when we had been placed in verbal exile (that is to say, Grandma had told us, in no uncertain terms, that we needed to get out of the house). Grandpa would mutter something about "they" not wanting us underfoot (although his application of a pronoun in place of Grandma's name, Minnie, never eased the brunt of her ready wrath), and we would retreat to the porch. It was a great setting, looking out over the river and close enough to hear the stream whisper and murmur as its waters rolled by in their long journey to the Little Tennessee and mighty Mississippi rivers before eventually entering the Gulf of Mexico.

There he would take his throne, a comfortable rocking chair made of locust and with a padded bottom. Before long I would have induced him to share tales of yesteryear. Grandpa was a natural, gifted storyteller and it didn't take much—just a request for a rerun of some oft-told tale such as the time he shot a "painter" (cougar)—and magic would unfold. I could sit enchanted for hours, doing little other than offering a bit of encouragement or tendering an occasional expression of rapt interest, as he relived what was clearly a rugged but exciting time in his life.

Add to that enjoyment of an icy watermelon or just a cold glass of water while resting after hours of hoeing corn, and the overall picture emerges of porches being a special retreat, a tiny piece of paradise. They were the perfect place for so many things. Family gatherings, courtships, music, relaxation, rest between periods of work, enjoying the soothing movement of a rocking chair, sensing and savoring the rhythm of a gentle rain, and more. Porches were a place where you could be at peace with the world, and as singer/songwriter Tracy Lawrence suggested years ago in a country hit, "If the World Had a Front Porch," they were a place to reduce stress, solve problems, and slow down life's often hectic pace.

Chapter 40

REMEMBERING GRANDPA JOE

As should be abundantly manifest by this point, I worshiped Grandpa Joe. His folksy wisdom, the wonderful times I enjoyed in his company as a youngster, and what he taught me when it came to living close to the good earth endeared him to me. He died a half century ago, and in fairness and from hindsight, I must acknowledge he was anything but a perfect man.

For reasons I'll never fully understand, his and Grandma Minnie's marriage was an unhappy one. He was stubborn and uncommunicative; she was sometimes angry and shrewish. Both treated me wonderfully well, generally got along with other people, and worked amazingly hard right into old age. Perhaps adult life's adversities affected their relationship, and there were plenty of them. The same may have been true for Grandma's childhood experiences as an indentured servant and the impact of a case of scarlet fever that almost killed Grandpa when he was in his twenties. Whatever the exact explanation, and I'm reasonably certain it was a complex tapestry woven from many factors, I never really thought much about their fractured, largely loveless relationship until long after both were gone. It seldom seemed to affect the way they interacted with me, and I mention the unfortunate situation only for the sake of complete accuracy and as a tiny bit of underpinning for the recollections that follow.

Joseph Hillbury Casada, known simply as Joe, was my paternal grand-father. Countless hours spent in his company during my halcyon days of youth served as foundational building stones for some key aspects of my life. In his inimitable fashion Grandpa Joe introduced me to storytelling, provided hands-on exposure to the traditional mountain way of life, and was a walking encyclopedia of Smokies folkways. A man I idolized, he was most certainly a character—at times exasperating to his wife and children, more than a bit out of touch with the mainstream in about any area you could think of, and obstinate as only the most stubborn of mountain folks can be. Yet with me he was seldom judgmental, never really critical, and seemingly always willing to listen to a pesky, eternally curious young boy.

He lived within shank's mare of our house, about a mile and a half walk, and as a boy I spent a world of time with him and Grandma Minnie. Grandpa was unquestionably quare, but if anything his idiosyncrasies only endeared him more to me. We were buddies in the special fashion only possible when a generation is skipped and those involved are, respectively, of appreciable age and quite young. In truth Grandpa's perspective and general approach to life closely resembled that of a youngster. He just had the misfortune of being a imprisoned in an old man's body. Offsetting the resultant physical constraints, however, was the decided advantage of being blessed with a lifetime of experience to go with his youthful zest for life.

Having now reached the approximate age Grandpa Joe was when my first recollections of him begin, I realize just how fortunate I was to spend so much time with him as a mentor. He was a man of infinite patience, at least with me, although he had no tolerance whatsoever for a fair portion of the adult world. Grandpa possibly had some mental problems, and there's no question that he was distrustful of most of mankind, highly individual-istic, perfectly comfortable in his own skin, religious after his own fashion, incredibly hardworking, self-sufficient, and possessor of an endless array of tricks.

Thanks to his tutelage I know how to make a slingshot and select the right type of wood for the task; have a solid understanding of down-to-earth subjects ranging from pulling weeds for pigs to dealing with free-range chickens; can find fishing worms; am able to store pumpkins, turnips, cabbage, apples, and other foodstuffs so they will keep for months; hold an advanced education in the finer points of fishing for knottyheads; have solid grounding in many of the elements of storytelling; realize that for-mal education is by no means the only measure of a man's intellect or his worth as a human being; am deeply permeated with traditional mountain culture; and most of all have an abiding appreciation of the meaning of seeking oneness with the natural world. To my way of thinking, in leaving me those qualities as well as many more, Grandpa Joe provided me with a mighty fine legacy.

Famed Tar Heel writer Robert Ruark, in reminiscing about his own "Old Man," wrote that when his maternal grandfather died, impoverished by medical bills and the economic toll taken by the Great Depression, "all he left me was the world." Pleas of poverty notwithstanding, his grandfather left him far more in terms of tangible things than Grandpa Joe did me. I have the rocking chair where he held storytelling court situated four feet from where these words are being written, a single photograph of him by himself, a few family snapshots where he is shown in the company of other family members, a push plow with which he worked his garden for decades, and nothing else you can hold in your hands or look upon with your eyes. That doesn't matter. I have a storehouse of memories filled with riches miles beyond the measure of material things.

Like anyone who has lived a sufficient span of time to develop some perspective I have plenty of regrets along with even more fond recollections. One was that I was unable to attend Grandpa Joe's funeral. He died in 1967, just short of his ninetieth birthday. I was twenty-five at the time and under different circumstances would have joined other grandsons as a pallbearer at his memorial service, which took place on a bitterly cold winter's day. By unhappy coincidence, though, his service and burial coincided with the date I was scheduled to take the Graduate Record Examination. I was teaching and coaching in a preparatory school in Virginia at the time and hoped to begin graduate studies once the spring semester ended. This was my final opportunity to sit the required examination if I was to start my graduate education that summer. Thus Grandpa's passing left me with an impossible choice—miss the funeral or mess up my future.

Fortunately I had in effect already said my goodbyes, not once but several times as we talked during his final years, so the decision was easier than it might otherwise have been. I was also fully aware of what he would have thought about the matter. "Son," he would have murmured, "funerals are for the living."

That was the first time I truly realized or thought about the truth inherent in that old adage. Looking back, my absence may have been a blessing, because not attending the funeral enabled me to remember the man and all he meant to me privately as opposed to being part of a wide circle of his extended family and friends in the local community. Since he was always a bit of a misanthrope, I have no doubt whatsoever Grandpa would have understood, indeed appreciated, my perspective in preferring to be alone with precious memories.

His death occurred in late February, which seemed to me somehow appropriate, because in our countless sessions of rocking chair relaxation in the heart of winter, as he eased close to the fire and muttered about what he simply styled "the miseries," Grandpa often philosophized about the month. "It's fittin' February is so short," he would say, "because twenty-eight days of it is about as much as a body can stand." He would then opine that the best of winter's hunting was over, "and besides, these gloomy days of rain and snow are a time for a spry young colt like you, not an old man like me, to be out and about."

I was often tempted to remind him that he had been "out and about" on just such a day when he slipped in snow while squirrel hunting and shattered his hip, but I knew better despite what was a pronounced penchant to speak when silence would have been advisable. I would have gotten a gentle but biting dose of verbal tea concluding with something to the effect that I didn't know what I was talking about, followed by his stern admonition, "But you'll learn." I reckon I'm still in the process of learning all those lessons that Grandpa figured ought to be a part of a mountain youngster's upbringing. Who knows, maybe I've now advanced to a point in my educational development that I am a bit beyond the kindergarten stage.

For all that he groused about weather, mistrusted mankind, and clung to his independence with ferocious tenacity, it was never in Grandpa's character to stay pessimistic for long. He had some pains associated with advancing age, but for the most part he ignored them while refusing to have anything to do with pain-relieving medications. "I reckon an old man's got a right to ache a bit," he'd say, "but it don't do to dwell on it."

Never mind that he had known poverty all his years and had ample reason to be morose or feel downtrodden, Grandpa was a dreamer. In some senses he spent his whole life dreaming, although his visions and wanderings in the realm of wishful thinking lay outside normal approaches. If financial affairs meant much to him, I never saw any real indication of it, although whenever the subject came up he always referred to "cash money." He had so little of it that the redundancy was richly deserved.

Grandpa could outwork men half his age and never shied from doing so, although he was constitutionally incapable of following orders if they involved so much as a hint of supervision or oversight. You could tell him a field needed hoeing, a lawn required mowing, or it was time for an orchard to be pruned. Just hire him to have at it and all would be fine. Look over his shoulder or make suggestions on how to perform the job, though, and it was time to seek someone else to handle the tasks. He was so completely his own man that no one, with the possible exception of Grandma Minnie on rare occasions, could tell him anything.

Grandpa's dreams focused not on money but on matters such as the American chestnut's return, the significance of planting black walnuts (he called them "grandchildren's trees" because of their slow growth), olden times when he often heard the scream of a "painter" and even killed one, hunting pheasants (his word for grouse) when they existed in large numbers, and indeed sport of any kind. He lived a life partly cast in the past and for the rest looking to the future rather than being preoccupied with the present.

Hunting took primacy of place in his reminiscences, but he also ventured into romantic realms on the fishing side of the sporting equation. I loved to hear him talk about a time when speckled trout were so plentiful you could easily catch a hundred in an afternoon of fishing. Similarly, every time he recounted an epic battle with a giant jackfish (muskellunge), I listened in enchantment. Despite hearing that particular tale times without number, I felt that it never grew old. That's a hallmark of a masterful weaver of words.

Sooner or later, and especially during the depths of winter when outside activities were limited by inclement weather, he would turn to a subject that brought me endless delight. Grandpa would abruptly switch from musing about matters dating back to the late nineteenth century and focus on the future. "I've always liked figurin'," he'd opine, "and it's high time the two of us got busy doing some." Or maybe he would suggest we needed to undertake a spell of dreamin' and schemin'. Whatever his choice of words, the point of it all was quite clear. He had decided to quit reflecting on the past and start musing on the near future. He reckoned a good dose of planning about events to come offered an ideal antidote for anything from cabin fever to Grandma being vexed with the two of us.

Grandpa would launch into a detailed plan of what we needed to do to get ready for spring fishing, or maybe decide it wasn't too late to make one more rabbit gum and set it in a likely spot. We might peruse that year's Sears & Roebuck catalog to compare mail order prices of essential items such as snelled fish hooks or the new-fangled monofilament line with what they cost at the local hardware store. Often Grandpa talked of trying a new fishing spot on the river or a journey up nearby Deep Creek, and if it was wintertime we would get several cane poles rigged and ready for our fishing forays come greening-up time. Year after wonderful year Grandpa showed me that dreaming is by no means the exclusive preserve of the young. You just had to be young at heart. That was one of his finest qualities.

Grandpa Joe never saw the ocean, but he fished pristine mountain streams and drank sweet spring water so icy it set your teeth on edge. He never drove a car, but he handled teams of horses and understood meaningful application of the words gee, haw, and whoa. I'm pretty sure he never left the state of North Carolina, but he lived a full life in the Smokies, mountains so lovely they make the soul soar. To my knowledge he never once ate in a restaurant, but he dined on sumptuous fare—pot likker, backbones and ribs, fried squirrel with sweet potatoes, country hams he cured from hogs he had raised and butchered, cathead biscuits with sausage gravy, cracklin' cornbread, and other fixin's the likes of which no high-profile chef ever prepared.

He never drank a soda pop, but he "sassered," sipped, and savored pepper tea he prepared from parched red pepper pods like a connoisseur of the finest wines. He never tasted seafood, but he dined on speckled trout battered with stone-ground cornmeal and fried in lard rendered from hogs he had raised. He never ate papayas or pomegranates, but he grew cannonball watermelons so sweet they'd leave you sticky all over and raised muskmelons so juicy you drooled despite yourself when one was sliced. He never had crepes Suzette, but he enjoyed buckwheat pancakes made with flour milled from grain he had grown, adorned with butter his wife churned, and covered with molasses made from cane he raised. He never ate eggs Benedict, but he dined daily on eggs from free-range chickens with yolks yellow as the summer sun. He was marginally literate, but he read the Bible faithfully every day. He didn't go to church, at least in the years I knew him, but he was an intensely religious man.

In short, Grandpa Joe was not, in the grander scheme of things, an individual who garnered fame, fortune, accolades, or grand achievements. His life was one of limitations in many ways—geographically, technologically, economically, in breadth of vision, and at least in the eyes of some, accomplishments. To my way of thinking, though, he epitomized love;

the magic of mentoring; liberal dispensation of that most precious of gifts, time; and sharing of the sort of down-to-earth wisdom redolent in singer/ songwriter John Prine's suggestion that "it don't make much sense that common sense don't make no sense no more."

I didn't quite think, to echo a refrain from a poignant Randy Travis song about his grandfather, that Grandpa Joe walked on water. Yet seldom has there been a day since his death, now encompassing the passage of half a century, I haven't thought about him. Invariably those thoughts bring a wry smile to my face even as they produce tightness in my throat. He blessed me with treasures beyond all measure, not the least of which was providing me an endless fund of anecdotes and tidbits of information to use in my writing. For that I owe him an enduring debt of gratitude. He was, in my small world, the most unforgettable character I've ever known or will likely ever know.

Chapter 41

MUSINGS ON TRADITIONAL MOUNTAIN CHARACTER TRAITS

In her often overlooked book, *Spirit of the Mountains*, Emma Bell Miles writes of residents of the Appalachian high country: "No amount of education ever quite rids the mountaineer of bull-headed contrariness." I would heartily and unashamedly concur with that statement. Indeed, my sister-in-law's reaction when she first heard those words, a spirited "Amen, brother," may well have included the "brother" part because she had me in mind. Of course my personal preference is to describe the trait of being born stubborn as one of proud independence, and anyone who doubts that such obduracy exists in traditional mountain ways simply lacks familiarity with them. A well-written book by Jim Webb, *Born Fighting: How the Scots-Irish Shaped America,* carries genetic obstinacy an extra step, and perhaps he is right. For my part, though, never mind a family history where words such as "affray" show up in court records, I prefer to think that "sot in his ways" goes to the heart of the matter.

Grandpa Joe was a grand example of many of the traits that defined traditional mountain people, and he certainly had sterling qualifications as a character. He embodied many of the pervasive traits that long defined people of the Smokies and surrounding regions. Grandpa would never work for another man, or at least not if the job involved any direct oversight, instruction, or over-the-shoulder observation. Call him mulish, obdurate, difficult, obstreperous, or downright ornery; it didn't matter. He was his own man and that was the long and short of it. He would not gee or haw to another's demands or commands, and many mountaineers shared his outlook. They were, in short, born stubborn, and if anything that obstinacy increased with advancing years.

Apparently Grandpa Joe's mentorship took holt, because more than once, with my good wife leading the list of accusers, I've been charged with rank stubbornness of the worst kind. Similarly, I'll confess to having a smidgen of reclusiveness in my outlook, and a desire for isolation has long been commonplace among folks living in the remote hills and hollows of Appalachia.

Indeed, in days gone by, and not all that far in the past, many folks living in the more rural areas of the Smokies were never happier than when their nearest neighbor lived two or three hollows away. Close enough to see tendrils of chimney smoke was "as near as you'd wanna be," was the way Grandpa put it. On the other hand, let a family fall on hard times or someone need a barn built, and willing hands were there to help. Corn shuckin's, taffy pulls, molasses makin', barn buildings, hog markin's, and a host of other activities meant togetherness. Neighborliness tempered by a keen awareness of the importance of space and ample opportunity to be alone distinguished the folks of Appalachian yesteryears.

Another area of commonality, and it is one that survives and even thrives today among some of the finest folks whose roots reach deep in the soil of the high country, is an ability to "make do." If I heard the phrase "make do with what you've got" once as a youngster, I heard it a thousand times. My family was fairly typical in that regard, inasmuch as we raised a big garden, fattened hogs every year for butchering in the fall, had an annual goal of 200 quarts of canned green beans and a like number of jars of apples, and supplemented our table fare to an appreciable degree with nature's rich bounty. That bounty took such forms as small game (squirrels, rabbits, grouse, quail, and on a couple of occasions ground hog or 'coon); wild berries including strawberries, dewberries, blackberries, and huckleberries; native nuts (especially black walnuts); poke salad; and trout. In today's fishing world it is de rigueur for the trout fisherman to practice catch-and-release, and in some streams (such as the delayed harvest sections of the Tuckaseigee and Nantahala) it is mandatory for several months each year.

Yet my mother considered turning fish loose just about the ultimate act of foolishness, as much at odds with "make do" as was humanly possible. Her approach was not catch-and-release but release-to-grease, and anyone who has yet to dine on fresh-caught trout dressed up in cornmeal dinner jackets and fried to a golden brown has lived a life of culinary deprivation. If it happens to be the spring of the year and those trout can be flanked by a kilt salad containing ramps and branch lettuce, so much the better.

Running closely parallel to "make do" was the concept of "waste not, want not." No nail or screw, no section of sawed lumber or fallen hardwood, not to mention table scraps, was thrown away. There was always going to be a use for anything made of metal; downed trees could be turned into fuel for wood-burning stoves or fireplaces; and scraps fed the chickens, went into hog slop, or offered food for the family's hunting dogs. Frugality, in short, was a byword for life. No one ever mentioned recycling, and I'm not sure it had even entered the Smokies lexicon. Yet the practice was universal.

Another phrase I heard uttered on a frequent basis was "poor but proud." The whole concept of welfare, dependence on government help, or regular reliance on others was pretty much alien. That isn't to suggest that mountains folks weren't of a giving inclination. When someone was down on their luck, lending a hand came as second nature. A philanthropic streak ran deep in Smokies souls even if the word "philanthropy" lay outside their vocabulary. By the same token, a sound work ethic was pretty much an expectation of everyday life, and any man or woman lacking that attribute was looked down upon. A lazy individual would normally be described as "trifling," "useless," or a "layabout," but those meriting such opprobrium were rare.

Examples of "making do" went well beyond the essentials of eking out a hardscrabble living. Youngsters didn't have and didn't need "play purties" bought with cash money. Instead, their playthings involved hands-on craftsmanship. This might mean the construction of cane fishing poles complete with the malleable lead coverings from roofing nails as sinkers or homemade toys in forms such as slingshots, corn shuck dolls, whimmy-diddles, flutter mills, and most anything an ample measure of ingenuity could conjure up. I remember Daddy making some dandy stilts out of sawn lumber scraps, and an electrical plug-in device he engineered would immediately bring enough worms to the surface for a long day's fishing.

Or, to compare youthful playthings then with what has become almost standard today, I feel reasonably certain that a boy with a slingshot he had handcrafted derived at least as much joy from that item as a youngster of today obtains from an iPhone. On top of that, the slingshot cost nothing, carried with it the pride of craftsmanship, and was almost indestructible.

Other character traits certainly merit mention. Loyalty, the ability to hate long and hold a grudge even longer, quick tempers, deep and abiding religious faith, susceptibility to suspicion sometimes verging on paranoia, and stoicism in the face of even the harshest adversity once formed standard components of mountain character.

If you are a child of the Smokies, ask yourself whether some or all of the above-mentioned traits typify your approach to life. Conversely, if you are an "outlander" (and with each passing year an increasing number of area residents fall into that category), maybe you will have at least a bit more insight on what comprises, to borrow again from Emma Bell Miles, the "spirit" that shapes mountain folkways and behavior. That spirit, conveyed by voices without number down through the generations, guides us even as it gives us a sacred responsibility. Our duty and destiny is to honor, protect, and perpetuate all that makes us distinctive and endows us with our unique identity. If this book has succeeded, in some small way, in accomplishing that then I'll consider it a success.

Glossary

Traditional "mountain talk" is dying. Words and phrases that were as common as pig tracks when I was a boy are seldom if ever heard today. Four-lane highways, electricity, cell towers, computers, the Internet, and all sorts of communication devices have brought the world to the Smokies and changed it irrevocably. Part of that change is a vanishing way of speech.

Frequently, without thinking, I will use a word or phrase in conversation that leaves others looking at me in amazement or sometimes with total incomprehension. It's invariably because I have unconsciously reverted to the language and expressions of my native heath. For that I make no apology. Indeed, I'm inordinately proud of my roots, the highly descriptive if sometimes quaint colloquialisms that were a part of my upbringing, and the joys of all that is special about traditional Appalachian speech.

Still, I'm aware of the fact that a number of words or phrases that appear in these pages fall outside the norms of spoken and written English. Accordingly, even though context frequently makes the meaning clear, the glossary that follows provides brief definitions of those that might possibly present stumbling blocks. For anyone wishing fuller information, there is a splendid reference source, based on an incredible amount of research, to offer guidance. This is Joseph S. Hall and Michael B. Montgomery's *Dictionary of Smoky Mountain English*. Its origins lay in Hall making a number of visits, always with a recorder in hand, to the Smokies in the two decades following creation of the GSMNP. Montgomery took his extensive notes and recordings, added a great deal by way of explanation, definitions, context, and examples of usage, to complete the book. It is, without question, one of the most important guides available to any student of Appalachian folkways, speech patterns, and life.

Adam's off ox—An unknown person or someone an individual cannot name. The phrase is usually preceded by "wouldn't know from."
bile or biled—Boil or boiled.
boomer—A small red squirrel, once common in the mountains but not so much anymore, most often found at higher elevations.

cash money—Bills or coins; the redundancy came from the fact that the expenditure of actual cash, as opposed to barter, was rare. Most commonly used by older folks.

cathead biscuit—A large biscuit, equivalent in size to the head of a cat; a biscuit cut from dough using the open end of a tin can.

catty-corner (also cater-corner or cattywampus)—At an oblique angle; askew or out of kilter

'coon's age—A long period of time

donnick—A rock, especially one of a size suitable for throwing.

dose of salts—Literally applied to Epsom salts or something similar used as a purgative, but more commonly a description of any type of purgative.

flutter mill—A tiny, toy-sized replica of a water wheel that could be turned by water, a breeze, or blowing on it.

gee—A plowing command to a horse or mule to make a right turn; haw is a command for a left turn. Gee haw was sometimes used to describe getting along well.

greasy beans—A particular type of green bean, so named because of its slick appearance.

hickory tea—A spanking or switching with a slender hickory limb—"a dose of hickory tea."

holp—Help or assist.

Jacob's ladder—A child's toy.

kilt—Killed; primarily used to describe the result of pouring hot grease over fresh lettuce or other greens.

laid holt or lay holt—Grabbed or seized.

leather britches—Dried green beans.

made—Usually applied to a crop that has matured.

mollygrubs—Doldrums or having low spirits.

mumblety-peg—A type of game played with pocket knives; there are many versions.

no shoulders—A snake.

peart—Perky or full of energy.

piddling—Messing around with no particular purpose; also, of insignificance or a description of urination.

poke—A paper bag; also, a wild vegetable eaten when sprouts first appear in the spring.

purt nigh—Almost or nearly.

quare (also sometimes rendered as quair)—Strange or different.

set pole—A fishing pole that is propped up and not handheld; most commonly associated with cane poles stuck in a muddy bank and propped up by a forked stick.

shank's mare—To go by foot; to walk.

sot in your ways—Stubborn or inflexible.

take holt—Seize, grab, or (in the case of plants) become well established.

vittles—Victuals or foodstuffs.

whimmy-diddle (or whammy-diddle)—Sometimes called a gee haw whimmy-diddle because operating the toy produces movement first in one direction and then the other. A common homemade child's "play purty."

yard birds—Any type of free-ranging domestic fowl, although most commonly applied to chickens.

Index